Eva Hope

New World Heroes. Lincoln and Garfield

The Life-Story of Two Self-Made Men, whom the People made Presidents

Eva Hope

New World Heroes. Lincoln and Garfield
The Life-Story of Two Self-Made Men, whom the People made Presidents

ISBN/EAN: 9783337191429

Printed in Europe, USA, Canada, Australia, Japan

Cover: Foto ©ninafisch / pixelio.de

More available books at **www.hansebooks.com**

New World Heroes.

LINCOLN AND GARFIELD:

The Life-Story of two self-made Men, whom the people made Presidents.

BY THE AUTHOR OF
"Our Queen," "Grace Darling," etc., etc.

"And moving up from high to higher,
Becomes on fortune's crowning slope,
The pillar of a people's hope,
The centre of a world's desire."

PRESTON:
JAMES ASKEW, 30 GRAFTON STREET,
1888.

CONTENTS.

ABRAHAM LINCOLN.

CHAP.
- I. A Hero's Birthplace
- II. The First Sorrow
- III. A New Mother
- IV. His Own Business
- V. Lawyer Lincoln
- VI. A Husband and a Father
- VII. Nominated and Elected President
- VIII. Congratulations
- IX. From Springfield to Washington
- X. War!
- XI. Emancipation
- XII. Life at the White House
- XIII. Re-elected
- XIV. Peace and Victory
- XV. Afterwards

CONTENTS.

JAMES A. GARFIELD.

CHAP.		PAGE
I.	A Forest Funeral	151
II.	Hard Times	158
III.	A Tow-Path Boy	168
IV.	"The Disciples of Christ"	177
V.	At Hiram as a Student	184
VI.	In College, and President of Hiram . . .	192
VII.	Garfield on College Education	202
VIII.	Senator Garfield at the War	217
IX.	General Garfield in Congress	226
X.	The New Home at Mentor	234
XI.	Elected President	243
XII.	Smitten Down	255
XIII.	The Wife and Mother	267
XIV.	A Fight for Life	279
XV.	The Funeral	290
XVI.	In Memory of Garfield	302
XVII.	Good out of Evil	317
XVIII.	The End of the Wicked	328
XIX.	Comrades	337
XX.	What Made them Heroes ?	346
XXI.	The Lessons of their Lives	358

Dedication.

O the boys and youths of Great Britain, whose only inheritance is the heritage of Work, this chronicle of two lives is affectionately dedicated, in the hope that it may inspire them with hope and courage for the race that is before them. The wish of the compiler is, that as it is read by British firesides, or in British playgrounds, many young eyes may brighten with new resolution—many hearts beat high with fresh determination. That which Abraham Lincoln and James Garfield were, others may become. Nearly, if not all, the possibilities that faced them stand waiting for those who have the power to win them. The tall

giant who emancipated the slaves, and the gentlemanly scholar whose guiding-star was Honesty, being dead yet speak; and their cry rings through the land—LIVE WORTHILY, NOT FOR THYSELF, BUT FOR THY FELLOW-MAN, AND FOR THY GOD! And it will surely reach the ears, and sink into the hearts of some whom the future shall crown as the New Heroes of the Old World!

ABRAHAM LINCOLN.

NEW WORLD HEROES.

CHAPTER I.

A HERO'S BIRTHPLACE.

"The short and simple annals of the poor."

T may seem to matter very little where a hero is born; but the birthplace of any man is perhaps of more importance than is generally thought. Beautiful scenery, fresh air, the simple habits of an honest people, are influences that affect more than a little the future of any child who is born into our world. It would be interesting to know how many of the great and good men of all ages first saw the light away from the busy town, and looked up to the blue skies through the interlacing boughs outside of some cottage home. Certainly we believe that a very large proportion of talented men and women had their birth, even in our crowded England, in the green country. It is little wonder that in America this should, in a very great degree, be the case. The boy of whom we write had for his early companions the birds and

the rabbits, and for his cradle-music the song of the brook and the winds, and the merry, dancing leaves; and though his after career lay in the midst of life and strife, and fulness of work and responsibility, we may well believe that he was the better and the stronger man because of the circumstances of his youth.

Abraham Lincoln was born on the 12th day of February 1809, at Nolin Creek, a place that is now known as La Rue country, about a mile and a-half from Hodgenville, in the State of Kentucky. His father and mother were Baptists; his early ancestors were English Quakers. His grandfather was one of the first to explore the rich and beautiful Kentucky valley. He was one of the pioneer frontiersmen to whom the States of America owe so much—a man stout of heart and strong of hand, a romantic adventurer, but God-fearing and faithful to conscience and duty. He had the courage, in spite of difficulty and danger, to establish his rude dwelling several miles away from any of his neighbours, and he paid the penalty of his temerity. He was at work one day some distance from home, when an Indian crept upon him unawares, and slew and scalped him. His widow was left with two daughters and three sons, who bore the names of Thomas, Mordecai, and Joseph.

Thomas, the father of Abraham Lincoln, the hero of our story, was six years old at the time of his father's death. When he was twelve years old he was a hard-working lad; and when he was twenty-eight he married Nancy Hanks, of Virginia, a woman who became a true help-meet to him in his backwoods life. She was pale and thin, and rather sad of countenance; he was broad-chested and well built, and of average height. She could read, but not write; he could manage, after a fashion, to write his own name. He was industrious and genial; she was possessed of excellent judgment and good sense, and particularly gentle and lovable. She was eminently a Christian woman, and supported the credit of her faith by a beautiful and irreproachable life. Every mother is the first and greatest teacher of her family; but on Mrs. Lincoln devolved for some years the sole training of her children. She had two sons and one daughter. Thomas, however, died while yet a baby, and Abraham and his sister Sarah were close friends and inseparable companions. Their home was a very poor one. English people can scarcely imagine the kind of residence that a log-cabin really was: there was no floor to it, except the ground; and no walls, except the rough ones made of logs; and there was almost no furniture in it. But the children had happy times, nevertheless. They had, as it seemed to them, the whole world for a play-ground. There were tall trees and thick undergrowth, green hills and running streams, woods full of wild flowers, places to hide in, places to swing from, plenty of cool, fresh water to drink, and plenty of rich, ripe berries to eat. Then in the evenings and on Sundays there were mother-talks for the children, which no child can miss without more or less of soul-starving. Mrs. Lincoln had only a few books, but she did the best she could with them. She read them, and told the children of their contents, and gradually taught them also to read. It is believed, indeed, that the only literature which belonged to the Lincoln cabin was two books—the Bible and the Catechism; but they were good books from which to get first lessons, especially in the hands of a gentle, pious mother. There were no places of worship to which the children could be taken, but their own log-hut became a sanctuary in which the children were told "the sweet Story of Old," and where right principles were inculcated. Abraham was never tired of listening to his mother, and in her children she had most attentive listeners, who stimulated her recitals with very eager questions.

"Mother, had the little Jew children black faces?"

"No, Abe, I suppose not."

"But they were like slaves in Egypt, were'nt they?"

"Oh yes, they were like slaves; and if they did not work hard enough to please their masters they were whipped."

"Were they like the slaves at Hodgen's mills and Elizabethtown, mother?"

"I suppose they were quite as badly off."

"But they were'nt always to be slaves, were they, mother?"

"No, for God sent a Deliverer."

"I know his name; it was Moses."

"Yes; the little boy, who was laid in the ark of rushes which his mother made, grew up to be the Deliverer of his people from bondage," said the mother, solemnly.

"Mother, do you think a Deliverer will come and set these slaves free?"

"Perhaps. Who knows? If it be God's will, He can raise some one up."

"You don't like slavery, do you, mother?"

"No, I do not. I cannot think it is right."

"I hope God will send a Moses to Kentucky some day, mother, to make all the little boys free."

And He did!

Abraham Lincoln was about seven years old when he had the opportunity of going to school. It was opened by Zechariah Reney, a Roman Catholic. We would like to have seen the school-room; what a contrast it would present to the beautiful and convenient edifices erected by the School Boards of our own land and times! At the end of three months Abraham and his sister went to either another school, or the same school kept by another master, whose name was Caleb Hazel, and there he remained another three months, making such rapid progress that at the end of the time he was able to read aloud to his parents some of the plain and easy parts of the Bible, a feat which astonished and delighted them, and caused them to feel more than a little proud of their boy.

A HERO'S BIRTHPLACE.

In the year 1816, when little Abraham Lincoln was nearly eight years old, his father decided to leave Kentucky for the wilds of Indiana. No one knows exactly why he did this. Perhaps he liked the excitement of a change. But it is more probable that as there was at the time a great deal of dispute about the titles to lands in Kentucky, he considered a residence there somewhat full of risk. And life in a slave state was always more or less unsatisfactory to the poor white man, who would be more likely to find better scope for himself and his children where free labour would not come into competition with slave labour, and he therefore made up his mind to go further west without loss of time.

As if to assure him that his decision was a right one, a man by the name of Colby came to the cabin.

"Are you going to move away from this?" he asked.

"I guess I am," replied Thomas Lincoln.

"I want to buy a farm, if you are inclined to sell," said Colby; "and I don't mind three hundred dollars for this real estate, if you are willing to make it over to me."

"I guess I'll do it," said Lincoln, with a look at his wife, who was more cautious and timid, perhaps because she was less strong than her husband. But she was willing to abide by his decision, and to make a home wherever her dear ones went.

Very strangely, as it seems to us, who live in the days when, happily, both in America and England, temperance principles are strong, Lincoln sold his farm for whisky. Ten barrels of whisky, of forty gallons each, valued at two hundred and eighty dollars, and twenty dollars in money, was the price which Colby paid, and Thomas Lincoln received for the farm and homestead! The whisky was for sale, and not to drink; and Abraham, when he grew to be a man, became a friend to Temperance.

The father of the family having sold his home, went off

to find a new one, leaving his wife and children in the old place while he did so.

He built a "flat-boat" (something like a gondola), and launched it on a little stream called "the Rolling Fork;" and in it he packed his ten barrels of whisky, and all the heavy articles of his home and farm. Then he went floating away down the Rolling Fork, out into the Ohio river, in which he came to grief, for his boat upset, and his cargo went into the water. Fortunately, however, he was near the shore, and succeeded, by the help of some friendly hands, in rescuing some of the whisky and other articles, which, if poor in themselves, were very valuable to him. He landed at a place called Thompson's Ferry, Indiana, and there he paid with his flat-boat for the services of a man and his team to take him and his possessions into the interior. It was slow travelling, for they had often to make the road before they could traverse it, by cutting down the trees and brushwood in the way. But at last they reached a spot of great beauty and fertility, and here Thomas Lincoln decided to make his future home.

The first thing to be done was clearly to go back at once and fetch his wife and children; and this, having given his goods into the care of the inhabitants of a house only two miles away, he started to do.

CHAPTER II.

THE FIRST SORROW.

"Friend after friend departs,
Who has not lost a friend?"

IT was no pleasant or easy task that was before Mrs. Lincoln and her children.

They welcomed with great glee the return of the husband and father, and tired though he was after his long walk, he had at once to begin answering their questions.

"Have you found a place, father? Will it be our own? Where is it? What is it like?"

They lost no time in starting on the journey. They bade good-bye to the little home, which, poor as it was, they all loved, with tears. Then they all went to look their last at the tiny grave of the baby who had died several years ago. When Abraham had grown to be both a tall and a great man, he used to speak of this incident with emotion.

But a long journey was before them, for a distance of a hundred miles separated the new home from the old, and it would take a week for them to go from one to the other. They had a cow, which, of course, they must take with them for the sake of her milk, three horses, and a waggon. They managed to pack in the waggon and on the horses all their household articles, which were very few; and as to themselves, Mrs. Lincoln and Sarah might ride if they liked, but the father and the son walked the greater part of the distance, for the horses had to be led and the cow to be driven. When they reached the proper part of the river Ohio, they were floated across in a flat-boat, and at the end of the seventh day they reached the spot which Thomas Lincoln had selected.

It was near the present town of Gentryville, in what was then Perry County, but is now Spencer County, that Mr. Lincoln and his son and a neighbour at once set to work to build a new log-cabin. It had two rooms, one downstairs, and a small attic or loft above. Sarah and her parents slept below, in what was the living room of the family; and Abraham slept in the loft, on the rough logs that made the floor. A bear-skin was spread for him to lie upon, and a blanket covered him. The bedstead of his father and mother was made of slabs nailed together against the side of the cabin, and their bed was a heap of dried leaves thrown upon the slabs. A rough table and three stools formed the rest of the furniture. There was always a good fire burning in the cabin, and when it was very cold, all the family slept around it; while skins were nailed over the doors to keep out the biting winds.

Winter was upon them, but Spring would follow; and Thomas Lincoln and his son began the hard work of clearing the forest, and preparing the land to receive the seed which they would put into it. Abraham, of course, helped him; and he proved the truth of the saying, "It is good for a man that he bear the yoke in his youth." He grew strong and hardy, self-denying and brave. He was very industrious; and when his day's work upon the forest or the farm was finished, he was free to spend some happy hours with his friends, and in the way he liked best.

EARLY HOME OF ABRAHAM LINCOLN, GENTRYVILLE, INDIANA. —*Page 8.*

Besides the Bible and the Catechism, there had been added to the family treasures an old copy of Dilworth's *Spelling Book*, and by the aid of this young Abraham Lincoln continued his education. Altogether he had enjoyed less than a year's schooling, but he had made as much as he could of the little; and he had begun to write and to "cipher." He practised well at home. Pens and ink and paper were luxuries unknown to, or at least unenjoyed by, the pioneer and his family; but Abraham did very well without them, for he managed to write letters or figures on the white surface of the bark of the birch-tree with charcoal. They had fine fun over the spelling and the reckoning, for Abraham tried to keep school at home, and change his parents and his sister into scholars.

About this time he came into possession of one or two other books. The first was *Æsop's Fables*, with which he was greatly delighted. It had pictures at which he never wearied of looking, and stories which interested him so deeply, that he read them over until they were firmly fixed in his own mind; and then he related them for the amusement and edification of his sister Sarah. About the next book that he read his mother took care often to talk to him. It was Bunyan's *Pilgrim's Progress*. The boy seemed to have the opportunity of reading it just at the time when he needed its instruction.

"You see, my boy, that there is another land, and a journey to be taken to the Celestial City," said his mother to him one day, little thinking that she was herself drawing very near to its gates.

"Yes, mother; and it must be a very beautiful city that!"

"Ah! my son, you cannot guess how lovely; and the best of it is that there we shall see Jesus, and the next best, that there will be no such thing known as sin."

"It will be a very wonderful place then, where everybody is good. I am afraid there is not much chance for me."

"Indeed there is! The King wishes to have my Abe in the beautiful city, and He will guide you if you ask Him. Only you must be willing to forsake sin here, and so be prepared for the holiness there."

And Abraham would say softly to his mother, and yet more earnestly to himself, that he meant to be good, and would really try to be.

Another book that he read was Weem's *Life of Washington*. It was a very exciting book, full of fighting and adventures, and it fired his young imagination greatly. Many years afterward he spoke of that book:—"I remember all the accounts there given of the battle-fields and struggles for the liberties of the country. I recollect thinking then, boy even though I was, that there must have been something more than common that these men struggled for."

The next book he read was also very useful to him; it was the *Life of Henry Clay*, who was at that time exceedingly famous. Since Abraham Lincoln was himself to become a politician and statesman, it was well for him to read of the brilliant speeches of this young orator, made on subjects that so nearly affected the interests of his country.

But Abraham had much to do besides read books. To get wood for his mother, to carry water for her, and help her in every way, was a pleasure to him; and he was besides learning to be a very useful help to his father. At that time he was dressed in coat and trousers made of buckskin, and was not afraid of either hard work or cold weather. On one occasion, too, he proved that he was not afraid to handle a gun. His father had taken his axe and gone away to work in the forest, when Abraham, looking through a crevice of the log-cabin, saw a flock of wild turkeys outside. He knew that these were worth having, for the family lived chiefly on game shot by the father. But the father was not there to shoot, and what was to be done? The boy, only about eight years old at the time, could not bear to let so good an opportunity pass; and so he called his mother.

"Could you load father's gun? Here is a flock of turkeys! If you can, I will have a shot."

Mrs. Lincoln peeped through the opening.

"They are beauties! Could you pull the trigger, Abe?"

"Yes, mother; load it and see."

In less than a minute the boy had fired into the midst of the birds, and hit one of the finest.

There was great glee when Mr. Lincoln returned.

"Father," said Sarah, "guess what there is for dinner to-morrow?"

"Fish?"

"No."

"Flesh?"

"No."

"Fowl?"

"Yes, a turkey."

"A turkey, indeed. Where is it to come from?"

"It has come already."

"You are joking. Let me see it."

It was drawn from its hiding-place with a triumphant "There!"

"But what does this mean. Who shot it?"

"Abraham."

"Did you really, Abe?" The boy stood blushing with pleasure. "It is a wonderful shot for a boy of your age," said Thomas Lincoln. "You will become a great hunter one of these days."

Abraham Lincoln, however, never became very fond of a gun.

But a shadow was gathering over the Lincoln's home.

They had only been in Indiana two years, when it became evident that Mrs. Lincoln was dying of consumption. It was some time before her husband and children could believe that so great a trouble was befalling them. But she knew it herself, and the coming separation made her love them more than ever.

"Let me do something for you, mother," Abraham would say; and she was glad to give up the work which she had done so long and so well.

"I am getting too weak to do it," she said.

At last she could not leave her bed; and it was Abraham's task to read to her the words which have comforted so many dying Christians. There was no minister; but the beautiful sayings of Jesus was not less powerful because they were conveyed by the clear tones of a boy's voice. "Let not your heart be troubled: ye believe in God, believe also in me. In my Father's house are many mansions. If it were not so I would have told you. I go to prepare a place for you."

And soon the place was hers.

There was great desolation in the log-cabin when the mother had died. Abraham keenly felt her loss; and he cried as if his heart would break when he and his sister stood with their father by the humble grave in the forest. A few friends came to the funeral, but there was not even an itinerant preacher—the only kind they ever had—in these parts.

But there had been one, Mr. Elkins, a Baptist, who sometimes conducted open-air services among the few settlers, and sometimes gave exhortations in their cabins. Mrs. Lincoln had known and respected him; and it was decided that a letter should be sent to ask him to come and preach a funeral sermon.

"I will write a letter," said Abraham, whose heart was

very much in the matter. And accordingly, with the feeling that he was doing a very great thing indeed, the boy wrote his first letter, telling the minister that his mother had died happily, trusting in Jesus, and that he, and his father, and his sister would be glad if Mr. Elkins would come and preach a funeral sermon. Thomas Lincoln praised the performance of his son, and the letter was despatched. As soon as possible the answer came, and it was to the effect that Mr. Elkins would be with them at a certain time. He had to journey a hundred miles to fulfil the engagement but he did so willingly, and found that young Abraham had been so busy making known the service, that there was quite a large congregation to hear the sermon. Mules and horses, ox-teams and waggons, had been pressed into service; and on a beautiful Sunday morning Parson Elkins stood at the head of the simple grave in the forest, and the people, old and young, pressed around to hear the words of life which he spoke. It was a simple service, but very solemn and beautiful. The hymn that rang through the air came from the hearts of the people; and they listened, as those who were in earnest, to the preacher's words, or joined with fervour in his prayer. Seeds were sown that day that brought forth fruit a hundred-fold.

When the congregation dispersed in silence, there remained, with his hat off, and his face full of serious resolve, the boy whom the dead woman had loved so dearly, and for whom she had prayed unceasingly. And who can tell what solemn vows, that were afterward fulfilled in the life, were made by young Abraham Lincoln, as he stood at his mother's grave on that never-to-be-forgotten day!

CHAPTER III.

A NEW MOTHER.

"Then spake the angel of mothers
To me in a gentle tone,
'Be kind to the children of others,
And God will bless thine own.'"

IT was a sad home in which Mr. Lincoln and his motherless children lived; but they made it as happy as they could. A school was opened in the neighbourhood by Mr. Crawford, who helped Abraham Lincoln in many things, and especially in arithmetic, of which the lad became very fond. He got to write so well that he became "the general letter-writer of the neighbourhood." His love of books grew upon him, and Mr. Crawford gratified it by lending him Ramsay's *Life of Washington*.

He ran home with it, and burst into the cabin in such a state of joyous excitement that his sister looked up in surprise.

"Why, Abe, what is the matter with you?"

"A new book! a new book!"

"Oh, capital!" said Sarah, who sympathised with everything that interested her brother. Indeed, the two, since their mother's death, had become more fond of each other than ever.

"What book is it?" cried the father, who was as rejoiced as his children over a new volume.

"It is another book about Washington; better than the other, because it has more solid facts, at least so Mr. Crawford says, and the writer's name is Ramsay."

"I will leave off my work then, and we will have some of it this evening."

So Thomas Lincoln sat by the fire-place in an attitude of rest and reflection, Sarah got her sewing or her knitting, and Abraham, with his back to the fire, so that the blaze might fall upon the book, read to his loving listeners hour after hour in such a way as to prove that he really entered into the spirit of the book. Indeed, he grew so interested in it that he did not wish to lay it aside either for sleep or for work. He read it the last thing at night and the first in the morning.

"Put down the book, Abe," his father would say, "and go and finish that wood."

"All right, father," said the lad; and immediately became so engrossed again in the book that he forgot everything else.

This was the case one night, and led to consequences that might have been very serious. He was reading after his father had retired to rest. Thomas, waking from a dream, to find his son still reading, became angry, and peremptorily ordered him to go to bed at once. Abraham laid down the book, and went off so hurriedly that he did not notice that he had placed it in the window. In the night a storm arose, and rain fell heavily. The next morning, when Abraham rose early, intending to have "one little read" before beginning the work of the day, he was dismayed to find that the rain had beaten in through the window, and the book was soaked through with water.

His heart sank at the remembrance of Mr. Crawford's assertion that that was the only copy of the book in the neighbourhood, and the thought that it had been spoiled through his carelessness. But he thought the best way would be to go to Mr. Crawford at once and confess the truth. So away he went to the schoolmaster, and with blushing face told his story.

"I am very sorry, sir, but I left your book near the window last night, and the rain came in and spoiled it."

"Let me look at it. Oh! what a pity. How could you be so careless, Abe?"

"I don't know, sir. I am ashamed of myself. I cannot pay for the damage, I know; no money could do it, and I have none; but if you will let me work out the cost I shall be very glad."

"I think you had better buy the book, Abe."

"Buy it, sir; how can I do that?"

"Come and pull fodder for me for two or three days, and the book shall be yours."

Very gratefully the boy set about the task; and Mr. Crawford had no reason to complain of the amount of work which he did in the time, and at the end of three days he went home, carrying the treasure that was now his own.

When Mrs. Lincoln had been dead a year, Mr. Lincoln married again. His second wife was a widow, Mrs. Sally Johnson of Elizabethtown, Kentucky. She had three children of her own, so that the family circle become considerably enlarged. Mrs. Lincoln proved a good and kind mother-in-law. She loved Abraham almost as much as if he were her own son. She pitied and admired him before she married his father; and it is said, indeed, that it was this love of the boy that was the chief reason of the union.

She soon set about making the home more comfortable.

"Cannot you make a puncheon floor, Thomas?" she asked of her husband.

A NEW MOTHER.

"I could, if I tried," said Mr. Lincoln.

"Then I wish you would try. The house would be so much more comfortable. We must make it as warm and cosy as we can for the children's sake. Abe is a great, strong fellow, who does not mind roughing it; but Sarah is only a delicate little girl, who needs taking care of."

And the good woman proceeded to take care of her excellently. She made warm, comfortable beds for both the children, and provided them with clothing thick and suitable for the cold weather; and made them both feel glad that they had once more a mother's loving care. Alas! Sarah did not live to enjoy it very long. She soon followed her own mother to heaven.

In the meantime Abraham Lincoln was growing in stature, and it seemed in favour also with God and man.

An incident occurred about this time which illustrated both his great strength and his kindness of heart. He and some other young men had been engaged in erecting the frame of a new house, when, as they were returning to their homes in the evening, they saw, standing by the roadside, a horse saddled and bridled.

"Hullo!" said young Lincoln, "here is Jim's horse. I suppose the stupid fellow is drunk, as usual. Let us see if we can find him."

A search was made, and presently the owner of the horse was discovered, chilled and unconscious.

"There let him lie, and serve him right," said one of the young men. "I hope it will teach him a lesson."

"It is more likely to kill him," said Abraham. "It is too bad to leave him here to die."

"Not at all. He has brought it on himself."

"Never mind. Here, lift him on my shoulders, will you? I will carry him to the nearest house."

And he did so. "Call and tell my father where I am,

please," he said to his companions; and then he remained with the drunken man until he became sober.

It was the first, but by no means the last life that Abraham Lincoln saved. It was the beginning of his career as a deliverer from slavery! It proved him to possess that kindness of heart which fits a man for any position, from the lowest to the highest.

His character was developing in many ways. Especially was he on the alert to obtain knowledge; and this perseverance helped him when another and less determined spirit would have failed.

The Rev. J. P. Gulliver once said to him in the afterward, when his high position was attained—" Mr. Lincoln, I very much want to know how you got your very unusual power of 'putting things.' No man has it by nature alone. What has your education been?"

Mr. Lincoln replied—" Well, as to education the newspapers are correct. I never went to school more than twelve months in my life. But, as you say, this must be a product of culture in *some* form. I have been putting the question you ask me to myself while you have been talking. I can say this, that among my earliest recollections, I remember how, when a mere child, I used to get irritated when anybody talked to me in a way I could not understand. I don't think I ever got angry at anything else in my life. But that always disturbed my temper, and has ever since. I can remember going to my little bed-room, after hearing the neighbours talk of an evening with my father, and spending no small part of the night walking up and down, and trying to make out what was the exact meaning of some of their, to me, dark sayings. I could not sleep, though I often tried to, when I got on such a hunt after an idea, until I had caught it; and when I thought I had got it, I was not satisfied until I had repeated it over and over—until I had put it in language plain enough, as I thought, for any boy I knew to comprehend. This was a kind of passion with me, and it has since stuck by me, for I am never easy now, when handling a thought, till I have bounded it north and bounded it south, bounded it east and bounded it west. Perhaps that accounts for the characteristics you observe in my speeches, though I never put the things together before."

Of his habits and deeds while he was still at home with his father and his stepmother we get a very good picture from Lamon's *Life of Abraham Lincoln:*—

"Abe never went to school again in Indiana or elsewhere. Mr. Turnham tells us that he had excelled all his masters, and it was no use for him to attempt to learn anything from them. But he continued his studies at home, or wherever he was hired out to work, with a perseverance which showed that he could scarcely live without some species of mental excitement. Abe loved to lie under a shade-tree, or up in the loft of the cabin, and read, cipher, and scribble. At night he sat by the chimney-'jamb,' and ciphered, by the light of the fire, on the wooden fire shovel. When the shovel was fairly covered he would shave it off with Tom Lincoln's knife, and begin again. In the daytime he used boards for the same purpose out of doors, and went through the shaving process everlastingly. His stepmother repeats often that he read every book he could lay his hands on. She says, 'Abe read diligently; and when he came across a passage that struck him, he would write it down on boards if he had no paper, and keep it there until he did get paper. Then he would re-write it, look at it, repeat it. He had a copy-book—a kind of scrap-book—in which he put down all things, and thus preserved them.'

"John Hanks came out from Kentucky when Abe was fourteen years of age, and lived four years with the Lincolns. We cannot describe some of Abe's habits better than John has described them for us:—When

Lincoln, Abe, and I returned to the house from work, he would go to the cupboard, snatch a piece of corn bread, take down a book, sit down in a chair, cock his legs up high as his head, and read. He and I worked barefooted, grubbed it, ploughed, mowed, and cradled together; ploughed corn, gathered it, and shucked corn. Abraham read constantly when he had opportunity; and he transferred extracts to the boards and the scrap-book. He had procured the scrap-book because most of his literature was borrowed; and he thought it profitable to take copious notes from the books before he returned them.

"At home, with his step-mother and the children, he was the most agreeable fellow in the world. He was always ready to do everything for everybody. When he was not doing some special act of kindness he told stories or cracked jokes. He was as full of his yarns in Indiana as ever he was in Illinois. Dennis Hanks was a clever hand at the same business, and so was old Tom Lincoln. Among them they must have made things very lively during the long winter evenings."

Mrs. Lincoln was never able to speak of Abe's conduct to her without tears. She spoke with deep emotion of her own son, but said she thought that Abe was kinder, better, truer than the other. Even the mother's instinct was lost as she looked back over those long years of poverty and privation in the Indian cabin, where Abe's grateful love softened the rigours of her lot, and his great heart and giant frame were always at her command. "Abe was a good boy," said she, "and I can say what scarcely one woman —a mother—can say in a thousand: Abe never gave me a cross word or look, and never refused, in fact or appearance, to do anything I asked him."

Abraham had another sorrow when his own mother had been dead four years. His sister Sarah died. She was married when she was only fourteen years old; and when she was fifteen she died. It was a great trouble to her brother, for the two had been not only brother and sister, but very close and dear friends.

When he was about eighteen years old, Abraham Lincoln left home on an expedition, and it came about in this wise:—

"We have more farm-produce than we shall require," said Thomas Lincoln.

"Let us sell it then," said his son.

"But how can we do that?"

"We will export it; that is the right thing to do with the over-abundance of any neighbourhood. Now, I will build a flat-boat, and take the produce down the river to the market, and there sell it."

"Could you build a boat?" asked his father.

"Yes, I'm sure I could, and I will too, if you only give me leave. I know the use of tools."

"But New Orleans is a long way off, and Abe is young," objected Mrs. Lincoln. "I don't think I could give my consent."

"I will not go unless you do, mother," said the lad; "but I should like to go very much. I want to see the world a little, and this will give me an opportunity."

"We could do a good deal better if we had more money," said Mr. Lincoln.

"Abe might get it this way."

"That is what I want to do, father. It is time I did more than I can do at home. You are not afraid to trust me, are you, mother?"

"Not at all, my boy; you will do what is right I know, for you are steady enough. You would not take to drinking whisky."

"Not I. I have never tasted it, and do not intend to do so."

"But if any harm should come to you, Abe, the extra money would do us very little good."

"But what harm will come? Let me try."

"Very well, you may try."

Abraham at once set to work. He had not many tools, but he was expert in the use of them, and was indeed rather fond of showing his mechanical skill. He lost no time in building a boat, and made it as complete as he could. When it was nearly finished, a steamer stopped opposite the place where he was at work. Two gentlemen wanted to be taken on board.

"Is that boat yours?" one inquired, looking at that which Abraham had made.

"Yes, sir."

"Will you take us and our luggage across to the steamer?"

"Certainly," said Abraham, beginning at once to shoulder the trunks. When they were placed on the flat-boat, the gentlemen sat on them. Abraham sculled them across. They sprang on the steamer, and the young man lifted the trunks on deck. Almost immediately the steamer started. But the gentlemen had forgotten to pay the young boatman, who had hoped to get some money. He thought he would remind them; he did not expect to get much; but he knew the service was worth something, and that he ought to get a little.

"You have forgotten to pay me," he said; and the two gentlemen, thus reminded, promptly threw each of them a silver half-dollar, which fell on the bottom of the boat. Abraham was delighted. He never forgot the pleasure it gave him, and he referred to the incident in after life. "It was the first dollar I had ever earned. I could scarcely believe my eyes. You may think it a very little thing, but it was a most important incident in my life. I could scarcely believe that I, a poor boy, had earned a dollar in less than a day. The world seemed wider and fairer before me. I was a more hopeful and confident being from that time."

When Abraham returned from the market, he settled down for a time to the ordinary work of the farm. He used to take the corn to the mill to get it ground. The mill was fifty miles away from where the Lincolns lived; so the grist was fastened to the back of a horse, and thus taken. The mill was driven by horse-power, and each customer had to use his own animal to grind his own corn, and each man had to wait his turn. On one occasion Abraham had fastened his mare to the lever, and he gave her a "cluck" and a cut with a switch: when she suddenly lifted her heels and kicked him. The blow sent him to the ground prostrate and insensible. As soon, however, as he came to himself, he finished the "cluck" that had been interrupted, and made the mare finish the work and carry the meal home.

He was fond of the water, and soon after took another trip. He was at this time nineteen years old, and was then six feet four high. All who knew him respected and trusted him.

"Abe," said a neighbour, "what do you say to a voyage down the Mississippi, and to take charge of my flat-boat and its cargo to the sugar plantation near New Orleans?"

"I should like it very much," said the young man, to whom a ride of eighteen hundred miles opened a delightful prospect of seeing the world.

"My son will go with you; but I shall trust the whole cargo, including him, to your care. I know that you have tact, ability, and honesty, and these will guide you. I shall invest a good round sum in the enterprise, but I am not afraid to trust you."

"I will go, and do the best I can for you," said the young man; and when the time for starting came, he set off in good spirits.

Sometimes the journey was easy and pleasant, the swift current of the "Father of Waters" bearing them along.

Sometimes they had to work hard with the long oars to keep the boat in safety. At night they tied-up alongside of the bank, and rested upon the hard deck, with a blanket for a covering; and during the hours of light—whether their lonely trip was cheered by a bright sun, or made disagreeable in the extreme by violent storms—their craft floated down the stream, its helmsmen never for a moment losing their spirits, or regretting their acceptance of the positions they occupied.

Some small adventures they had on their journey, talks with settlers and hunters, and other flat-boat men; but they had an adventure that was not small when they had come near to the end of their journey.

They had reached a sugar plantation between Natchez and New Orleans, and had pulled their boat in and fastened it to the shore for the night. But when they had lain down on their hard bed in the little cabin, they heard a scuffling. Abraham called out "Who's there?" Receiving no answer he went up on deck, and found seven negroes bent on plunder. He caught up a handspike and knocked one into the water; the second, third, and fourth were served the same way. The rest began to see that they had no ordinary assailant to deal with, and tried to run away; but Abraham and his companion leaped on shore and pursued them. The white young men were exhausted and hurt, though not seriously; but they drifted down the river for a few miles further before they again betook themselves to sleep.

The expedition was a very successful one; the cargo and the boat were disposed of advantageously, and Abraham Lincoln received ten dollars a-month for his services.

CHAPTER IV.

HIS OWN BUSINESS.

"Whatsoever thy hand findeth to do, do it with thy might."

THE father of Abraham Lincoln liked change, and by this time he had begun to grow tired of Indiana. In March 1830, when Abraham had just completed his majority, the family moved away from Indiana farm to the fertile prairie lands of Illinois. Dennis Hanks had been sent to see if the stories told were true ones; and as he brought back a good report, Thomas Lincoln sold his land, and they started. Their goods were packed in ox waggons, one of which was driven by Abraham. The journey occupied fifteen days; and in consequence of the heavy rain, which had swollen the rivers, was often very difficult. At one time, when they were crossing the lands by Kaskaskia River, the men had to wade through water that was several feet in depth. After a journey of two hundred miles they entered Macon County, in the State of Illinois; and Mr. Lincoln selected for his home a pleasant spot on the north side of the Sangamon River, where the prairie land was bordered by trees, about ten miles west of Decatur.

There they halted, and there a home was made. They first cleared a space for it, and next built a log-cabin. Forest trees were hewn down for the purpose, and then split. It took about four days to build the house, Abraham working harder than anyone until it was finished. It was "nine logs" high, and about eighteen feet by sixteen in size. It had a peaked roof. The trees used in the manufacture were hickory, hackberry, red elm, walnut, basswood, honey, locust, and sassafras. A half sheet of oiled paper let in the light. John Hanks afterwards exhibited this cabin with great pride, showing how he and Abraham Lincoln had worked together building and splitting rails. The only tools they had were a common axe, a broad axe, a hand-saw, and a "drawer" knife. The cabin is now in the museum of Mr. Barnum in New York.

When the house was finished, the young "rail-splitter,' as he was afterwards called, split rails enough to enclose a ten-acre lot; and having done that, he helped to plough and plant the ten-acre field, and then announced his intention of leaving his father's house, and beginning on his own account.

The author of the *Athens of America* speaks thus eloquently of Abraham Lincoln as he was at this time:— "His youth was now spent, and at the age of twenty-one he left his father's house to begin the world for himself. A small bundle, a laughing face, and an honest heart—these were his visible possessions, together with that unconscious character and intelligence which his country afterwards learned to prize. In the long history of 'worth depressed' there is no instance on record of such a contrast between the depression and the triumph . . . No academy, no university, no *alma mater* of science or learning had nourished him. No government had taken him by the hand, and given to him the gift of opportunity. No inheritance of land or money had fallen to him. No friend stood by his side. He was alone in poverty, and yet not all alone. There was God above, who watches all, and does not desert the lowly. Simple in life and manners, and knowing nothing of form or ceremony, with a village schoolmaster for six months as his only teacher, he had grown up in companionship with the people, with nature, with trees, with the fruitful corn, and with the stars. While yet a child his father had borne him away from a soil wasted by slavery, and he was now the citizen of a free state, where free labour had been placed under the safeguard of irreversible compact and fundamental law. And thus closed the youth of the future President, happy at least that he could go forth under the day-star of Liberty."

He began by hiring himself to a farmer in the neighbourhood. With four yoke of oxen he broke up fifty acres of prairie land. During the winter he was engaged in splitting rails and chopping wood.

A curious story was told to the Rev. A. Hale about him by Mrs. Brown. Mr. Lincoln's name was mentioned, and she said, "Well, I remember Mr. Linken. He worked with my old man thirty-four year ago, and made a crop. We lived on the same farm where we live now, and he worked all the season and made a crop of corn, and the next winter they hauled the crop all the way to Galena, and sold it for two dollars and a half a bushel. At that time there was no public-houses, and travellers were obliged to stay at any house at night that could take them in. One evening a right smart-looking man rode up to the fence, and asked my old man if he could take him in. 'Well,' said Mr. Brown, 'we can feed your critter and give you something to eat; but we can't lodge you unless you can sleep on the same bed with the hired man.' The man hesitated, and asked, 'Where is he?' and Mr. Brown took him round to where, in the shade of the house,

Mr. Lincoln lay his full length on the ground, with an open book before him. 'There he is,' said Mr. Brown. The stranger looked at him a minute, and then said, 'Well, I think he'll do,' and he stayed and slept with the future President of the United States."

George Cluse, who used to work with Abraham Lincoln at that time, says he was the roughest-looking young man he ever saw. He was tall, and angular, and ungainly. He was very badly dressed ; his trousers, which were made of flax and tow, were cut tight at the ankle, and were out at both knees. He split rails to get some better clothing, entering into a contract with Mrs. Nancy Miller "to split four hundred rails for every yard of brown jeans, dyed with white walnut bark, that would be necessary to make him a pair of trousers." He was not afraid of work, and often walked six or seven miles to get it.

His father and stepmother, and his half-brothers and sisters, had again removed from the Sangamon to Coles County, for they had all suffered from ague and fever. But although Abraham did not go with them, he always kept up a very loving connection with his family, showing many kindnesses to his father, who lived to complete his seventy-third year, and to see his son one of the most honoured men in the land.

The winter, which plunged the family into all the discomforts of ague, was a very severe one ; and as soon as the snow was melted Abraham was asked to join John D. Johnson, his stepmother's son, and John Hanks, a relative of his own mother, in another trip to New Orleans, for Mr. Dentun Offutt, a trader. When they joined Offutt they found that he had not been able to buy a boat as he expected, and although they were disappointed, they were unwilling to give up in despair, and so they decided to build a boat first. Every plank of their boat was sawed by hand with a ship saw ; and for building it the men received

HIS OWN BUSINESS.

twelve dollars a-month each. It was launched and taken to a spot where a drove of hogs were to be taken on board. Some of these were wild and difficult to manage. They were securely penned, but they could not be made to move towards the boat. They tried every plan they could think of to get them on board in vain, and at last Abraham Lincoln took them one by one into his long arms and carried them on board!

The expedition proved a very successful one; and when it was ended Offutt was so impressed with the honesty and capacity of Abraham Lincoln, that he invited him to become a clerk in his pioneer store, and take the management of it and a mill. This he did, and though he had not the graces and accomplishments of some modern young men, he speedily became a favourite, and was trusted and esteemed by all who knew him. The year that he spent in Mr. Offutt's store was of great service to him; and several characteristic tales are told of him having reference to this time.

On one occasion he sold some goods to a woman for which he charged her two dollars and six cents, which she accordingly paid him. After she had left he reckoned up the items again and found that he had charged her six cents too much. He knew he would not sleep with that on his mind; so when he had closed the store for the night he walked two or three miles to the house of the customer, and there handed back her change.

At another time, when it was nearly dark, a woman came in as the store was being closed, and asking for half-a-pound of tea. Lincoln weighed the tea and took the money; but the next morning as soon as he opened the shop he found that he had made a mistake the night before, and put a four-ounce instead of a half-pound weight on the scale. So he at once started, and without waiting for his breakfast took the woman the quarter of a pound of tea that belonged to her.

Abraham had some fighting to do while he was in Offutt's store. He was once serving some ladies, when a rough looking, rough-mannered fellow came in and began talking in very coarse and insulting language. Lincoln said quietly, " Don't you see there are ladies here ? If you have anything of this kind to say to me, cannot you wait until they have gone ? " " No," said the man, in a loud voice, "this is my time, and I shall say what I please." " You had better not," answered the store-clerk.

"You come on," said the man, threateningly ; " I will fight any man who presumes to tell me what I shall say."

"Very well," said Lincoln. "Wait a minute ; if you must be whipped I suppose I may as well whip you as any other man."

As soon as the ladies had left, Lincoln went out and punished the bully as he deserved. He threw him on the ground, and held him there while he rubbed his face with some " smart-weed " that grew near, until the man bellowed for mercy. Then Lincoln washed his face, and did what he could to alleviate the pain. He not only cured the man of his folly, but turned him into a friend.

There were living in the neighbourhood of Offutt's store at this time a number of roystering young men known as " The Clary Grove Boys." They called themselves " Regulators," and beat into submission those who refused to obey their rule. They were all very strong, very swift runners, and very unscrupulous. They made every new-comer try his skill with one of their number, and either fight, or wrestle, or run a race. They selected Jack Armstrong, their champion, to oppose Abraham Lincoln, who was nothing loth to try his strength. But it soon became evident that Abe was more than a match for their favourite ; and then, rather than allow their side to lose, they all set on the young man, struck and disabled him, and then Armstrong, by " legging " his opponent, managed to get him on his back. They quite expected that this would make Lincoln angry, in which case they would have beaten him severely; but Abe took the whole thing as a joke, and getting up from the ground with a smile of good-humour on his face, proved that he was as much master of his temper as of his right arm.

This so delighted the "boys" that they wished to make him one of their number, but he declined. His heart was set upon other and higher things. He read all the books he could get, and became especially anxious to be acquainted with the rudiments of grammar. Some one told him that a man who lived eight miles from New Salem had a copy of Kirkham's Grammar; so Lincoln walked the eight miles and borrowed it. He found it an excellent text book, and he had plenty of time to study it, for just then Offut's store was closed, and Lincoln was for the time out of employment. He used to take the book to the top of a hill outside of the village, and lie there studying with all his might until he had mastered it.

"If this is what is called science," he remarked to a friend, "I think I could subdue another."

About this time he joined some debating clubs, often walking seven or eight miles to attend a meeting. He called it "practising polemics."

John Hanks told a story (reproduced in Mudge's book) of how at this time he was one day at Decatur, when a political meeting was being addressed out of doors by a grey-headed man on the subject of the legislature of Vandalia. Lincoln and Hanks stopped to listen.

"Abe, you can beat that," said John; but Lincoln shook his head. Next a genteel young man spoke, and Hanks whispered, "Abe, I *know* you can beat that;" but the reply was "Oh, no, John, I guess not."

But Hanks excited some interest on Abraham's behalf, and presently there was a call for "Abraham Lincoln."

Abraham was without shoes or stockings, and the roads were muddy. He had coarse trousers, and his jacket was not too tidy; but just as he was he ascended a salt-box which served for a platform, and began to speak as if he were master of the subject in hand. The people listened with pleasure and astonishment.

"Young man, where did you learn all that?" demanded one.

"In my father's log-cabin," was the reply.

Lincoln lost no time in increasing his store of knowledge. He used to lie on a trundle bed, and rock the cradle in which his landlady's baby reposed, and read, and study, and think with all his power. He was willing to turn his hands and his head to any good work; and we give two little bits of his speeches, that it may be seen what were his ideas in regard to work, though they were not uttered until a later period of his history:—

"My understanding of the hired labourer is this: A young man finds himself of an age to be dismissed from parental control; he has for his capital nothing save two strong hands that God has given him, a heart willing to labour, and a freedom to choose the mode of his work and the manner of his employer; he has no soil nor shop, and he avails himself of the opportunity of hiring himself to some man who has capital to pay him a fair day's wage for a fair day's work. He is benefited by availing himself of that privilege; he works industriously, he behaves soberly, and the result of a year or two's labour is a surplus of capital. Now he buys land on his own hook, he settles, marries, begets sons and daughters, and in course of time he, too, has enough capital to hire some new beginners.

"Our government was not established that one man might do with himself what he pleased, and with another man too. . . . I say, whereas God Almighty has given every man one mouth to be fed, and one pair of hands adapted to furnish food for that mouth, if anything can be proved to be the will of heaven it is proved by this fact— that that mouth is to be fed by those hands, without being interfered with by any other man, who has also his mouth to feed and his hands to labour with. I hold that if the Almighty had ever made a set of men that should do all the eating and none of the work, He would have made them with mouths only and no hands; and if He had ever made another class that he intended should do all the work and none of the eating, He would have made them without mouths and with all hands."

Abraham Lincoln was known to be an honest workman, and he was employed by those whose trust he had secured; but he was at this time miserably poor, and looking out for some means of subsistence. But he had faith in God; and was beginning to feel that the life which was before him would be a grander thing than he had dreamed in his boyhood. He still lacked confidence in himself, but he was biding his time, and waiting for opportunities which were certain to come.

CHAPTER V.

LAWYER LINCOLN.

" It was a link from youth to age—
A harbinger of good presage,
With youth, and age, and heaven allied,
With liberty on virtue's side."
—BLANCHARD.

IN the spring of 1832 Black Hawk, a celebrated Indian chief, came down the Mississippi, and declared his intention of ascending the Rock River to the territory of the Winnebagoes. As this was in direct opposition to the terms of the treaty, which confined him to the western bank of the Mississippi, Governor Reynolds called for volunteers to fight him. Abraham Lincoln was the first to enlist, and he was soon followed by other men from New Salem and Clary's Grove. A meeting was held at Richland for the election of officers. The Clary Grove Boys told Lincoln that he must be their captain, which, however, he felt was too great an honour. He was compelled, however, to become one of the candidates, and the other was a Mr. Kirkpatrick, one of Lincoln's former employers. The election was conducted in a very simple fashion. The two candidates were told to stand apart, and the men were to range themselves beside the man of their choice. Three out of every four went at once to Lincoln, who felt much gratified at that which proved him to have gained the good-will of so many who knew him.

Captain Lincoln's company and others were ordered to rendezvous at Beardstown, and here he met for the first time the Hon. John T. Stewart, a lawyer and a gentleman. General Samuel Whiteside was in command, and the men had some severe marching, but the Black Hawk war was remarkable for nothing.

Mr. Lincoln spoke of it afterwards in the following humorous terms, when the friends of General Cass were endeavouring to prove him a hero:—"By the way, Mr. Speaker, did you know I am a military hero? Yes, sir, in the days of the Black Hawk war I fought, bled, and came away. Speaking of General Cass's career reminds me of my own. I was not at Stillman's defeat, but I was about as near it as Cass to Hull's surrender. It is quite certain I did not break my sword, for I had none to break. If Cass broke his sword, the idea is he broke it in desperation. I bent my musket by accident. If General Cass went in advance of me in picking whortleberries, I guess I surpassed him in charges upon the wild onions. If he saw any live fighting Indians, it is more than I did; but I had a good many bloody struggles with the mosquitoes, and though I never fainted from loss of blood, I can truly say I was often very hungry. Mr. Speaker, if I should ever conclude to doff whatever our Democratic friends may suppose there is of black-cockade Federation about me, and thereupon they should take me up as a candidate for the Presidency, I protest they shall not make fun of me, as they have of General Cass, by attempting to write me into a military hero."

His military campaign, if it did nothing else for Abraham Lincoln, must have given him a great increase of self-confidence, for on his return he became a candidate for representative in the State Legislature, an election being near. He was then twenty-three, and comparatively unknown. Party feeling ran very high between the friends of General Jackson and Henry Clay. Lincoln was for the latter. He was not elected; but such was his popularity in his own neighbourhood that two hundred and seventy-seven out of the two hundred and eighty-four votes taken in the precincts were given to him.

His defeat in no wise discouraged him. He turned his attention to business. He became a partner in a store; but he was less successful than he had been in his political essay. Holland, in his admirable *Life of Lincoln*, says:—
" About this time Mr. Lincoln was appointed postmaster by President Jackson. The office was too insignificant to be considered politically; and it was given to the young man because everybody liked him, and because he was the only man willing to take it who could make out the returns. He was exceedingly pleased with the appointment, because it gave him a chance to read every newspaper that was taken in the vicinity. He had never been able to get half the newspapers he wanted before, and the office gave him the prospect of a constant feast. Not wishing to be tied to the office, as it gave him no revenue that would reward him for the confinement, he made a post-office of his hat. Whenever he went out the letters were placed in his hat. When an anxious looker for a letter found the postmaster he found his office; and the public officer, taking off his hat, looked over his mail wherever the public might find him. He kept the office until it was discontinued, or removed to Petersburgh."

An interesting story is told in connection with this. Some years afterwards he was suddenly called upon to settle his account with the Post-Office Department. Seeing a look of perplexity upon his face, a friend said—"Lincoln, if you are in want of money, let us help you." But he went to a little old trunk hidden away under some books, opened it, and took out a little parcel of coin, counting the seventeen dollars, which was the exact sum required. Hardly pressed by poverty as he was, he had not used the money that did not belong to him, but had carefully kept it until it should be asked for.

About this time, hearing that there was a chance of work as an assistant surveyor, he began the study, and procured a compass. At first he was too poor to buy a chain, and so he used a grape-vine. Sometime afterward, having become a surety for a debt, his compass and chain were sold, but subsequently returned to him.

Lincoln had some good friends—Mr. Greene, Major Stewart, and others. The latter strongly advised him to study the law, and nothing loth, he at once set about it. He bought a copy of Blackstone at a book auction in Springfield, and the major lent him others. He was once asked by the Rev. J. P. Gulliver—"Did you not have a law education? How did you prepare for your profession?"

He replied—"Oh, yes; I 'read law'—as the phrase is; that is, I became a lawyer's clerk in Springfield, and copied tedious documents, and picked up what I could of law in the intervals of other work. But your question reminds me of a bit of education I had, which I am bound in honesty to mention. In the course of my law-reading I constantly came upon the word *demonstrate*. I thought at first that I understood its meaning, but soon became satisfied that I did not. I said to myself—What do I do when I demonstrate more than when I *reason* or *prove?* How does demonstration differ from any other proof? I consulted *Webster's Dictionary*. That told of 'certain proof'—'proof beyond the possibility of doubt;' but I could form no idea what sort of proof that was. I thought a great many things were proved beyond a possibility of doubt without recourse to any such extraordinary process of reasoning as I understood 'demonstrate' to be. I consulted all the dictionaries and books of reference I could find, but with no better results. You might as well have defined *blue* to a blind man. At last I said, 'Lincoln, you can never make a lawyer if you do not understand what *demonstrate* means;' and I left my situation in Springfield, went home to my father's house, and stayed there till I could give any propositions in the six books of *Euclid* at sight. I then found out what 'demonstrate' meant, and went back to my law-studies."

Dr. Brockett says—"He was compelled to prosecute his studies somewhat at a disadvantage, both from the necessity of supporting himself meanwhile by his own labour, and the time and attention which his position obliged him to give to politics. But nothing could prevent the consummation of his purpose; and having completed the preliminary studies, he was admitted to practice in 1836. He was what is called in the West 'a rising man,' and he commenced practice with a reputation which speedily brought him plenty of business, and placed him in the front rank of his profession. He displayed remarkable ability as an advocate in jury trials, and a ready perception and sound judgment of the turning legal points of a case. Many of his law arguments were masterpieces of logical reasoning. His forensic efforts all bore the stamp of masculine common sense, and he had a natural, easy mode of illustration that made the most abstruse subjects appear plain. Indeed, clear, practical sense, and skill in homely or humorous illustration, were the especially noticeable traits in his arguments. The graces of a polished rhetoric he certainly had not, nor did he aim to acquire them. His style of expression and the cast of his thought were his own, having all the native force of a genuine originality."

Dr. Brockett mentions, as several of Lincoln's biographers do, an incident told by one who wrote from personal knowledge. It was in connection with a son of the man named Armstrong, the champion of the Clary Grove Boys, who had proved himself a kind friend to Lincoln, and who was now dead. This young man was accused of murder. The public mind was in a state of great excitement, and the mob would have slain young Armstrong without a trial if he had not been kept securely in prison. At the preliminary examination the accuser swore so positively that it seemed there could be no hope for the young man, who abandoned himself to despair. "At this juncture," says the narrator, "the widow received a letter from Mr. Lincoln, volunteering his services in an effort to save the youth from the impending stroke. Gladly was his aid accepted, although it seemed impossible for even his sagacity to prevail in such a desperate case; but the heart of the attorney was in his work, and he set about it with a will that knew no such word as fail. Feeling that the poisoned condition of the public mind was such as to preclude the possibility of impannelling an impartial jury in the court having jurisdiction, he procured a change of *venue* and the postponement of the trial. He then went studiously to work, unravelling the history of the case, and satisfied himself that his client was the victim of malice, and that the statements of the accuser were a tissue of falsehoods.

"When the trial was called on, the prisoner, pale and emaciated, with hopelessness written on every feature, and accompanied by his half-hoping, half-despairing mother—whose only hope was in a mother's belief in a son's innocence—in the justice of the God she worshipped, and in the noble counsel who, without hope of fee or reward upon earth, had undertaken the cause—took his seat in the prisoner's box, and with a 'stony firmness' listened to the reading of the indictment. Lincoln sat quietly by, whilst the large auditory looked on him as though wondering what he could say in defence of one whose guilt they regarded as certain. The examination of the witnesses for the State was begun, and a well-arranged mass of evidence, circumstantial and positive, was introduced, which seemed to impale the prisoner beyond the possibility of extrication. The counsel for the defence propounded but few questions, and those of a character which excited no uneasiness on the part of the prosecutor—merely in most cases requiring the main witnesses to be definite as to time and place. When the evidence of the prosecution was ended, Lincoln introduced a few witnesses to remove some erroneous impressions in regard to the previous character of his client, who, though somewhat rowdyish, had never been known to commit a vicious act; and to show that a greater degree of ill-feeling existed between the accuser and the accused than between the accuser and the deceased.

"The prosecutor felt that his case was a clear one, and his opening speech was brief and formal. Lincoln arose, while a deathly silence pervaded the vast audience, and, in a clear and moderate tone, began his argument. Slowly and carefully he reviewed the testimony, pointing out the hitherto unobserved discrepancies in the statements of the principal witness. That which had seemed plain and plausible he made to appear crooked as a serpent's path. The witness had stated that the affair took place at a certain hour in the evening, and that by the aid of the brightly shining moon he saw the prisoner inflict the death-blow with a sling-shot. Mr. Lincoln showed that at the hour referred to the moon had not yet appeared above the horizon, and consequently the whole tale was a fabrication.

"An almost instantaneous change seemed to have been wrought in the minds of his auditors, and a verdict of *Not Guilty* was at the end of every tongue. But the orator was not content with this intellectual achievement, his whole being had for months been bound up in this work of gratitude and mercy, and as the lava of the overcharged crater bursts from its imprisonment, so great thoughts and burning words leaped forth from the soul of the eloquent Lincoln. He drew a picture of the perjurer so horrid and ghastly that the accuser could sit under it no longer, but reeled and staggered from the court-room, whilst the audience fancied they could see the brand upon his brow. Then in words of thrilling pathos Lincoln appealed to the jurors as fathers of some who might become fatherless, and as husbands of wives who might be widowed, to yield to no previous impressions, no ill-founded prejudice, but to do his client justice; and as he alluded to the debt of gratitude which he owed the boy's sire, tears were seen to fall from many eyes unused to weep.

"It was near night when he concluded by saying that if justice was done—as he believed it would be—before the sun should set, it would shine upon his client a free man. The jury retired, and the court adjourned for the day. Half-an-hour had not elapsed, when, as the officers of the court and the volunteer attorney sat at the tea-table of their hotel, a messenger announced that the jury had returned to their seats. All repaired immediately to the court-house, and while the prisoner was being brought from the jail, the court-room was filled to overflowing with citizens from the town. When the prisoner and his mother entered, silence reigned as though the house were empty. The foreman of the jury, in answer to the usual inquiry from the court, delivered the verdict of *Not Guilty*. The widow dropped into the arms of her son, who lifted her up, and told her to look upon him as before, free and innocent. Then, with the words, 'Where is Mr. Lincoln?' he rushed across the room and grasped the hand of his deliverer, whilst his heart was too full for utterance. Lincoln turned his eyes towards the west, where the sun still lingered in view, and then, turning to the youth, said, 'It is not yet sundown, and you are free.' I confess," adds the narrator, "that my cheeks were not wholly unwet by tears, and I turned from the affecting scene. As I cast a glance behind, I saw Abraham Lincoln obeying the divine injunction by comforting the widow and fatherless."

There are other stories told of him which prove him to have been both kindly and just. He was employed by a Mr. Cogdal, who had been unfortunate in business, to manage the winding-up of his affairs. Mr. Cogdal gave him a note promising to pay. Sometime after the man met with an accident, and lost the use of his arm through an explosion of gunpowder. Mr. Lincoln met him one day and inquired kindly how he was. "I am getting along poor enough," was the reply, "and I have been thinking about that note." Mr. Lincoln put the note at once into Cogdal's hand. "There, think no more about it," he said, and went quickly away so as to give the man no time to express his thanks.

A poor woman once came to Mr. Lincoln's office in great trouble. "My husband was a revolutionary soldier," she said, "and I have had to employ a pension-agent to get my claim to a pension settled by the government."

"Has he done it?"

"Yes, but he has made me pay him two hundred dollars for his services. It is all the money I have. It has ruined me. I have not even enough to pay my fare home."

"His charge was wicked and exorbitant," said Lincoln. "I will make him pay some of it back to you."

He gave that poor widow the money to pay her fare home, and commenced a suit against the dishonest agent, which was successful. Mr. Lincoln stood by at the end of the suit, and watched, with great glee, while a hundred dollars were returned to the widow.

There were two classes of persons with whom, as will be readily imagined, he had great sympathy, and for whom his services were always available—the negroes, and their friends who had helped them to escape. It made a lawyer very unpopular to undertake the defence of the latter, but Lincoln was never afraid to risk his reputation and lose his money by helping the cause of the workers on " the underground railroad," as the system was called which sheltered slaves who were trying to escape.

Mr. Mudge tells the following story of a negro mother who came to Abraham Lincoln in her trouble:—"She and her family were brought by her master from Kentucky into Illinois, and set free. Her oldest son, upon whom she was dependent, had gone down the Mississippi on a steamboat as a waiter. On his arrival at New Orleans, he unwisely went ashore, and was arrested and thrown into prison, for no reason, except that he was a free negro, from a non-slaveholding State. This outrage was further aggravated by a threatened sale into slavery to pay his jail expenses. The feelings of Mr. Lincoln were aroused. He went at once to the Governor to inquire if he could render any official aid to the young man. The Governor replied that he was sorry to say he could do nothing. The powerful passions of Mr. Lincoln lost their usual restraint, and found expression in language he seldom used. He declared he would have the negro back or have a twenty years' agitation in Illinois; the people should be stirred up until the Governor was invested with constitutional authority in such matters. But it was well for the young coloured man that he was not compelled to wait the result of a twenty years' agitation. Upon a sober second thought Mr. Lincoln and his partner made up a purse, and sent it to a New Orleans correspondent, who procured the negro's release, and returned him to his mother."

CHAPTER VI.

A HUSBAND AND A FATHER.

> "Then earth takes on a livelier hue,
> And heaven distils her pearly dew;
> And life and beauty crown the heath
> With genial summer's emerald wreath."

EVEN before Abraham Lincoln had gained his reputation as a lawyer, he had again tried to obtain a seat in the Legislature, and this time had succeeded. This was in 1834. A writer says of him—"He had not yet acquired position. At this time he was very plain in his costume, as well as rather uncourtly in his dress and appearance. His clothing was of homely Kentucky jean, and the first impression made upon those who saw him was not specially prepossessing. He had not outgrown his hard backwood experience, and showed no inclination to disguise or to cast behind him the honest and manly, though unpolished characteristics of his early days. Never was a man further removed from all snobbish affectation. As little was there, also, of the demagogue art of assuming an uncouthness or rusticity of manner and outward habit, with a mistaken motive of thus securing particular favour as one of the masses. He chose to appear then, as he has at all times since, precisely what he was. His deportment was unassuming, though without any awkwardness or reserve. During this, his first session in the Legislature, he was taking lessons, as became his youth and inexperience, and preparing himself for the future by close observation and attention to business, rather than by a prominent participation in debate. He seldom or never took the floor to speak, although before the close of this and the succeeding special session of the same Legislature, he had shown, as previously in any other capacity in which he was engaged, qualities that clearly pointed to him as fitted to act a leading part."

In 1836 he was again a candidate for the Legislature, and was re-elected. The election was a very exciting one, and he both wrote to the papers and gave addresses. His first remarkable speech was made on behalf of a friend on this occasion. Holland thus describes it:—"Lincoln took his turn upon the platform. Embarrassed at first, and speaking slowly, he began to lay down and fix his propositions. His auditors followed him with breathless attention, and saw him enclose his adversary in a wall of fact, and then weave over him a network of deductions, so logically tight in all its meshes that there was no escape for the victim. He forgot himself entirely as he grew warm at his work. His audience applauded; and with ridicule and wit he riddled the man whom he had made helpless. Men who remember the speech allude particularly to the transformation which it wrought in Mr. Lincoln's appearance. The homely man was majestic; the plain, good-natured face was full of expression; the long, bent figure was straight as an arrow; and the kind and dreamy eyes flashed with the fire of true inspiration. His reputation was made, and from that day to the day of his death he was recognised in Illinois as one of the most powerful orators in the State." "The Sangamon County Delegation," which consisted of nine representatives, was remarkable for the height of its members. Mr. Lincoln was the tallest, but not a man of them was less than six feet high. They used to be called "the Long Nine." Lincoln had the second place on the Committee on Public Accounts and Expenditure. He was thrown into contact with some of the best and most able men of this new State. They were chiefly occupied with measures for public improvements. Mr. Lincoln, during this session, became acquainted with Stephen A. Douglass, who was characterised by Lincoln as "the least man he ever saw." He was both slight and short. They worked together in this session, which saw Mr. Lincoln take, for the first time, his stand on the Anti-Slavery side. He was careful, however, to avoid identifying himself with the theoretical Abolitionists of the day, and declared that he thought them illegal; but he announced his belief that "the institution of slavery was founded on both injustice and bad policy."

He was still very poor. He had walked to Vandalia, where the House met, which was a hundred miles from his home, and when the session was over he walked home again. He was the only one of the "Long Nine" who did not possess a horse; and, of course, at that time there were no railways. He was very thinly clad; and when he complained of the cold, one of his companions remarked, looking down at the large feet of the future President, "It is no wonder you are cold, Abe, there is so much of you on the ground."

In 1838 he was elected for the third, and in 1840 for the fourth time to a seat in the Legislature; and in 1840 Mr. Lincoln engaged to fight a duel.

The quarrel was originally none of his, but he made it so. It arose out of the publication of a sarcastic poem in the *Sangamon Journal*, which was understood to refer to Mr. James Shields. He called on the editor, and demanded the name of the writer. This the editor refused to give, as the writer was a lady. But the lady was a friend of Lincoln's, and he told Shields that he held himself responsible for the poem. So a duel was decided upon, which was to take place in a neutral territory on the Mississippi, called Bloody Island. But no blood was shed there on that occasion. A reconciliation was effected, and the duel was happily prevented.

In 1842, and when he was thirty-three years old, Mr. Lincoln was married to Miss Mary Todd, daughter of the Hon. Robert S. Todd of Kentucky. He wrote to a friend, J. F. Speed, Esq., just after:—" We are not keeping house, but boarding at the Globe Tavern, which is very well kept now by a widow lady of the name of Beck. Our rooms are the same Dr. Wallace occupied there, and boarding only costs four dollars a-week. . . . I most heartily wish you and your family will not fail to come. Just let us know the time a week in advance, and we will have a room prepared for you, and we will all be merry together for a while."

After his marriage Mr. Lincoln remained several years in private life, practising law with considerable success. He was too conscientious a man, however, to try to shield those whom he knew to be guilty from the punishment which they deserved.

Mr. Lincoln became the father of four children, all sons— Robert Todd, Edward, who died in infancy, William, who died in Washington during the presidency of his father, and Thomas, nicknamed by his father "Tadpole," and generally called Tad. Their home was in a pleasant house at Springfield, very different from the log-cabin in which their father was born. He was a very loving parent, never impatient with the restlessness of the children, but always kind, tender, and indulgent. He used to be seen wheeling them about in a child's gig, up and down the path in front of the house, often without hat or coat on, with his hands behind, holding the little carriage, and his thoughts evidently far away. He was very absent-minded: some people used to say he was crazy, he seemed to be so full of thought; but all the while he was preparing for his future work and responsibility. His wife was a good woman, of the Presbyterian Church, and Mr. Lincoln, though not a member, attended with her. The Sunday-school and all benevolent institutions found in him a good friend and helper. But he was especially the friend and teacher of his own children. He used to say to them when they exhibited any unlovely tendencies in temper and disposition, "You break my heart when you act like this."

In the meantime great events were occurring, and Abraham Lincoln was known to be a man who would serve his party well. There was a growing feeling against slavery, and he had taken a very decided stand on the side of its enemies. Soon after his marriage he was expecting a nomination to Congress; but the convention of his county sent him as a delegate to nominate another man. He referred to this in his own playful manner—"In getting Baker the nomination, I shall be fixed a good deal like a fellow that is made groomsman to the man who has cut him out, and is marrying his own dear gal." But he behaved loyally to his rival, and supported him with sincerity and zeal. And Lincoln bided his time.

In 1854 a new political era opened. Holland, in his *Life of Lincoln*, thus describes the crisis:—" Events occurred of immeasurable influence upon the country; and an agitation of the slavery question was begun, which was destined not to cease until slavery itself should be destroyed. Disregarding the pledges of peace and harmony, the party in the interest of slavery effected in Congress the abrogation of the Missouri Compromise of 1820—a compromise which was intended to shut slavery for ever out of the north-west; and a bill organising the territories of Kansas and Nebraska was enacted, which left them free to choose whether they would have slavery as an institution or not. The intention, without doubt, was to force slavery upon those territories—to make it impossible for them ever to become free States—as the subsequent exhibitions of "border ruffianism" in Kansas sufficiently testified. This great political iniquity aroused Mr. Lincoln as he had never before been aroused. It was at this time that he fully comprehended the fact that there was to be no peace on the slavery question until either freedom or slavery should triumph. He knew slavery to be wrong. He had always known and felt it to be so. He knew that he regarded the institution as the Fathers of the Republic had regarded it; but a new doctrine had been put forward. Slavery was right. Slavery was entitled to equal consideration with freedom. Slavery claimed the privilege of going wherever, into the national domain, it might choose to go. Slavery claimed national protection everywhere. Instead of remaining contentedly within the territory it occupied under the protection of the Constitution, it sought to extend itself indefinitely—to nationalise itself.

"Judge Douglas, of Illinois, was the responsible author of what was called the Kansas-Nebraska bill—a bill which he based upon what he was pleased to denominate 'popular sovereignty'—the right of a people of a territory to choose their own institutions: and between Judge Douglas and Mr. Lincoln was destined to be fought 'the battle of the giants' on the questions that grew out of this great political crime. Mr. Lincoln's indignation was an index to the popular feeling all over the North. The men who, in good faith, had acquiesced in the compromise measures, though with great reluctance, and only for the sake of peace—who had compelled themselves to silence by biting their lips—who had been forced into silence by their love of the Union, whose existence the slave power had threatened—saw that they had been overreached and foully wronged."

It was on the occasion of a visit which Mr. Douglas paid to Springfield that the two men first measured swords in the great war of words which followed. The State Fair was being held at that time, and it had brought together a large number of representative men from all parts of the state. Mr. Douglas had been before the public all the time which Lincoln had spent in retirement, and he expounded his principles and policy with the bearing of a man who was all assurance and self-confidence; and the next day in answer to his speech Lincoln put forth all his powers. The *Springfield Journal* thus described the speaker and the scene:—

"He quivered with feeling and emotion. The whole house was as still as death. He attacked the Kansas-Nebraska bill with unusual warmth and energy, and all felt that a man of strength was its enemy, and that he intended to blast it if he could by strong and manly efforts. He was most successful; and the house approved the glorious triumph of truth by loud and long continued huzzas. Women waved their white handkerchiefs in token of woman's silent but heartfelt consent. . . . Mr. Lincoln exhibited Douglas in all the attitudes he could be placed in in a friendly debate. He exhibited the bill in all its aspects, to show its humbuggery and falsehoods, and when thus torn to rags, cut into slips, held up to the gaze of the vast crowd, a kind of scorn was visible upon the face of the crowd, and upon the lips of the most eloquent speaker." The editor in concluding his account says—"At the conclusion of the speech, every man felt that it was unanswerable—that no human power could overthrow it, or trample it under foot. The long and repeated applause evinced the feeling of the crowd, and gave tokens of universal assent to Lincoln's whole argument; and every mind present did homage to the man who took captive the heart, and broke like a sun over the understanding."

The fight thus commenced was a long one. Mr. Lincoln

during the campaign thus expressed his ideas in regard to the Declaration of Independence:—"These communities, the thirteen colonies, by their representatives in the old Independence Hall, said to the world of men, 'We hold these truths to be self-evident, that all men are born equal; that they are endowed by their Creator with inalienable rights; that among these are life, liberty, and the pursuit of happiness.' This was their interpretation of the economy of the universe. This was their lofty, and wise, and noble understanding of the justice of the Creator to His creatures. Yes, gentlemen, to all His creatures, to the whole great family of man. In their enlightened belief, nothing stamped with the divine image and likeness was sent into the world to be trodden on, and degraded, and embruted by its fellows. They grasped not only the race of men then living, but they reached forward and seized upon the furthest posterity. They created a beacon to guide their children, and their children's children, and the countless myriads who should inhabit the earth in other ages. Wise statesmen as they were, they knew the tendency of prosperity to breed tyrants, and so they established these great self-evident truths that when, in the distant future, some man, some faction, some interest should set up the doctrine that none but rich men, or none but white men, or none but Anglo-Saxon white men, were entitled to life, liberty, and the pursuit of happiness, their posterity might look up again to the Declaration of Independence, and take courage to renew the battle which their fathers began, so that truth, and justice, and mercy, and all the humane and Christian virtues, might not be extinguished from the land; so that no man would hereafter dare to limit and circumscribe the great principles on which the temple of liberty was being built.

"Now, my countrymen, if you have been taught doctrines conflicting with the great landmarks of the Declaration of Independence; if you have listened to suggestions which would take away from its grandeur, and mutilate the fair symmetry of its proportions; if you have been inclined to believe that all men are not created equal in those inalienable rights enumerated by our chart of liberty, let me entreat you to come back—return to the fountain whose waters spring close by the blood of the Revolution. Think nothing of me, take no thought for the political fate of any man whomsoever, but come back to the truths that are in the Declaration of Independence.

"You may do anything with me you choose, if you will but heed these sacred principles. You may not only defeat me for the Senate, but you may take me and put me to death. While pretending no indifference to earthly honours, I *do claim* to be actuated in this contest by something higher than an anxiety for office. I charge you to drop every paltry and insignificant thought for any man's success. It is nothing; I am nothing; Judge Douglas is nothing. *But do not destroy that immortal emblem of humanity—the Declaration of American Independence.*"

From 1858 Lincoln and Douglas were engaged in a grand fight. Debates were held at Ottawa, Freeport, Jonesborough, Charleston, Galesburg, Quincy, and Alton, and they were said to be unsurpassed in campaign annals for eloquence, ability, earnestness, adroitness, and comprehensiveness. The two rivals often travelled together in the same car or carriage, and were friendly so far as the manifestation of good feeling was concerned, though each fought the other with uncompromising vigour. Douglas once pronounced this graceful eulogy upon his opponent, at Springfield :—" I take great pleasure in bearing my testimony to the fact that Mr. Lincoln is a kind-hearted, amiable, good-natured gentleman, with whom no man has a right to pick a quarrel, even if he wanted one. He is a worthy gentleman. I have known him for twenty-five years; and there is no better citizen, and no kinder-hearted man. He is a fine lawyer, possesses high ability; and there is no objection to him, except the monstrous revolutionary doctrines with which he is identified."

Perhaps the greatest of Lincoln's speeches was made at New York, at the Cooper Institute, on the 27th of February 1860. William Cullen Bryant presided, and the crowded audience received Mr. Lincoln with demonstrations of the greatest enthusiasm. He closed with these words:— " Neither let us be slandered from our duty by false accusations against us, not frightened from it by measures of destruction to the government, nor of dangers to ourselves. Let us have faith that right makes might, and in that faith let us to the end dare to do our duty as we understand it."

He stood now at the close of his old life and the beginning of the new; and of his appearance at the time a writer gives the following pen-portrait:—" Mr. Lincoln stands six feet and four inches high in his stockings. His frame is not muscular, but gaunt and wiry; his arms are long, but not unreasonably so for a person of his height; his lower limbs are not disproportioned to his body. In walking, his gait, though firm, is never brisk. He steps slowly and deliberately, almost always with his head inclined forward, and his hands clasped behind his back. In matters of dress he is by no means precise. Always clean, he is never fashionable; he is careless, but not slovenly. In manner he is remarkably cordial, and at the same time simple. His politeness is always sincere, but never elaborate or oppressive. A warm shake of the hand, and a warmer smile of recognition, are his methods of greeting his friends. At rest, his features, though those of a man of mark, are not such as belong to a handsome man; but when his fine dark grey eyes are lighted up by any emotion, and his features begin their play, he would be chosen from among a crowd as one who had in him not only the kindly sentiments which women love, but the heavier metal of which full-grown men and presidents are made. His hair is black, and though thin, is wiry. His head sits well on his shoulders, but beyond that it defies description. It nearer resembles that of Clay than that of Webster; but it is unlike either. It is very large, and, phrenologically, well proportioned, betokening power in all its developments. A slightly Roman nose, a wide-cut mouth, and a dark complexion, with the appearance of having been weather-beaten, complete the description.

"In his personal habits Mr. Lincoln is as simple as a child. He loves a good dinner, and eats with the appetite which goes with a good brain; but his food is plain and nutritious. He never drinks intoxicating liquors of any sort, not even a glass of wine. He is not addicted to tobacco in any of its shapes. He was never accused of a licentious act in all his life. He never uses profane language. He never gambles; we doubt if he ever indulges in any game of chance. He is particularly cautious about incurring pecuniary obligations for any purpose whatever, and in debt he is never content until the score is discharged. We presume he owes no man a dollar. He never speculates. The rage for the sudden acquisition of wealth never took hold of him. His gains from his profession have been moderate, but sufficient for his purposes. While others have dreamed of gold, he has been in pursuit of knowledge. In all his dealings he has the reputation of being generous, but exact; and, above all, religiously honest. He would be a bold man who would say that Abraham Lincoln ever wronged any one out of a cent, or ever spent a dollar that he had not honestly earned. His struggles in early life have made him careful of money, but his generosity with his own is proverbial. He is a regular attendant upon religious worship, and though not a communicant, is a pew-holder and liberal supporter of the Presbyterian Church in Springfield, to which Mrs. Lincoln belongs. He is a scrupulous teller of the truth—too exact in his notions to suit the atmosphere of Washington as it is now. His enemies may say that he tells black Republican lies; but no man could ever say that, in a professional capacity, or as a citizen dealing with his neighbours, he would depart from the Scriptural command. At home he lives like a gentleman of modest means and simple tastes. A good-sized house of wood, simply but tastefully furnished, surrounded by trees and flowers, is his own, and there he lives, at peace with himself, the idol of his family, and, for his honesty, ability, and patriotism, the admiration of his countrymen."

CHAPTER VII.

NOMINATED AND ELECTED TO THE PRESIDENTIAL CHAIR.

"God cares, and humanity cares, and I care; and with God's help I shall not fail."

IN May 1859, at the Illinois State Republican Convention, an incident occurred which was amusing. Abraham Lincoln attended as a spectator, and his entrance was greeted with applause. He had scarcely taken his seat, when the Governor of the State arose, and said that an old democrat wished to make a presentation to the Convention. Leave was granted, and in came Lincoln's old friend Hanks, bearing with him two old fence-rails, gaily decorated, and bearing this inscription:—

"ABRAHAM LINCOLN,
The Rail Candidate for the Presidency in 1860. Two Rails from a lot of three thousand made in 1830, by
THOMAS HANKS AND ABE LINCOLN,
Whose father was the first pioneer of Macon County."

The effect of the introduction of these rails upon an audience already excited was to increase enthusiasm, as such melo-dramatic incidents often do. One would have thought that to have been a rail-splitter was the greatest and best training for a President, according to the ideas of the people. It is said that they cheered and shouted for a quarter-of-an-hour, and compelled Mr. Lincoln to tell them the story of those rails. He did so; they were some of the rails he had split for his father's log-cabin. He himself thought it would have been better if, instead of splitting rails, he had been preparing by work in school or college for future duties and responsibilities; but the people loved him all the more because he had been one of themselves. They raised a cry which was taken up by the toilers in all parts of the West!—"The rail-splitter of Illinois is the people's choice for the Presidency." His enemies despised him for his lowly youth; some of his friends regretted that the name of "rail-splitter" should be associated with him; but he, never ashamed of the circumstances of his birth, and never parading his poor origin, went steadily onward and upward in his course.

Mr. Buchanan, the President of the United States, had not seen his way to oppose slavery, and the tenure of his office would expire in March 1861. It was time to fix upon a President-elect, and on the 18th of May 1860 there was a meeting of the Republican National Convention, "in an immense building which the people of Chicago had put up for the purpose, called the Wigwam. There were four hundred and sixty-five delegates. The city was filled," says Raymond, "with earnest men who had gathered to press the claims of their favourite candidates, and the halls and corridors of all the hotels swarmed and buzzed with an eager crowd, in and out of which darted or pushed their way the various leaders of party politics." J. H. Holland, in his *Life of Abraham Lincoln*, thus describes the exciting scene:—

"On the assembling of the Convention everybody was

anxious to get at the decisive work, and as a preliminary, the various candidates in the field were nominated by their friends. Mr. Evarts of New York nominated Mr. Seward, and Mr. Judd of Illinois named Abraham Lincoln. Afterwards Mr. Dayton of New Jersey, Mr. Cameron of Pennsylvania, Mr. Chase of Ohio, Edward Bates of Missouri, and John McLean of Ohio, were formally nominated, but no enthusiasm was awakened by the mention of any names except those of Mr. Seward and Mr. Lincoln. Caleb B. Smith of Indiana seconded the nomination of Mr. Lincoln, as did also Mr. Delano of Ohio; while Carl Schurz of Wisconsin, and Mr. Blair of Michigan, seconded the nomination of Mr. Seward. It was certain that one of these two men would be nominated. On every pronunciation of their names, their respective partisans raised their shouts, vieing with each other in the strength of their applause. The excitement of this mass of men at that time cannot be measured by those not there, or by men in their sober senses.

"The ballot came. Maine gave nearly half her vote for Lincoln; New Hampshire seven of her ten for Lincoln. Massachusetts was divided. New York voted solid for Mr. Seward, giving him her seventy votes. Virginia, which was expected also to vote solid for Mr. Seward, gave fourteen of her twenty-two votes for Lincoln. Indiana gave her twenty-six votes for Lincoln without a break. Thus the balloting went on, amid the most intense excitement, until the whole number of four hundred and sixty-five votes was cast. It was necessary to a choice that one candidate should have two hundred and thirty-three. William H. Seward had one hundred and seventy-three and a half, Abraham Lincoln one hundred and two, Edward Bates forty-eight, Simon Cameron fifty and a half, Salmon P. Chase forty-nine. The remaining forty-two votes were divided among John McLean, Benjamin Wade, William

L. Dayton, John M. Reed, Jacob Collamer, Charles Sumner, and John C. Fremont—Reed, Sumner, and Fremont having one each.

On the second ballot the first gain for Lincoln was from New Hampshire. Then Vermont followed with her vote, which she had previously given to her senator, Mr. Collamer, as a compliment. Pennsylvania came next to his support, with the votes she had given to Cameron. On the whole ballot he gained seventy-nine votes, and received one hundred and eighty-one, while Mr. Seward received one hundred and eighty-four and a half votes, having gained eleven. The announcement of the votes given to Mr. Seward and Mr. Lincoln was received with deafening applause by their respective partisans. Then came the third ballot. All felt that it was likely to be the decisive one, and the friends of Mr. Seward trembled for the result. Hundreds of pencils were in operation, and before the result was announced, it was whispered through the immense and excited mass of people that Abraham Lincoln had received two hundred and thirty-one and a half votes, only lacking one vote and a half of an election. Mr. Carther of Ohio was up in an instant, to announce the change of four votes of Ohio from Mr. Chase to Mr. Lincoln. That finished the work. The excitement had culminated. After a moment's pause, like the sudden and breathless stillness that precedes the hurricane, the storm of wild, uncontrollable, and almost insane enthusiasm descended. The scene surpassed description. During all the ballotings a man had been standing upon the roof communicating the results to the outsiders, who in surging masses far outnumbered those who were packed in the Wigwam. To this man one of the secretaries shouted—"Fire the salute! Abe Lincoln is nominated!" Then, as the cheering inside died away, the roar began on the outside, and swelled up from the excited masses like the noise of many waters. This the insiders heard, and to it they replied. Thus deep called to deep with such a frenzy of sympathetic enthusiasm that even the thundering salute of cannon was unheard by many upon the platform.

"When the multitudes became too tired to cheer more, the business of the Convention proceeded. Half-a-dozen men were on their feet announcing the change of votes of their States, swelling Mr. Lincoln's majority. Missouri, Iowa, Kentucky, Minnesota, Virginia, California, Texas, District of Columbia, Kansas, Nebraska, and Oregon insisted on casting unanimous votes for Mr. Lincoln, before the vote was declared. While these changes were going on, a photograph of the nominee was brought in and exhibited to the Convention. When the vote was declared, Mr. Evarts, on behalf of the New York delegation, expressed his grief that Mr. Seward had not been nominated, and then moved that the nomination of Mr. Lincoln should be made unanimous. John A. Andrew of Massachusetts, and Carl Schurz of Wisconsin, seconded the motion, and it was carried. Before the nomination of a vice-president, the Convention adjourned for dinner. It is reported that such had been the excitement during the morning session that men who never tasted intoxicating liquors staggered like drunken men on coming into the open air. The nervous tension had been so great that, when it subsided, they were as flaccid and feeble as if they had but recently risen from a fever."

In the meantime, two hundred miles away from the scene of all this excitement, Abraham Lincoln was quietly waiting in the office of the *Springfield State Journal.* He could not but be anxious, but he kept masterly control over himself, and talked to his friends while his fate seemed to hang in the balance. The news of the first and second ballots had been telegraphed to him, and he waited the result of the third.

Presently a boy entered the room, and went at once to Mr. Lincoln.

"Well?"

"The nomination has taken place, and Mr. Seward—is not the highest."

The Superintendent wrote on a slip of paper, "Mr. Lincoln, you are nominated on the third ballot."

Mr. Lincoln said not a word.

Then some one belonging to the *Journal* cried, "Three cheers for the new President, Abraham Lincoln of Springfield," and a storm of applause answered the suggestion.

Then Mr. Lincoln spoke, trying hard to steady his voice, and this is what he said :—

"There is a little woman down at our house in Twelfth Street who would like to hear this. I'll go down and tell her."

And in the sacred privacy of his happy home the man was able to pour forth his emotion in the most natural way. A wave of solemn feeling came over him. He was not exultant, for he knew that an awful responsibility was laid upon him; but in prayer and thanksgiving he found courage.

He was left alone for a time, that he might be able to bear the rush of thoughts. We wonder if a picture of the log-cabin, in which his first days were spent, did not flash across his mind; and if he had not a wish that his dearly-beloved "angel-mother" could know how wonderfully her prayers had been answered, and how greatly God had honoured her son. Even if his father had only lived to see the beginning of his prosperity; but he had now been dead eight years.

However, he had soon other matters to employ his mind. A deputation from the Convention arrived, and the Hon. George Ashmum formally notified him of his nomination :—

"I have, sir, the honour, in behalf of the gentlemen who are present, a committee appointed by the Republican Convention, recently assembled at Chicago, to discharge a most pleasant duty. We have come, sir, under a vote of instructions to that committee, to notify you that you have been selected by the Convention of the Republicans at Chicago for President of the United States. They instruct us, sir, to notify you of that selection; and that committee deem it not only respectful to yourself, but appropriate to the important matter which they have in hand, that they should come in person and present to you the authentic evidence of the action of that Convention; and, sir, without any phrase which shall either be considered personally laudatory to yourself, or which shall have any reference to the principles involved in the questions which are connected with your nomination, I desire to present to you the letter which has been prepared, and which informs you of the nomination, and with it the platform resolutions and sentiments which the Convention adopted. Sir, at your convenience we shall be glad to receive from you such a response as it may be your pleasure to give us."

Mr. Lincoln listened with a countenance grave and earnest almost to sternness, regarding Mr. Ashmum with the profoundest attention, and at the conclusion of that gentleman's remarks, after an impressive pause, he replied in a clear, but subdued voice, with that perfect enunciation which always marked his utterances, and a dignified sincerity of manner suited to the man and the occasion, in the following words:—

"Mr. Chairman and gentlemen of the committee—I tender to you, and through you to the Republican National Convention, and all the people represented in it, my profoundest thanks for the high honour done me, which you now formally announce. Deeply, and even painfully sensible of the great responsibility which I could almost wish had fallen upon some one of the far more eminent men and experienced statesmen whose distinguished names were before the Convention, I shall, by your leave, consider more fully the resolutions of the Convention, denominated the platform, and, without unnecessary or unreasonable delay, respond to you, Mr. Chairman, in writing, not doubting that the platform will be found satisfactory, and the nomination gratefully accepted.

"And now I will not longer defer the pleasure of taking you, and each of you, by the hand."

It was thought by Mr. Lincoln's friends that such an occasion ought to be one of feasting and drinking; and knowing that he was an abstainer from intoxicating liquors, one of them sent him a quantity to be used on that day.

"What am I to do?" he asked a friend. "I do not want to be inhospitable, but I believe that strong drink does harm every way. I have never had a drink of whisky in my life, and do not want to have anything to do with it now."

"Very well then, don't."

"But I am afraid my good friend who sent it will consider it very ungracious of me not to have it used."

"But you know, Mr. Lincoln, this is a matter of principle with you, and you have been elected on purpose that you may abide by principle."

"So I have, and so I will."

"Then send the liquor back—'Declined with thanks.'"

The President-elect did so; and at the close of his interview with the State delegations he said, "Gentlemen, I do not offer you wine, because I never drink it. Can we pledge each other better than in clear cold water?" With that he lifted a glass of Nature's beverage to his lips, and all the gentlemen did the same.

One of the committee was called "Tall Judge Kelly of Pennsylvania." When it came to his turn to shake hands with Mr. Lincoln, he so evidently measured him with his eyes, that Lincoln said, "Judge, how tall are you?"

"Six feet three," was the answer. "How tall are you, Mr. Lincoln?"

"Six feet four!"

"Then, sir," said the Judge, "Pennsylvania bows to Illinois. My dear man, for years my heart has been aching for a President that I could *look up to*, and I've found him at last in a land where we thought there was none but *little giants*."

CHAPTER VIII.

CONGRATULATIONS.

"The good State has broken the cords for her spun ;
Her oil-springs and water won't fuse into one ;
The Dutchman has seasoned with freedom his krout ;
And slow, late, but certain, the Quakers are out.

Give the flag to the winds, set the hills all aflame,
Make way for the man with the patriarch's name ;
Away with misgiving, away with all doubt,
For Lincoln goes in when the Quakers come out."
—WHITTIER.

FROM the moment that he was made President until the day of his death, Mr. Lincoln had no more leisure. From henceforth he was the property of the nation, and the nation was determined to have its rights. Some amusing stories are told by his biographers. The *Portland Press* told of a gentleman who had been at the Chicago Convention, and who, when the nomination was made, at once started to see the candidate at his house.

Arriving at Springfield, he put up at a public-house, and loitering at the front door, had the curiosity to inquire where Mr. Lincoln lived.

"There is Mr. Lincoln now, coming down the sidewalk; that tall, crooked man, loosely walking this way; if you wish to see him, you will have an opportunity by putting yourself in his track."

In a few moments the object of his curiosity reached the point which our friend occupied, who, advancing, ventured to accost him thus :—

"Is this Mr. Lincoln?"

"That, sir, is my name."

"My name is R., from Plymouth County, Massachusetts, and learning that you have to-day been made the public property of the United States, I have ventured to introduce myself, with a view to a brief acquaintance, hoping you will pardon such patriotic curiosity in a stranger."

Mr. Lincoln received his salutation with cordiality, told him no apology was necessary for his introduction, and asked him to accompany him to his residence. He was introduced to Mrs. Lincoln and the two boys. After some conversation concerning the Lincoln family of the Plymouth colony, and the history of the Pilgrim Fathers, with which Mr. Lincoln seemed familiar, Mr. R. desired the privilege of writing a letter to be despatched by the next mail. Mr. Lincoln very kindly and promptly provided him with the necessary means. As he began to write, Mr. Lincoln approached, and tapping him on the shoulder, expressed the hope that he was not a spy who had come thus early to report his faults to the public.

"By no means, sir," protested Mr. R. "I am writing home to my wife, who, I dare say, will hardly credit the fact that I am writing in your house."

"Oh, sir," exclaimed Mr. Lincoln, "if your wife doubts your word, I will cheerfully endorse it, if you will give me permission."

He took the pen, and wrote in a clear hand upon the blank page of the letter as follows :—

"I am happy to say that your husband is at the present time a guest in my house, and in due time I trust you will greet his safe return to the bosom of his family.

"A. LINCOLN."

He was always most kind and patient. On one occasion he noticed two young men waiting about his door, as if wishing to speak to him, and yet feeling too timid to call.

"How do you do, my good fellows? What can I do for you? Will you sit down?" One sat, and the other said bashfully, "Mr. Lincoln, I and my companion have been having a talk about your height. He is very tall. I think he is as tall as you are: he doesn't think he is; and we just came in to see."

"Oh," said Mr. Lincoln, reaching a cane, "come here, young man, and stand against the wall."

The young man did so.

"Now come out and let me stand under it. There you see, we are exactly of the same height. Are you satisfied?"

The young men said they were; and immediately thanking Mr. Lincoln, who shook hands with them, they went away.

Directly afterwards an old woman called.

"How do you do, Mr. Lincoln? Do you remember me?"

"No, I cannot say I do."

"But, sir, I know you very well, and I have walked ten miles to congratulate you."

She then reminded him of certain incidents connected with his rides upon the circuits, until he recollected who she was and where she lived.

"I believe that I dined at your house several times, did I not?"

"Yes, sir; and once when I had nothing to give you but bread and milk."

"I don't remember that; I think I always dined well at your place."

"No; once you did not, and you said a very remarkable thing. You came along after we had got through dinner, and had eaten everything up, and I could give you nothing but a bowl of bread and milk. But you ate it and seemed satisfied; and when you got up to leave you said, 'I have had a good dinner, *good enough for the President of the United States.*'"

"Did I, indeed?"

"Yes, you did; and now, sure enough, you are the President."

"The President-elect," he said; and he had a very pleasant talk with his old friend.

But he found the frequent calls and interviews rather disturbing. He wanted peace and quiet in his home; and so the Executive Chamber, a large room in the State House, was fitted up for him, and here he held his receptions until he should depart for Washington. "Here he met the millionaire and the menial, the priest and the politician, women and children, old friends and new friends, those who called for love, and those who sought for office. From morning until night this was his business, and he performed it with conscientious care, and the most unwearying patience."

Adjoining and opening into the Executive Chamber was a room occupied by Mr. Newton Bateman, Superintendent of Public Instruction for the State of Illinois, a friend of Mr. Lincoln, with whom he often had a quiet talk. On one of these occasions he uttered these significant words, afterwards given to the public by his biographer, Holland—"I know there is a God, and that He hates injustice and slavery. I see the storm coming, and I know that His hand is in it. If He has a place and work for me—and I think He has—I believe I am ready. I am nothing, but truth is everything. I know I am right, because I know that liberty is right, for Christ teaches it, and Christ is God. I have told them that a house divided against itself cannot stand, and Christ and reason say the same ; and they will find it so. Douglas don't care whether slavery is voted up or voted down, but God cares, and humanity cares, and I care ; and with God's help I shall not fail. I may not see the end ; but it will come, and I shall be vindicated; and these men will find that they have not read their Bibles aright."

These words were spoken when he was feeling very sad, because some ministers· had voted against him, and for slavery. Mr. Bateman was surprised at the religious feeling they expressed, and Lincoln said, " I think more upon these subjects than upon all others, and have done so for years."

Generally he hid these deeper feelings from others ; and was full of the grotesque, the witty, and the funny. He was a good tale-teller, and gave himself up to mirth like a boy.

But a little story is told of an address in a Sunday-school, in connection with his visit to New York, already referred to as the occasion of his speech at Cooper Institute, which gives additional evidence that his heart was right.

" One Sunday morning I saw a tall, remarkable-looking man enter the room and take a seat among us. He listened with fixed attention to our exercises, and his countenance expressed such genuine interest that I approached him, and suggested that he might be willing to say something to the children. He accepted the invitation with evident pleasure ; and, coming forward, began a simple address, which at once fascinated every little hearer, and hushed the room into silence. His language was strikingly beautiful, and his tones musical, with intense feeling.

The little faces would droop into sad conviction as he uttered sentences of warning, and would brighten into sunshine as he spoke cheerfully words of promise. Once or twice he attempted to close his remarks, but the imperative shout of 'Go on! Oh, do go on!' would compel him to resume. As I looked upon the gaunt and sinewy frame of the stranger, and marked his powerful head and determined features, now touched into softness by the impressions of the moment, I felt an irrepressible curiosity to learn something more about him, and while he was quietly leaving the room I begged to know his name. He courteously replied, 'It is Abraham Lincoln, from Illinois.'"

During this visit, too, Abraham Lincoln attended divine service at the church of the Rev. Henry Ward Beecher. The place was packed, but Mr. Nelson Sizer, recognising Lincoln, gave up his own seat to the President-elect, who evidently enjoyed the sermon exceedingly. He told the Rev. M. Field of New York that "he thought there was not upon record, in ancient or modern biography, so *productive* a mind as had been exhibited in the career of Henry Ward Beecher."

As the months passed away between the nomination and the election, Abraham Lincoln was exalted by his friends, and cruelly slandered by his enemies. The mental strain upon him was so great that he "saw visions," and was a little disturbed by them. A settled sadness at one time seemed to come over him; and he told his wife that he felt a pang, as though something dreadful had happened. She sympathised with him, and said that though he might be elected to a second term of office, she was afraid he would not live to complete it, though on the other hand she said the thing he had seen might be a sign of a good career.

"On the 6th November the election took place throughout the whole country, and the result was Mr. Lincoln's triumph, not by a majority of the votes cast, but by a handsome plurality. The popular vote for him was 1,857,610; while Stephen A. Douglas received 1,365,976 votes, John C. Breckinridge 847,953, and John Bell 590,631. In the electoral college Mr. Lincoln had 180, Mr. Douglas received 12, Mr. Breckinridge 72, and Mr. Bell 39."

Mr. Lincoln was in quiet retirement while the election went on. He knew that though many were rejoicing in the North, in the South thick storms of rebellion were gathering. Mr. Stephens, the Vice-President of the Rebel Confederacy, said—" The question that presents itself is, Shall the people of the South secede from the Union in consequence of the election of Mr. Lincoln? My countrymen, I tell you candidly, frankly, and earnestly, that I do not think they ought. In my judgment the election of no man, constitutionally chosen to that high office, is sufficient cause for any state to separate from the Union. It ought to stand by and aid still in maintaining the constitution of the country. To make a point of resistance to the government, to withdraw from it because a man has been constitutionally elected, puts us in the wrong. . . . We went into the election with this people. The result was different from what we wished; but the election has been constitutionally held. Were we to make a point of resistance to the Government, and go out of the Union on this account, the record would be made up hereafter against us."

These were wise words, but the people were not willing to accept and abide by them.

The time came for Mr. Lincoln to leave the old life and enter upon the new. His progress from Springfield to the White House at Washington was full of incidents. Everywhere he was met by crowds at the railway stations, and everywhere he was expected to make addresses. It was not without regret that he left the old house in which he had been very happy, and the neighbours who had been kind to him, and his farewell words to them are full of pathos :—

"My friends—No one not in my position can appreciate the sadness I feel at this parting. To this people I owe all that I am. Here I have lived more than a quarter of a century. Here my children were born, and here one of them lies buried. I know not how soon I shall see you again. A duty devolves upon me which is perhaps greater than that which has devolved upon any other man since the days of Washington. He never would have succeeded except for the aid of Divine Providence, upon which he at all times relied. I feel that I cannot succeed without the aid of the same Divine aid which sustained him, and in the same Almighty Being I place my reliance for support; and I hope you, my friends, will all pray that I may receive that Divine assistance, without which I cannot succeed, but with which success is certain. Again I bid you all an affectionate farewell."

The spirit of this little address shows Abraham Lincoln at his best. It was noticed by his biographers that no two persons spoke of him in the same terms. His acquaintances did not see him with the same eyes; he revealed one part of himself to one person and quite another to the next individual with whom he came in contact.

"He visited Chicago after his election, and met with a magnificent welcome. One or two little incidents of this trip will illustrate especially his consideration for children. He was holding a reception at the Tremont House. A fond father took in a little boy by the hand who was anxious to see the new President. The moment the child entered the parlour door, he, of his own notion, and quite to the surprise of his father, took off his hat. and giving it a swing, cried, 'Hurrah for Lincoln!' There was a crowd, but as soon as Mr. Lincoln could get hold of the little fellow, he lifted him in his hands, and tossing him towards the ceiling, laughingly shouted, 'Hurrah for you!' To Mr. Lincoln it was evidently a refreshing episode in the dreary work of hand-shaking. At a party in Chicago during this visit he saw a little girl timidly approaching him. He called her to him, and asked her what she wished for. She replied that she wanted his name. Mr. Lincoln looked back into the room and said, 'But here are other little girls— they would feel badly if I should give my name only to you!' The little girl replied that there were only eight of them in all. 'Then,' said Mr. Lincoln, 'get me eight sheets of paper, and a pen and ink, and I will see what I can do for you!' The paper was brought, and Mr. Lincoln sat down in the crowded dining-room and wrote a sentence upon each sheet, appending his name; and thus every little girl carried off her souvenir."

He must have found some of the congratulations, both from their number and their force, more than a little irksome.

"People plunged at his arms with frantic enthusiasm, and all the infinite variety of shakes, from the wild and irrepressible pump-handle movement to the dead-grip, was executed upon the devoted dexter and sinister of the President. Some glanced at his face as they grasped his hand; others invoked the blessing of heaven upon him; others affectionately gave him their last gasping assurance of devotion; others, bewildered and furious, with hats crushed over their eyes, seized his hand in a convulsive grasp, and passed on, as if they had not the remotest idea who, what, or where they were."

CHAPTER IX.

FROM SPRINGFIELD TO WASHINGTON.

" Forever then their visions see
The dawn of rising liberty,
Reflecting through the morning air
In answer to their earnest prayer:
And Freedom's virgin fires flame
Within their hearts in Lincoln's name."
—BLANCHARD.

LINCOLN'S journey was, as we have said, made from stage to stage the opportunity of declaring his sentiments in the different towns through which he passed; and these were delivered in his own masterly style. Everywhere he was welcomed with the greatest loyalty and hopefulness, and nowhere did he disappoint those who trusted him.

At Indiana he said :—" Fellow-citizens of the State of Indiana—I am here to thank you for this magnificent welcome, and still more for the very generous support given by your State to that political cause which, I think, is the true and just cause of the whole country and the whole world. Solomon says, 'There is a time to keep silence;' and when men wrangle by the mouth, with no certainty that they mean the same thing while using the same words, it perhaps were as well if they kept silence.

"The words 'coercion' and 'invasion' are much used in these days, and often with some temper and hot blood. Let us make sure, if we can, that we do not misunderstand the meaning of those who use them. Let us get the exact definition of these words, not from dictionaries, but from the men themselves, who certainly deprecate the things they would represent by the use of the words. What, then, is 'coercion?' What is 'invasion?' Would the marching of an army into South Carolina, without the consent of her people, and with hostile intent toward them, be invasion? I certainly think it would, and it would be coercion also if the South Carolinians were forced to submit. But if the United States should merely hold and retake its own forts and other property, and collect the duties on foreign importations, or even withhold the mails from places where they were habitually violated, would any or all of these things be invasion or coercion? Do our professed lovers of the Union, who spitefully resolve that they will resist coercion and invasion, understand that such things as these, on the part of the United States, would be coercion or invasion of a State? If so, their ideas of means to preserve the object of their great affection would seem to be exceedingly thin and airy. If sick, the little pills of the homœopathist would be much too large for it to swallow. In their view the Union, as a family relation, would seem to be no regular marriage, but rather a sort of free-love arrangement, to be maintained on passional attraction.

"By the way, in what consists the special sacredness of a State? I speak not in the position assigned to a State in the Union by the Constitution, for that is a bond we all recognise. That position, however, a State cannot carry out of the Union with it. I speak of that assumed primary right of a State to rule all which is less than itself, and to ruin all which is larger than itself. If a State and a county in a given case should be equal in number of inhabitants, in what, as a matter of principle, is the State better than the county? Would an exchange of name be an exchange of rights? Upon what principle, upon what rightful principle, may a State, being no more than one-fiftieth part of the nation in soil and population, break up the nation and then coerce a proportionably large sub-division of itself in the most arbitrary way? What mysterious right to play tyrant is conferred on a district or county, with its people, by simply calling it a State? Fellow-citizens, I am not asserting anything: I am merely asking questions for you to consider. And now allow me to bid you farewell."

At New Jersey he concluded his speech by saying—"I shall endeavour to take the ground I deem most just to the North, the East, the West, and the South, and the whole country. I take it, I hope, in good temper, certainly with no malice towards any section. I shall do all that may be in my power to promote a peaceful settlement of all our difficulties. The man does not live who is more devoted to peace than I am; none who would do more to preserve it. But it may be necessary to put the foot firmly down; and if I do my duty, and do it right, you will sustain me, will you not? Received as I am by the members of a Legislature, the majority of whom do not agree with me in political sentiment, I trust that I may have their assistance in piloting the ship of State through this voyage, surrounded by perils as it is; for, if it should suffer shipwreck now, there will be no pilot needed for another voyage."

Both at New Jersey and New York his reception was most enthusiastic, and when he reached Philadelphia he was warmly received by the Mayor. In his reply he said —" It were useless for me to speak of details of plans now. I shall speak officially next Monday week, *if ever*. If

I should not speak then, it were useless for me to do so now."

Mrs. Lincoln and their two sons were travelling with the President during the eventful journey, which was less eventful than some of his foes meant to make it. He had known that all along the route were some men seeking to take his life. An endeavour was made to throw the train off the track soon after it left Springfield; and at Cincinatti a hand grenade was found concealed upon the train. At Philadelphia the whole plot was unfolded to him. A detective of great skill and experience undertook to ferret out the conspiracy, and he got several persons to assist him. He found that the conspirators were resolved that Mr. Lincoln should not pass through Baltimore alive; that in case he should reach Baltimore, he should be shot by one of a party that was to gather round the carriage in the guise of friends. A hand grenade was to complete the work which the pistol had begun.

The detective had an interview with the President on his arrival at Philadelphia. Mr. Lincoln told him that he had two engagements—the one was to raise the American flag on Independence Hall the next morning, which happened to be the anniversary of Washington's birthday; and that he had accepted an invitation to a reception by the Pennsylvanian Legislature the same afternoon. "Both of these engagements I will keep," said he, "if it costs me my life."

In the meantime General Scott and Senator Seward, who were in Washington, sent Mr. Frederick W. Seward to Philadelphia to warn Mr. Lincoln that his life was in danger, and it would be wise to come to Washington in the quietest possible way. He knew, therefore, that the slave-power was in active revolt, and the friends of slavery were seeking his life. But he did not shrink from the performance of his duty. He uttered these words in Independence Hall:—

"I am filled with deep emotion at finding myself standing here in this place, where were collected the wisdom, the patriotism, the devotion to principle from which sprang the institutions under which we live. You have kindly suggested to me that in my hands is the task of restoring peace to the present disturbed state of the country. I can say in return, sir, that all the political sentiments I entertain have been drawn, as far as I have been able to draw them, from the sentiments which originated in, and have been given to the world from this Hall. I have never had a feeling politically that did not spring from the sentiments embodied in the Declaration of Independence. I have often pondered over the dangers that were incurred by the men who assembled here, and framed and adopted that Declaration of Independence. I have pondered over the toils that were endured by the officers and soldiers of the army who achieved that independence. I have often inquired of myself what idea or principle it was that kept this confederacy so long together. It was not the mere matter of the separation of the colonies from the mother-land, but that sentiment that gave liberty not alone to the people of this country, but to the world for all future time. It was that which gave promise that in due time the weight would be lifted from the shoulders of all men. This is a sentiment embodied in the Declaration of Independence. Now, my friends, can this country be saved upon this basis? If it can, I will consider myself one of the happiest men in the world if I can help to save it. If it cannot be saved upon that principle, it will be truly awful. But if this country cannot be saved without giving up that principle, I was about to say I would rather be assassinated on this spot than surrender it. Now, in my view of the present aspect of affairs, there need be no bloodshed or war. There is no necessity for it. I am not in favour of such a course; and I may say in advance that there will be no bloodshed, unless it be forced upon the Government, and then it will be compelled to act in self-defence."

At the close of the speech Mr. Lincoln went, as invited, on the platform outside, and with a few words to the people, ran up the beautiful flag to the top of the staff, amid the hearty cheers of many thousands.

Abraham Lincoln was not lacking in courage, but the fact remains that he entered the capital about six o'clock in the morning, and when only a few of his friends expected him. It was considered absolutely necessary for the safety of his life that special precautions should be taken. His family remained behind, and went on by the special train that was prepared for the President; but the news was telegraphed that Lincoln himself had safely arrived, and was staying with Senator Seward at Willard's Hotel. Two days later he was serenaded by the Republican Association, and waited upon by the Mayor and municipal authorities, who gave him a cordial welcome. He suitably replied to both deputations.

Holland says—"The days that preceded the inauguration were rapidly passing away. In the meantime, although General Scott had been busy and efficient in his military preparations for the occasion, many were fearful that scenes of violence would be enacted on that day, even should Mr. Lincoln be permitted to escape assassination until then. It was a time of fearful uncertainty. The leading society of Washington hated Mr. Lincoln and the principles he represented. If it would be uncharitable to say that they would have rejoiced at his death, it is certainly true that they were in perfect sympathy with those who were plotting his destruction. His coming and remaining would be death to the social dominance of slavery in the national capital. This they felt, and nothing would have pleased them better than a revolution which should send Mr. Lincoln back to Illinois, and instal Jefferson Davis in the White House.

There was probably not one man in five in Washington, at the time Mr. Lincoln entered the city, who, in his heart, gave him welcome. It is not to be wondered at that his friends all over the country looked nervously forward to the 4th of March.

But the inaugural day broke beautifully clear, and the true friends of the new President surged into the city by thousands. There was an unusual display of soldiers, but all beside looked as usual on these occasions. Most of the schools and places of business were closed, and the stars and stripes floated from every flagstaff. Those who were in the hall regarded with the profoundest interest the entrance of President Buchanan and the President-elect—the outgoing and the incoming man. Judge Taney administered the oath to Mr. Lincoln, and the judge was exceedingly agitated as he did so. Every one listened with an absorbed interest, so profound as to be almost painful, to the inaugural address of the President. It was moderate and conciliatory, marked by respectful friendliness to the South, and clear and wise throughout.

"Fellow-citizens of the United States—In compliance with a custom as old as the Government itself, I appear before you to address you briefly, and to take in your presence the oath prescribed by the constitution of the United States to be taken by the President before he enters on the execution of his office . . . I take the official oath to-day with no mental reservations, and with no purpose to construe the constitution or laws by any hypocritical rules; and while I do not choose now to specify particular acts of Congress as proper to be enforced, I do suggest that it will be much safer for all, both in official and private stations, to conform to and abide by all those acts which stand unrepealed, than to violate any of them, trusting to find impunity in having them held to be unconstitutional . . . Such of you as are now dissatisfied still have the old constitution unimpaired, and, on the sensitive point, the laws of your own framing under it; while the new administration will have no immediate power, if it would, to change either. If it were admitted that you, who are dissatisfied, hold the right side in the dispute, there is still no single reason for precipitate action. Intelligence, patriotism, Christianity, and a firm reliance on Him who has never yet forsaken this favoured land, are still competent to adjust in the best way all our present difficulties. In your hands, my dissatisfied fellow-countrymen, and not in mine, is the momentous issue of civil war. The Government will not assail you. You can have no conflict without being yourselves the aggressors. You have no oath registered in heaven to destroy the Government, while I shall have the most solemn one to preserve, protect, and defend it. I am loth to close. We are not enemies but friends. We must not be enemies. Though passion may have strained, it must not break our bond of affection. The mystic cord of memory, stretching from every battle-field and patriot-grave to every living heart and hearthstone all over this broad land, will yet swell the chorus of the Union when again touched, as surely they will be, by the better angels of our nature."

"This address," says Dr. Brockett, "was delivered in tones distinctly audible to the vast throng who surrounded the President; and almost before the echo of his voice had faded from their hearing, the telegraph and the printing-press carried it to the homes and the hearts of his countrymen in other parts of the Union. To the people it brought the welcome assurance that imbecility, double-dealing, and treachery no longer held sway over the nation; that the new President was determined to maintain the national integrity; and that, while faithful to his official oath, he would use every lawful and reasonable means to avert the evils of domestic war. . . . Men felt that a new political era had dawned, and breathed more freely even in the face of dangers that encompassed the Republic."

Mr. Lincoln's first duty was to appoint his Cabinet, and this he proceeded at once to do. The position occupied by Mr. Seward before the country was such as to point him out as the person to occupy the highest point of honour under the executive, and Mr. Lincoln had no hesitation in asking him to become the Secretary of State. Judge Bates of Missouri was made Attorney-General; Salmon P. Chase of Ohio was appointed to the Treasury; and Simon Cameron of Pennsylvania became Secretary of War. Mr. Wells of Connecticut was Secretary of the Navy; Mr. Montgomery Blair of Maryland, Postmaster-General; and Mr. Caleb Smith of Indiana was Secretary of the Interior.

A more disagreeable and irksome duty followed; but it was necessary to sift out all the disloyal men who filled responsible positions. Lieutenant-General Scott, the head of the army, tendered his advice and services. At the time of the inauguration seven States had revolted, and there was treason everywhere; but Mr. Lincoln was determined that if a first shot were fired it should be by the rebels and not the Government. The rebels had taken some forts; but a gallant little band in Fort Sumter, Charleston Harbour, refused to surrender. There was a bombardment of thirty-three hours "sustained by Anderson and his little band of heroes, only seventy in number," and the fort had to be evacuated on Sunday morning, the 14th of April 1861.

These were dark days for Abraham Lincoln. Trouble and treachery met him in unexpected places. He was for peace, but his enemies were determined to have war, and it was evident that force must be met with force.

CHAPTER X.

WAR!

"'Come to the rescue!' The cry went forth
Through the length and breadth of the loyal North,
For the gun that startled Sumter heard
Wakened the land with its fiery word.
The farmer paused with his work half done,
And snatched from the nail his rusty gun;
And the smart mechanic wiped his brow,
Shouting 'There's work for my strong arm now!'
And the parson doffed his gown, and said—
'Bring me my right good sword instead!'
And the scholar paused in his eager quest,
And buckled his belt on with the rest;
And each and all to the rescue went
As unto a royal tournament;
For the loyal blood of a nation stirred
To the gun that startled Sumter heard."
—CAROLINE A. MASON.

ON the 15th of April, the day after the evacuation of Fort Sumter, the President issued his first proclamation:—

"Whereas the laws of the United States have been for some time past, and are now, opposed, and the executive thereof obstructed in the States of South Carolina,

Georgia, Alabama, Florida, Mississippi, Louisiana, and Texas, by combinations too powerful to be suppressed by the ordinary course of judicial proceedings, or by the power vested in the marshals by law; now, therefore, I, Abraham Lincoln, President of the United States, in virtue of the power in me vested by the Constitution and the laws, have thought fit to call forth, and hereby do call forth, the militia of the several States of the Union, to the aggregate number of 75,000, in order to suppress said combinations, and to cause the laws to be duly executed.

"The details of this object will be immediately communicated to the State authorities through the War Department. I appeal to all loyal citizens to favour, facilitate, and aid this effort to maintain the honour, the integrity, and existence of our national Union, and the perpetuity of popular government, and to redress wrongs already long enough endured. I deem it proper to say, that the first service assigned to the forces hereby called forth will probably be to repossess the forts, places, and property which have been seized from the Union; and in every event the utmost care will be observed, consistently with the objects aforesaid, to avoid any devastation, any destruction of, or interference with property, or any disturbance of peaceful citizens of any part of the country; and I hereby command the persons composing the combinations aforesaid to disperse and return peaceably to their respective abodes within twenty days from this date. Deeming that the present condition of public affairs presents an extraordinary occasion, I do hereby, in virtue of the power in me vested by the constitution, convene both Houses of Congress. The senators and representatives are, therefore, summoned to assemble at their respective chambers at twelve o'clock noon, on Thursday, the fourth day of July next, then and there to consider and determine such measures as, in their wisdom, the public safety and interest seem to demand.—In witness whereof, I hereunto set my hand, and cause the seal of the United States to be affixed.

"Done at the City of Washington, this fifteenth day of April, in the year of our Lord one thousand eight hundred and sixty-one, and of the Independence of the United States the eighty-fifth.

"ABRAHAM LINCOLN.

"By the President:
  "WILLIAM H. SEWARD, *Secretary of State.*"

"The utterance of this proclamation," says a historian, "was so clearly a necessity, and was so directly a response to the uprising of the people, that not a voice was raised against it. It was received with no small degree of excitement, but it was a healthy excitement. It was a necessity, and loyal men felt everywhere that the great struggle between slavery and the country was upon them. 'Better that it should be settled by us than by our children,' they said; and in their self-devotion they were encouraged by their mothers, sisters, and wives. The South knew that war must come, and they were prepared. Nearly all the Southern ports were already in their hands. They had robbed the Northern arsenals through the miscreant Floyd. They had cut off the payment of debts due to the North. They had ransacked the mails so that the Government could have no communication with its friends and forces. They had been instructing officers for years, and drilling troops for months. They knew that there were not arms enough in the North to furnish an army competent to overcome them. When, therefore, Mr. Lincoln called for his seventy-five thousand men, they met the proclamation with a howl of derision."

But they did not know the North! Under the influence of the insult to the national flag all the patriotism of the North was aroused, and there was a universal desire to avenge the fall of Sumter. Every Northern State responded, and from private persons as well as from the Legislatures men, arms, and money were offered with a profusion that was absolutely lavish. Massachusetts was first, for it had troops already at hand. Governor Banks had said years before, that "troops would be called upon to suppress a slaveholders' rebellion." He had gone out of office now, but his prediction was fulfilled, and his successor, Governor Andrew, promptly despatched the troops which were ready. The "Massachusetts Sixth" marched off at once, completely equipped, and within forty-eight hours two other regiments also left Boston, on their way to Washington. As the "Sixth" passed through Baltimore it was met by a mob, carrying a secession flag, and a free fight ensued, by which several men were killed and wounded. This raised the excitement of the people to boiling point. The entire section of the Union in the North felt outraged that troops should be assailed and murdered while going to protect the capital of the nation. Governor Hicks of Maryland, and Major Brown of Baltimore, urged that no more troops should pass through Baltimore; and the men burnt down the bridges so that the troops should not have access to the town. Governor Hicks proposed that the matter should be referred to Lord Lyons, the British Minister, for arbitration; but Mr. Seward replied for the President that they ought not to refer their domestic contentions to any foreign power for settlement. Eventually the troops were forwarded by way of Annapolis.

A pleasant ray of light in the darkness of the trouble that hung over President Lincoln was the reconciliation effected by Mr Ashmum between Lincoln and Douglas. At first Douglas hesitated, but his wife being called in, threw all the weight of her influence into the scale. "He gave up all his enmity and resentment, cast every unworthy sentiment behind him, and cordially declared his willingness to go to Mr. Lincoln and offer him his earnest and hearty support." Mr. Lincoln welcomed him, and the two were faithful friends until the death of Mr. Douglas.

The secession of the States of Virginia, Tennessee, North Carolina, and Arkansas, was soon proclaimed. Then Washington, which was in great danger, was the scene of important military operations. Fortress Monroe, commanding the gateway of Virginia, was reinforced and held, and Harper's Ferry was blown up.

Mr. Lincoln had no longer his old antagonist Mr. Douglas to deal with, but he had instead Mr. Jefferson Davis, who convened his Congress at Montgomery, and issued a document which declared the rightfulness of his position, and tried to shift the blame to the shoulders of Abraham Lincoln.

Fighting now began in earnest. On the 10th of June was fought the battle of Big Bethel. A young officer, Major Winthrop, a man of great bravery and literary ability, whose loss was severely felt, was killed in the fight, and greatly mourned by Lincoln. So was another man, Colonel Ellsworth, who died under the following circumstances:—A secession flag had been planted on a building in Alexandria, in sight of the capitol at Washington. Colonel Ellsworth went personally to the Marshal House, kept by James Jackson, and mounting to the top, pulled down the secession flag. James Jackson at once shot him dead. His body was borne to the White House, and the sight of it filled Mr. Lincoln with grief.

"This was a friend of mine; I knew him well," he said, in broken accents. "He was a student in my office when I and Herndon were together. Poor young martyr! One of the first, but how many are to follow!"

When the young man whose death had so affected the President was buried, Mr. Lincoln himself attended the funeral as chief mourner.

The trouble of Mr. Lincoln was greatly increased by that which came next. "On the 16th of July the national army, of about thirty thousand men, under General McDowell, moved forward and attacked the enemy at Bull Run on the twenty-first, the result being the defeat, with a loss of four hundred and eighty killed, and one thousand wounded, of our forces, who fell back on Washington in the greatest confusion and disorder. Had the rebel forces closely followed the panic-stricken fugitives, the capitol would have been their easy prey." The result of this battle was naturally exceedingly disappointing to the country; but the people did not lose heart: their courage and determination only became stronger. We are not writing a history of the American War, and do not therefore describe the battles. But we give, in the words of the Hon. George Bancroft, in his memorable address, a condensed account of the spirit in which it was carried on by Mr. Lincoln and the loyal people:—

"When it came home to the consciousness of the Americans that the war which they were waging was a war for the liberty of all the nations of the world, for freedom itself, they thanked God for giving them strength to endure the severity of the trial to which He put their sincerity, and nerved themselves for their duty with an inexorable will.

"The President was led along by the greatness of their self-sacrificing example; and, as a child in a dark night, on a rugged way, catches hold of the hand of its father for guidance and support, he clung fast to the hand of the people, and moved calmly through the gloom. While the statesmanship of Europe was mocking at the hopeless vanity of their efforts, they put forth such miracles of energy as the history of the world had never known. The contributions to the popular loans amounted in four years to twenty-seven and a-half hundred millions of dollars; the revenue of the country from taxation was increased seven fold. The navy of the United States, drawing into the public service the willing militia of the seas, doubled its tonnage in eight months, and established an actual blockade from Cape Hatteras to the Rio Grande. In the course of the war it was increased fivefold in men and in tonnage, while the inventive genius of the country devised more effective means of ordnance, and new forms of naval architecture in wood and iron. There went into the field, for various terms of enlistment, about two millions of men, and at the close of the war the men in the army exceeded a million.

. . . "In one single month one hundred and sixty-five thousand men were recruited into service. Once, within four weeks, Ohio organised and placed in the field forty-two regiments of infantry, nearly thirty-six thousand men; and Ohio was like other States in the east and in the west. The well-mounted cavalry numbered eighty-four thousand of horses and mules: there were bought, from first to last, two-thirds of a million. In the movements of the troops science came in aid of patriotism, so that, to choose a single instance out of many, an army twenty-three thousand strong, with its artillery, trains, baggage, and animals, was moved by rail from the Potomac to the Tennessee, twelve hundred miles, in seven days. On the long marches wonders of military construction bridged the rivers, and wherever an army halted ample supplies awaited them at their ever-changing base. The vile thought that life is the greatest blessing did not rise up. In six hundred and twenty-five battles and severe skirmishes blood flowed like water. It streamed over the grassy plains, it stained the rocks; the undergrowth of the forest was red with it; and the armies marched on with majestic courage from one conflict to another, knowing that they were fighting for God and liberty. The organisation of the medical department met its infinitely multiplied duties with exactness and despatch. At the news of a battle the best surgeons of our cities hastened to the field to offer the untiring aid of the greatest experience and skill. The gentlest and most refined of women left homes of luxury and ease to build hospital-tents near the armies, and serve as nurses to the sick and dying. Besides the large supply of religious teachers by the public, the congregations spared to their brothers in the field the ablest ministers. The Christian Commission, which expended more than six million and a quarter of dollars, sent nearly five thousand clergymen, chosen out of the best, to keep unsoiled the religious character of the men, and made gifts of clothes, food, and medicine. The organisation of private charity assumed unheard-of dimensions. The Sanitary Commission, which had seven thousand societies, distributed, under the direction of an unpaid board, spontaneous contributions to the amount of fifteen millions in supplies or money, a million-and-a-half in money from California alone, and dotted the scene of war, from Paducah to Port Royal, from Belle Plain, Virginia, to Brownsville, Texas, with homes and lodges."

CHAPTER XI.

EMANCIPATION.

"Emancipation is proclaimed,
The shackles fall—the slave's unchained."

MR. LINCOLN was always careful to insist on the truth that the war was entered into to preserve the Union, and not for the abolition of slavery. But events pointed to this as the great result; and Abraham Lincoln, whose soul hated slavery, could not but be thankful to have been the man chosen by God to set the slaves free.

In the meantime the terrible war and its miseries pressed on no heart more heavily than that of the President. He had lived among the people, and knew many of them, and when he heard of the losses of the men he frequently shed tears. "Poor fellows! I am thinking of our poor fellows," he would say.

Of course he had many advisers. He was too cautious and deliberate for some people, who wondered why he did not at once declare the emancipation of the slaves. But there are two sides to every question, and Mr. Lincoln never limited his view to one of them. At last a good deal of pressure was brought to bear upon him, especially in the press; and a long letter from Horace Greeley, printed in the *New York Tribune*, though somewhat intemperate and severe, put the case of the slaves very earnestly before the President and the public. Mr. Lincoln replied to it, declaring that his first desire was to save the Union, as he had sworn by oath to do.

"People wish to hurry me," he said to a friend, "but I must wait until I see that the time has come. Many point out to me what they consider my duty, and say that divine Providence has revealed it. May not I hope that light will be given to me?"

At length it seemed to him that the exigencies of the army called for the emancipation of the slaves. News of the battle of Antietam came to the President while he was on a visit to the Soldier's Home. He had already written the draft of a preliminary proclamation, and he at once went back to Washington and called a Cabinet, at which he said the time for emancipation had come.

"I believe that public sentiment will support it," he said. "Many of my warmest friends and adherents have demanded it, and I have promised my God that I will do it." The last words were uttered very reverently, and in low tones.

"Did I understand you correctly, Mr. President?" asked Mr. Clay, who sat nearest him, in surprise.

And Lincoln replied—"I made a solemn vow before God that if General Lee should be driven back from Pennsylvania, I would crown the result by a declaration of freedom to the slaves."

Accordingly, on the 22d of September the proclamation was issued:—

"I, Abraham Lincoln, President of the United States of America, and Commander-in-Chief of the Army and Navy thereof, do hereby proclaim and declare that hereafter, as heretofore, the war will be prosecuted for the object of practically restoring the constitutional relation between the United States and the people thereof in those States in which that relation is or may be suspended or disturbed; that it is my purpose, upon the next meeting of Congress, to again recommend the adoption of a practical measure tendering pecuniary aid to the free acceptance or rejection of all the slave States so called, the people whereof may not then be in rebellion against the United States, and which States may then have voluntarily adopted, or thereafter may voluntarily adopt, the immediate or gradual abolishment of slavery within their respective limits, and that the effort to colonise persons of African descent, with their consent, upon the continent or elsewhere, with the previously-obtained consent of the Government existing there, will be continued; that on the first day of January, in the year of our Lord one thousand eight hundred and sixty-three, all persons held as slaves within any State, or any designated part of a State, the people whereof shall then be in rebellion against the United States, shall be then, thenceforward, and for ever free." When this was followed by the other proclamation on New Year's Day 1863, he added these words:—"And I hereby enjoin upon the people so declared to be free to abstain from all violence, unless in necessary self-defence; and I recommend to them that, in all cases when allowed, they labour faithfully for reasonable wages.

"And I further declare and make known that such persons, of suitable condition, will be received into the armed service of the United States, to garrison forts, positions, stations, and other places, and to man vessels of all sorts in said service.

"And upon this act, sincerely believed to be an act of justice, warranted by the Constitution upon military necessity, I invoke the considerate judgment of mankind, and the gracious favour of Almighty God.

"In testimony whereof, I have hereunto set my name, and caused the seal of the United States to be affixed.

"Done at the City of Washington, the first day of January, in the year of our Lord one thousand eight hundred and sixty-three, and of the independence of the United States the eighty-seventh.

"By the President :   ABRAHAM LINCOLN.

"WILLIAM H. SEWARD, *Secretary of State*."

Two days after the issue of the proclamation a large body of men assembled in front of the White House with music, and called for the President, to congratulate him on what he had done. He courteously appeared, and addressed a few words to them—"What I did," he said, "I did after a very full deliberation, and under a heavy and solemn sense of responsibility. I can only trust in God I have made no mistake." The President remarked to Mr. Colfax, the same evening, that the signature appeared somewhat tremulous and uneven. "Not," said he, "because of any uncertainty or hesitation on my part, but it was just after the public reception, and three hours hand-shaking is not calculated to improve a man's chirography." Then changing his tone, he added—"The South had fair warning that if they did not return to their duty I should strike at this pillar of their strength. The promise must now be kept, and I shall never recall one word."

How did the slaves themselves receive the news? They were overwhelmed with joy; and Mr. Lincoln followed up the great kindness by many smaller ones, such as inviting a host of coloured Sunday school children to the White House. No public testimonial of regard, it is safe to say, gave Mr. Lincoln more sincere pleasure during his entire public life than that presented by the coloured people of the city of Baltimore, in the summer of 1864, consisting of an elegant copy of the Holy Bible. The volume was of the usual pulpit size, bound in violet-coloured velvet. The corners were bands of solid gold, and carved upon a plate also of gold, not less than one-fourth of an inch thick. Upon the left-hand cover was a design representing the President in a cotton-field knocking the shackles off the wrists of a slave, who held one hand aloft as if invoking blessings upon the head of his benefactor—at whose feet was a scroll, upon which was written "Emancipation." Upon the cover was a similar plate, bearing the inscription :—

TO

Abraham Lincoln,

PRESIDENT OF THE UNITED STATES, THE FRIEND OF UNIVERSAL FREEDOM,

From the loyal coloured people of Baltimore, as a token of respect and gratitude. Baltimore, 4th July 1864.

The presentation was made by a committee of coloured people, consisting of three clergymen and two laymen, who were received by the President in the most cordial manner, after which the Rev. F. W. Chase, on the part of the committee, said :—

"Mr. President—The loyal coloured people of Baltimore have delegated to us the authority to present this Bible, as a token of their appreciation of your humane part towards the people of our race. While all the nation are offering their tributes of respect, we cannot let the occasion pass by without tendering ours. Since we have been incorporated in the American family we have been true and loyal, and we now stand by ready to defend the country. We are ready to be armed and trained in military matters, in order to defend and protect the star-spangled banner!"

A coloured nurse in one of the hospitals, who had once been a slave, prepared, as an expression of love and reverence, a collection of wax-fruits, and went with her minister to present it to Mr. Lincoln. In the *Anti-Slavery Standard* the account of the visit was published in her own words—"The Commissioner, Mr. Newton, received us kindly, and sent the box to the White House, with directions that it should not be opened until I came. The next day was reception-day, but the President sent me word that he would receive me at one o'clock. I went and arranged the table, placing it in the centre of the room. Then I was introduced to the President and his wife; he stood next to me, then Mrs. Lincoln, Mr. Newton, and the minister, the others outside. Mr. Hamilton, the minister, made an appropriate speech, and at the conclusion said, 'Perhaps Mrs. Johnson would like to say a few words?' I looked down to the floor and felt that I had not a word to say, but after a moment or two the fire began to burn" (laying her hand on her breast), "and it burned and burned till it went all over me. I think it was the Spirit, and I looked up to him and said, 'Mr. President, I believe God has hewn you out of a rock, for this great and mighty purpose. Many have been led away by bribes of gold, of silver, of presents, but you have stood firm, because God was with you, and if you are faithful to the end He will be with you!' With his eyes full of tears he walked round and examined the present, pronounced it beautiful, thanked me kindly, but said, 'You must not give me the praise: it belongs to God.'"

These stories are given in an interesting book by a painter, Mr. F. B. Carpenter, called *Six months at the White House with Abraham Lincoln: the Story of a Picture*. The book gives a pleasing account of the home-life of the President, and we are sure our readers will be gratified to read some extracts:—

"My first interview with the President took place at the customary Saturday afternoon public reception. Never shall I forget the thrill which went through my whole being as I first caught sight of that tall, gaunt form through a distant doorway, bowed down, it seemed to me, even then, with the weight of the nation he carried upon his heart, as a mother carries her suffering child, and thought of the place he held in the affection of the people, and the prayers ascending constantly, day after day, in his behalf. The crowd was passing through the rooms, and presently it was my turn and name to be announced. Greeting me very pleasantly, he soon afterwards made an appointment to see me in the official chamber directly after the close of the 'reception.' The hour named found me at the well-remembered door of the apartment, that door watched daily with so many conflicting emotions of hope and fear, by the miscellaneous throng gathered there. The President was alone and already deep in official business, which was always pressing. He received me with the frank kindness and simplicity so characteristic of his nature, and after reading Mr. Lovejoy's note, said, 'Well, Mr. Carpenter, we will turn you in loose here, and try to give you a good chance to work out your idea!' . . . The President seemed much interested in my work from the first, but as it progressed his interest increased. I occupied for a studio the spacious 'state dining-room' of the White House, in the south-western corner of the mansion. He was in the habit of bringing many friends in to see what advance I was making from day to day. I have known him to come by himself as many as three or four times in a single day. It seemed a pleasant diversion to him to watch the gradual progress of the work, and his suggestions, though sometimes quaint and homely, were almost invariably excellent. Seldom was he heard to allude to anything which might be construed into a personality in connection with any member of the Cabinet. On one occasion, however, I remember with a sly twinkle of the eye he turned to a senatorial friend whom he had brought in to see the picture, and said, 'Mrs.

Lincoln calls Mr. Carpenter's group *The Happy Family.*' . . . There was a satisfaction to me simply in sitting in the room with him, though no words might be uttered, perhaps, for long intervals. Apparently absorbed with my pencil, and he with his papers, he would sometimes seem to forget my presence entirely. It was at such times that I loved to study him. Frequently, when persons were admitted on business, before entering upon confidential discussions, they would turn an inquiring eye upon me, which Mr. Lincoln would meet by saying, 'Oh, you need not mind him; he is but a painter!' There was never a feeling of restraint or constraint on my part; his personal magnetism was so great, to hear him was like getting into the sunshine. As I now look back upon these privileged days, my heart is stirred with affection for the just and noble man, second only to the filial regard due to a parent. It has been my fortune to mingle quite freely, in my professional life, with many distinguished public men. I have said repeatedly to friends, that I never knew one so utterly unconscious of distinction or power as Mr. Lincoln. He seemed to forget himself in the magnitude of his responsibilities. Under all circumstances he was precisely the same—plain, unostentatious, truth-loving, pure and good. Dr. Stone, his family physician in Washington, once said to me, 'I tell you, Mr. Lincoln *is the purest hearted man I ever saw.*'"

CHAPTER XII.

LIFE AT THE WHITE HOUSE.

"And when the griefs of life are past,
And safe in heaven your lot is cast,
Then you shall see the good and ill
That human destinies fulfil,
Though oft in hidden footsteps trod,
The path that marks the will of God."
—BLANCHARD.

AS will be seen from the interesting account of *Life in the White House*, by Mr. Carpenter, the painter, Mr. Lincoln had brought the old sincerity and homeliness of taste into the President's official residence. Other biographers tell tales scarcely less interesting. Mr. Mudge, especially, tells one of John Hanks, which he got from his own lips :—

"Soon after Mr. Lincoln's first inauguration I called at the White House, and sent up my name. I trembled a little bit, but said to myself, 'Don't I know Abe Lincoln, and don't he know John Hanks?' Still the thought kept crowding into my mind, 'Abe's a long way out of sight of John now.' Soon the messenger returned, saying, 'The President says, Come up.' I entered the office where Mr.

Lincoln was sitting, surrounded, it seemed to me, by all the great men of the country. Rising from his seat, and stepping forth to meet me, he seized my extended hand with both of his, exclaiming, 'John, I'm glad to see you. How do you do? How is your family?' It was the welcome of other years, and I forgot that he was President, and replied, 'I'm pretty well, I thank you, Abe: how's you rfolks?' After we had chatted a while, he asked me to come again, and I did call upon him several times, and he never seemed to feel above his old friend of the Illinois log-cabin."

Mr. Lincoln on one occasion invited a former friend and his wife to take a drive in the presidential carriage, which, naturally, was gladly accepted.

"Must I wear gloves?" asked the friend.

"Oh, yes, of course you must," replied his wife.

"But we never used to do so in the old days, unless because the weather was cold."

"But things are different now. You must wear gloves out of respect to the President."

"Lincoln used not to like them any better than I. However, I suppose I must put them on."

At the same time the President was asking Mrs. Lincoln, "Must I wear gloves?"

"Yes, I think you had better."

"I'll put a pair in my pocket, and we will see."

When they were seated in the carriage, Mr. Lincoln began slyly to pull his gloves on, and his friend just as quietly to pull his off. It was too absurd; and as soon as each saw what the other was doing, both burst into a hearty laugh; and they had their drive in an ungloved condition.

When the President could get a little respite he was always glad to do so. "He entered the White House a healthy man, with a frame of iron, and without indulgence in a single debilitating vice, he became a feeble man, weary-worn beyond the reach of rest." But he was fond of music and singing, and often found relief in story-telling.

Carpenter says that once a man known as "Jeems Pipes of Pipesville" begged Mr. and Mrs. Lincoln to give him half-an-hour in their presence to go through his performance. The man gave comic illustrations of various characters, and among the rest that of a stammering man, which greatly amused Mr. Lincoln. At the close the President told him that he had once known a stammering man who *whistled* with his stammering, and advised Pipes to add that touch of nature to his performance. Pipes practised it several times, trying to imitate the whistle as performed by the President, and then went away greatly delighted.

Sometimes the determination of Mr. Lincoln to have his bit of fun annoyed those who came to him on serious business. A Congressman once went to him, and Lincoln began, as usual, to tell him an amusing story.

"Mr. President," said his visitor, warmly, "I did not come hear to listen to stories. The times are too serious for that." Lincoln at once became grave. "My dear sir," he said, "do you suppose that I do not feel the gravity of the situation as deeply as you? I assure you the trouble is with me night and day; but if I did not sometimes find *vent* I should die."

The fact is that he took his fun as other over-burdened statesmen take their wine, and it helped him, if not in the same, in a better way.

It is said that when he had prepared the draft of the Emancipation proclamation, and had the members of the Cabinet together, that he might read it to them, he commenced proceedings by reading a chapter of *Artemus Ward;* and when he had read it, he went on with the solemn business in hand.

When General Grant came into chief command of the

armies, Mr. Stanton, the Secretary of War, at their first interview, could not agree with him as to the number of troops to be left for the defence of Washington, while the main army marched on Richmond. A correspondent of the *New York Herald* thus gives the conversation, and the happy turn given to the dispute between the high officials:—

"Well, General," remarked the Secretary, "I suppose you have left enough men to strongly garrison the forts round Washington?"

"No," said Grant, coolly, "I couldn't do that."

"Why not?" cried Stanton, nervously; "why not? why not?"

"Because I have already sent the men to the front," replied Grant, calmly.

"That won't do," cried Stanton, more nervously than before. "It's contrary to my plans. I can't allow it. I'll order the men back."

"I shall need the men there, and you can't order them back," answered Grant.

"Why not?" inquired Stanton, again. "Why not? why not?"

"I believe that I rank the Secretary in this matter," was the quiet reply.

"Very well," said Stanton, a little warmly, "we'll see the President about that. I'll have to take you to the President."

"That's right," politely observed Grant. "The President ranks us both."

Arrived at the White House, the General and Secretary asked to see the President upon important business, and in a few moments the good-natured face of Mr. Lincoln appeared.

"Well, gentlemen," said the President, "what do you want of me?"

"General," said Stanton, stiffly, "state your case."

LIFE AT THE WHITE HOUSE. 103

"I have no case to state," replied General Grant. "I am satisfied as it is;" thus outflanking the Secretary, and displaying the same strategy in diplomacy as in war.

"Well, well," said the President, laughing, "state your case, Secretary."

Secretary Stanton obeyed; General Grant said nothing; the President listened very attentively. When Stanton had concluded, the President crossed his legs, rested his elbow on his knee, twinkled his eyes quaintly, and said, "Now, Secretary, you know we have been trying to manage this army for two years and a-half, and you know we hav'n't done much with it. We sent over the mountains and brought *Mister* Grant, as Mrs. Grant calls him, to manage it for us, and now I guess we had better let *Mister* Grant have his own way."

A German paper publishes the following:—"A lieutenant, whom debts compelled to leave the Fatherland and the service of his country, succeeded in being admitted to President Lincoln, and by reason of his commendable and winning deportment, together with his intelligent appearance, was promised a lieutenant's commission in a cavalry regiment. He was so enraptured with his success that he deemed it his duty to inform the President that he belonged to one of the oldest families of the nobility of Germany. 'Oh, never mind that,' said Mr. Lincoln; 'you will not find that to be an obstacle in the way of your promotion.'"

Mr. Lincoln's kindness of heart showed itself in many ways. A young man had been sentenced to be shot for falling asleep at his post as a sentinel. Mr. Lincoln was to sign the death warrant.

"How many hours has this young man been on duty?" he asked.

"He was on duty some time, sir, for he had relieved a friend who was ill. But nothing can excuse so great a fault as sleeping at his post."

"I shall pardon him," said the President. "I could not think of going into eternity with the blood of the young man on my skirts. It is not to be wondered at that a boy raised on a farm, probably going to bed at dark, should, when required to watch all night, fall asleep; and I cannot consent to shoot him for such an act."

So the young man was pardoned; but Mr. Lincoln thought so much about him that he became nervous lest, after all, through some mistake, the pardon should not find its way to the proper authorities in time to stay execution, and he could not sleep that night until some one had been sent to see that all was right.

The gratitude of the young man was proved in a very pathetic manner. He fought in the battle of Fredericksburg, and was found among the slain. When the body was examined it was discovered that he was wearing next his heart a photograph of his friend and preserver, and underneath were written the words "*God bless President Lincoln.*"

The Rev. Newman Hall was told a story by an officer to the effect that twenty-four deserters had been tried by court-martial, and sentenced to be shot. Lincoln refused to sign the warrant for their execution. The officer then went to Washington himself to try to prevail on the President.

"It will not do to forgive those men," he said.

"It will not do to shoot them," said the President.

"Mr. President, unless these men are made an example of, the army itself is in danger. Mercy to the few is cruelty to the many," pleaded the officer.

But Lincoln replied, "Mr. General, there are already too many weeping widows in the United States. For God's sake don't ask me to add to the number, for I won't do it."

In the midst of his kindliness, his love of fun was constantly creeping up. A friend from Illinois once called to plead for a neighbour. On the march he had fallen out of the ranks, and entered a drinking saloon. There he stayed, indulging his taste for liquor, until his regiment had left the town. Failing to join it at the proper time, he was sentenced to be shot as a deserter.

"He may as well be pardoned," said Lincoln; "I guess he will do us more good above the ground than under the ground."

He took the order to sign the pardon, but the table was so full of papers of all kinds that he could find no room.

"By-the-by," he said, "do you know how the Patagonians manage about their oysters? They open them, and throw the shells out of the window, until the pile gets higher than the house, and then they move."

Having told the story, he signed the pardon, and sent the man away rejoicing.

Holland says:—"Yet Mr. Lincoln could be severe. Towards crimes resulting from sudden anger, or untoward circumstances, or sharp temptations—the long catalogue of vices growing out of human weakness—towards these he was always lenient; but towards a cool, calculating crime against the race, or any member of it, from ambitious or mercenary motives, he was severe. The systematic, heartless oppression of one man by another man always aroused his indignation to the highest pitch. An incident occurred soon after his inauguration which forcibly illustrates this point. The Hon. John B. Alley of Lynn, Massachusetts, was made the bearer to the President of a petition for pardon, by a person confined in the Newburyport jail, for being engaged in the slave trade. He had been sentenced to five years' imprisonment, and the payment of a fine of one thousand dollars. The petition was accompanied by a letter to Mr. Alley, in which the prisoner acknowledged his guilt, and the justice of his sentence. He was very penitent—at least on paper—and had received the full measure of his punishment so far as it related to the term of his imprisonment; but he was still held because he could not pay his fine. Mr. Alley read the letter to the President, who was much moved by its pathetic appeals, and when he had himself read the petition, he looked up, and said, 'My friend, that is a very touching appeal to our feelings. You know my weakness is to be, if possible, too easily moved by appeals for mercy, and if this man were guilty of the foulest murder that the arm of man could perpetrate, I might forgive him on such an appeal; but the man who could go to Africa, and rob her of her children, and sell them into interminable bondage, with no other motive than that which is furnished by dollars and cents, is so much worse than the most depraved murderer, that he can never receive pardon at my hands. No! He may rot in jail before he shall have liberty by any act of mine.' A sudden crime, committed under strong temptation, was venial in his eyes, on evidence of repentance; but the calculating, mercenary crime of man-stealing and man-selling, with all the cruelties that are essential accompaniments of the business, could win from him, as an officer of the people, no pardon."

Mr. Lincoln had not only the troubles of state to bear, but his own domestic griefs as well; and in February 1862 he had a very severe one. Sickness entered his house. Both Willie and "Tad" were ill; and as his children were very dear to him, this added trouble perplexed and distressed him greatly. A good Christian lady of Massachusetts, who was giving her services in one of the hospitals, went to the White House to help Mr. and Mrs. Lincoln in nursing the children. She said afterwards that Mr. Lincoln often watched with her, and this gave her an opportunity of speaking to him.

He was always patient when people exhorted him, but he took the few serious words of this lady better than some from other people. It is reported that once when a minister was introduced, he provided him a seat, and sitting opposite, said, "Now, sir, I am ready to hear what you have to say."

"Oh, bless you, sir," said the minister, "I have nothing special to say; I merely called to pay my respects to you, and, as one of the million, to assure you of my hearty sympathy and support."

"My dear sir," said the President, rising with a sigh of relief, "I am very glad to see you indeed; *I thought you had come to preach to me.*"

But he did not mind being preached to sometimes.

He said to the lady who was nursing his children, "This is the hardest trial of my life; why is it? why is it?"

The lady did not know that she could do better than tell Mr. Lincoln a little of her own history.

"I used to ask, 'How is it?' when my troubles came," she said.

"Ah, you have had troubles like the rest of us, I suppose."

"Yes, indeed, very sore troubles. I am a widow, and have two children in heaven. But I have seen the hand of God in it all, and can say that I never loved or trusted Him so much as since my affliction."

"But how was that brought about?"

"Simply by trusting in God, and feeling that He does all things well," she replied.

"Did you submit fully under the first loss?" he asked.

"No, not wholly," she replied; "but as blow came upon blow, and all was taken, I could and did submit, and was very happy."

"I am glad to hear you say that," responded the President; "your experience will help me to bear my afflictions."

If sympathy could have helped the President he would have been helped; but there are some troubles that are too great for anything human to alleviate; only God can bind up a bruised and broken heart. Willie Lincoln died. The Cabinet addressed these words to Congress :—" The President of the United States was last evening plunged into affliction by the death of a beloved child. The heads of departments, in consideration of this distressing event, have thought it would be agreeable to Congress, and to the American people, that the official and private buildings occupied by them should not be illuminated on the evening of the twenty-second."

It was a time of joy, but the President and the people were full of sorrow. Willie Wallace Lincoln was buried in a vault in the Oak-Hill Cemetery at Georgetown; but the funeral services were conducted at the White House. His friends were allowed to pass through and take a last look at him. He was dressed in his accustomed jacket and trousers, with white stockings and low shoes, and white collar and wristband turned over his dark jacket. A wreath of flowers was on his breast, and in his hand a beautiful bouquet of camelias, while his body was covered with azalias and sprigs of mignonette. There were present Members of the Cabinet, Foreign Ministers, Members of Congress, Officers of the Army and Navy, and many citizens and ladies. The Rev. Dr. Gurley, the President's chaplain, performed the service in a very impressive manner. The President said some time afterwards to a friend, "Since Willie's death I catch myself every day involuntarily talking with him, as if he were with me."

That the loss of his child was blessed and sanctified to him there can be no doubt. The author of *The Forest Boy* says, that when a gentleman was going on business to the White House, a number of Christian friends said to him, " We want you to ask Mr. Lincoln if he loves Jesus." He promised that he would do so. When he had finished his interview with the President, he said, "At the solicitation of some Christian friends, I have a question to propose to you, if you will allow me, Mr. Lincoln."

"Certainly," was the courteous reply.

"It is this :—'*Do you love Jesus?*'"

The President burst into tears, buried his face in his handkerchief, and for a time was unable to speak. At length he said, "When I left Springfield I said to my fellow-citizens, 'Pray for me,' but I was not then a Christian. When my child died my heart was still rebellious against God. But when I walked the battle-field of Gettysburg, and saw the wounded and the dying, and felt that by that victory our cause was saved, I then and there resolved, and gave my heart to Jesus. *I do love Jesus.*"

On 19th November 1863 the Gettysburg Cemetery was opened, and on that occasion Mr. Lincoln said—

"Fourscore and seven years ago our fathers brought forth upon this Continent a new nation, conceived in liberty, and dedicated to the proposition that all men are created equal. Now we are engaged in a great civil war, testing whether that nation, or any nation so conceived and dedicated, can endure. We are met on a great battle-field of that war. We are met to dedicate a portion of it as the final resting-place of those who here gave their lives that a nation might live. It is altogether fitting and proper to do this.

"But in a larger sense we cannot dedicate, we cannot consecrate, we cannot hallow this ground. The brave men, living or dead, who struggled here, have consecrated it far above my power to add or detract. The world will little note or long remember what we say here. It is for us, the living rather, to be dedicated here to the unfinished work that they have so nobly carried on. It is rather for us to be dedicated here to the great task remaining before us— that from these honoured dead we take increased devotion to the cause for which they died, resolved that the dead shall not have died in vain ; that the nation shall, under

God, have a new birth of freedom, and that the government of the people, by the people, and for the people, shall not perish from the earth.'

Mr. Carpenter tells of a poem of which the President was very fond, and which he had learnt by heart. We give the first and last stanzas—

> "Oh, why should the spirit of mortal be proud ?
> Like a fast-flitting meteor, a fast flying cloud,
> A flash of the lightning, a break of the wave,
> He passes from life to his rest in the grave.
>
> 'Tis the twink of an eye, 'tis the draught of a breath,
> From the blossom of health to the paleness of death,
> From the gilded saloon to the bier and the shroud :
> Oh, why should the spirit of mortal be proud ?"

To Mrs. Gurney, the widow of the London banker, and well-known friend and philanthropist, Mr. Lincoln wrote :— "My esteemed friend, I have not forgotten, never shall forget, the very impressive occasion when you and your friends visited me on a Sabbath forenoon two years ago. Nor had your kind letter, written nearly a year later, ever been forgotten. In all it has been your purpose to strengthen my reliance upon God. I am much indebted to the good Christian people of the country for their constant prayers and consolations, and to none more than to yourself. The purposes of the Almighty are perfect, and must prevail, though we erring mortals may fail accurately to perceive this in advance. We hoped for a happy termination of this terrible war before this ; but God knows best, and has ruled otherwise. We shall yet acknowledge His wisdom, and our own errors therein ; meanwhile we must work earnestly in the best lights He gives us, trusting that so working still conduces to the great end He ordains. Surely He intends some great good to follow this mighty commotion, which no mortal could make, and no mortal could stay."

More and more Abraham Lincoln was learning to trust

in God. He spent an hour every morning in reading the Scriptures and in prayer. Once, when a great battle was in progress, he said, "I have done all that I could. There is nothing that I can do."

"Yes," said a lady, "you can pray."

He went away to his own room; and while he was there, a telegram came to say that a Union victory had been won. He came into the room crying, "Good news! Good news! The victory is ours. God is good." "Nothing like prayer," suggested the lady. "Yes," said Lincoln, "there is praise: prayer and praise."

Dr. Brockett gives the account of the daily routine of the life at the White House in the narrative of "One who Knew":—"Mr. Lincoln is an early riser, and he is thus able to devote two or three hours each morning to his voluminous private correspondence, besides glancing at a city paper. At nine he breakfasts; then walks over to the War Office, to read such war telegrams as they give him (occasionally some are withheld), and to have a chat with General Hallick on the military situation, in which he takes a great interest. Returning to the White House, he goes through with his morning's mail, in company with a private secretary, who makes a minute of the reply which he is to make, and others the President retains that he may answer them himself. Every letter receives attention, and all which are entitled to a reply receive one, no matter how they are worded, or how inelegant the chirography may be.

"Tuesdays and Fridays are Cabinet days, but on other days visitors at the White House are requested to wait in the ante-room, and send in their cards. Sometimes before the President has finished reading his mail, Louis will have a handful of pasteboard, and from the cards laid before him Mr. Lincoln has visitors ushered in, giving precedence to acquaintances. Three or four hours do they pour in, in rapid succession, nine out of ten asking offices, and patiently does the President listen to their application. Care and anxiety have furrowed his rather homely features, yet occasionally he is reminded of an anecdote, and good-humoured glances beam from his clear grey eyes, while his ringing laugh shows that he is not 'used up' yet. The simple and natural manner in which he delivers his thoughts make him appear to those visiting him like an earnest, affectionate friend. He makes little parade of his legal science, and rarely indulges in speculative propositions, but states his ideas in plain Anglo-Saxon, illuminated by many lively images and pleasing allusions, which seem to flow as if in obedience to a restless impulse of nature. Some newspaper admirer attempts to deny that the President tells stories. Why, it is rarely that anyone is in his company for five minutes without hearing a good tale appropriate to the subject talked about. Many a metaphysical argument does he demolish by simply telling an anecdote, which exactly overturns the verbal structure.

"About four o'clock the President declines seeing any more company, and often accompanies his wife in her carriage to take a drive. He is fond of horseback exercise. The President dines at six, and it is rare that some personal friends do not grace the round dining-table, where he throws off the cares of office, and reminds those who have been in Kentucky of the old-school gentleman who used to dispense generous hospitality there. From the dinner-table the party retire to the crimson drawing-room, where coffee is served, and where the President passes the evening, unless some dignitary has a special interview. Such is the almost unvarying life of Abraham Lincoln, whose administration will rank next in importance to that of Washington in our national annals."

CHAPTER XIII.

RE-ELECTED.

"Not lightly fall beyond recall
  The written scrolls a breath can float;
The crowning fact, the kingliest act
  Of freedom, is the freeman's vote.

So shall our voice of sovereign choice
  Swell the deep bass of duty done,
And strike the key of time to be,
  When God and man shall speak as one."
—WHITTIER.

"I SHALL NEVER BE GLAD AGAIN," said Abraham Lincoln to a lady who waited upon him for six days, to persuade him to give an order for the erection of hospitals in the North. But when he said that, he was thinking of the dead soldiers whose lives had been poured out as water. Other things there were that certainly gave him pleasure, and among them was the fact that from the working men of England came addresses of sympathy and confidence. England's sufferings were only second to those of America during the long war, which deprived the Lancashire mills of cotton, and made hundreds of thousands idle, and plunged nearly half the homes of England into poverty and distress. Yet so clearly did the

people understand that this was no fault of the wise and kindly, but hard-pressed President, that the working men of Manchester sent him words of cheer. He said, among other things, in reply—" I know and deeply deplore the sufferings which the working men of Manchester and in all Europe are called to endure in this crisis. It has been often and studiously represented that the attempt to overthrow this Government, which was built upon the foundation of human rights, and to substitute for it one which should rest exclusively on the basis of human slavery, was likely to obtain the favour of Europe. Through the action of our loyal citizens, the working men of Europe have been subjected to severe trial, for the purpose of forcing their sanction to that attempt. Under the circumstances I cannot but regard your decisive utterances upon the question as an instance of sublime Christian heroism, which has not been surpassed in any age or in any country. It is indeed an energetic and reinspiring assurance of the inherent power of truth, and of the ultimate and universal triumph of justice, humanity, and freedom. I do not doubt that the sentiments you have expressed will be sustained by your great nation ; and, on the other hand, I have no hesitation in assuring you that they will excite admiration, esteem, and the most reciprocal feelings of friendship among the American people. I hail this interchange of sentiment, therefore, as an augury that whatever else may happen, whatever misfortune may befall your country or my own, the peace and friendship which now exist between the two nations will be, as it shall be my desire to make them, perpetual.

"ABRAHAM LINCOLN."

The working men of London held a similar meeting about the same time, and took substantially the same action. The President made the following response to their address:—

"Executive Mansion, Washington, 2nd Feb. 1863.

"*To the Working Men of London—*

"I have received the New Year's Address which you have sent me, with a sincere appreciation of the exalted and humane sentiments by which it was inspired.

"As these sentiments are manifestly the enduring support of the free institutions of England, so I am sure also that they constitute the only reliable basis for free institutions throughout the world.

"The resources, advantages, and powers of the American people are very great, and they have consequently succeeded to equally great responsibilities. It seems to have devolved upon them to test whether a Government established on the principles of human freedom can be maintained against an effort to build one upon the exclusive foundation of human bondage. They will rejoice with me in the new evidences which your proceedings furnish, that the magnanimity they exhibit is justly estimated by the true friends of freedom and humanity in foreign countries.

"Accept my best wishes for your individual welfare, and for the welfare and happiness of the whole British people.

"Abraham Lincoln."

In connection with England, an amusing story, culled from Carpenter's book, may here be given:—

"Upon the betrothal of the Prince of Wales to the Princess Alexandra, Queen Victoria sent a letter to each of the European sovereigns, and also to President Lincoln, announcing the fact. Lord Lyons, her ambassador at Washington, requested an audience of Mr. Lincoln, that he might present the document in person. At the time appointed he was received at the White House, in company with Mr. Seward.

"'May it please your Excellency,' said Lord Lyons, 'I

hold in my hand an autograph letter from my royal mistress, Queen Victoria, which I have been commanded to present to your Excellency. In it she informs your Excellency that her son, His Royal Highness the Prince of Wales, is about to contract a matrimonial alliance with Her Royal Highness the Princess Alexandra of Denmark.'

"After continuing in this strain for a few minutes, Lord Lyons tendered the letter to the President, and awaited his reply. It was short, simple, and expressive, and must have astonished the ambassador (who was a bachelor), for it consisted of these words, '*Lord Lyons, go thou and do likewise.*'"

Mr. Carpenter wonders what success he met with in putting the reply in diplomatic words when he reported it to Her Majesty.

The year 1864 was a very remarkable one in the annals of the United States. It became evident, when the year had only half passed, that, in regard to the election of a President, which had in due course now to be made, the people were already resolved.

A great convention was held at Baltimore, at which a ballot was taken, the result of which proved that Lincoln was again the choice of the people. The chairman went to Washington to tell the President, and he replied :—

"Having served four years in the depth of a great and yet unended national peril, I can view this call to a second term in nowise more flattering to myself than as an expression of the public judgment that I may better finish a difficult work, in which I have laboured from the first, than could any one less severely schooled to the task. In this view, and with assured reliance on that Almighty Ruler who has so graciously sustained us thus far, and with increased gratitude to the generous people for their continued confidence, I accept the renewed **trust, with its yet onerous and perplexing duties and responsibilities.**"

But between the writing of this letter and the election there came a trial to Mr. Lincoln. He did not approve a bill which Congress brought forward, and this roused part of the press to very offensive attacks.

Mr. Horace Greeley wrote to Mr Lincoln to say that two ambassadors were in Canada, with powers from the South to negotiate a peace; and Lincoln replied, "If you can find any person anywhere, professing to have any proposition of Jefferson Davis *in writing*, embracing the restoration of the Union and abandonment of slavery, whatever else it embraces, say to him that he may come to me with you." He also wrote the following letter:—

"EXECUTIVE MANSION, WASHINGTON, 18th July 1864.

"TO WHOM IT MAY CONCERN:—

"Any proposition which embraces the restoration of peace, the integrity of the whole Union, and the abandonment of slavery, and which comes by and with an authority that can control the armies now at war against the United States, will be received and considered by the Executive Government of the United States, and will be met on liberal terms, on substantial and collateral points; and the bearer or bearers thereof shall have safe-conduct both ways.

"ABRAHAM LINCOLN."

Some of Lincoln's friends were uneasy lest the best that could be done was not done; but he said to a deputation from Maryland:—

"Something said by the Secretary of State, in his recent speech at Auburn, has been construed by some into a threat that, if I shall be beaten at the election, I will, between then and the constitutional end of my term, do what I may be able to ruin the Government. Others regard the fact that the Chicago Convention adjourned not *sine die*, but to meet again, if called to do so by a particular individual, as the intimation of a purpose that, if their nominee shall be elected, he will at once seize control of the Government. I hope the good people will permit themselves to suffer no uneasiness on either point. I am struggling to maintain the Government, not to overthrow it. I am struggling especially to prevent others from overthrowing it. I therefore say, that, if I live, I shall remain President until the fourth of next March, and that whoever shall be constitutionally elected in November shall be duly installed as President on the fourth of March; and, in the interval, I shall do my utmost that whoever is to hold the helm for the next voyage shall start with the best possible chance of saving the ship."

The presidential election took place on the 8th November 1864, and resulted in the triumph of Mr. Lincoln in every loyal State except Kentucky, New Jersey, and Delaware. In some of the States their soldiers in the field were allowed to vote, and the military vote was almost invariably cast for Lincoln and Johnson. The official returns for the entire vote polled summed up 4,034,789. Of these Mr. Lincoln received 2,223,035, and Mr. M'Clellan received 1,811,754, leaving a majority of 411,281 on the popular vote. Mr. Lincoln was elected by a plurality in 1860. In 1864 his majority was decided and unmistakable.

Of course Mr. Lincoln was gratified. "I am thankful to God for this approval of the people," said he on the night of his election, to a band of Pennsylvanians who had called upon him; and he added, "But while deeply grateful for this mark of their confidence in me, if I know my heart, my gratitude is free from any taint of personal triumph. I do not impugn the motives of any one opposed to me. It is no pleasure to me to triumph over any one; but I give thanks to the Almighty for this evidence of the people's resolution to stand by free government and the rights of humanity." A German soldier said—"I goes for Fader

Abraham; he likes the soldier boy. Ven he serves tree years, he gives him four hundred dollars, and re-enlists him von veteran. Now, Fader Abraham, he serve four years. We re-enlist him for four years more, and make von veteran of him."

Congratulations poured in upon him from all quarters. There was a pressure upon him, almost greater than he could sustain; but he found time in the midst of all the excitement to write the following :—

"EXECUTIVE MANSION, WASHINGTON, 21st Nov. 1864.

"DEAR MADAM—I have been shown, on the files of the War Department, a statement of the Adjutant-General of Massachusetts, that you are the mother of five sons who have died gloriously on the field of battle. I feel how weak and fruitless must be any words of mine which should attempt to beguile you from the grief of a loss so overwhelming. But I cannot refrain from tendering to you the consolation that may be found in the thanks of the Republic they have died to save. I pray that our Heavenly Father may assuage the anguish of your bereavement, and leave you only the cherished memory of the loved and lost, and the solemn pride that must be yours to have laid so costly a sacrifice upon the altar of freedom.

"Yours very sincerely and respectfully,

"ABRAHAM LINCOLN.

"To MRS. BRIXBY, Boston, Massachusetts."

A clergyman once said to the President that he hoped "the Lord was on our side." Lincoln replied, "I am not at all concerned about that, for I know that the Lord is always on the side of the *right*. But it is my constant anxiety and prayer that I and this nation should be on the Lord's side."

It seemed that at last He who was on the side of the right was about to send peace again. The crisis had come. Mr. Lincoln was himself in a tent at City Point, on the James' River, and he telegraphed the results of the battles as news were brought to him. The strain upon his nervous system was very great; but he found some relief in tending a cat and a family of kittens that had just been born. On Monday morning, 3rd April, the news came that the rebels had left Richmond, and that the Union forces were occupying the city. He started to go, but paused—" Little kitten," he said, taking up one of the tiny creatures, " I must perform a last act of kindness for you before I go. I must open your eyes ;" and this he did as tenderly as a woman could have done it. When the kitten blinkingly looked around in wonder, he said, "Oh, that I could open the eyes of my blinded fellow-countrymen as easily as I have those of that little creature."

On the same afternoon, 3rd April, Mr. Lincoln, attended by his son "Tad," who held his father's hand in awe and wonder, visited the city of Richmond. The visit is thus described by C. C. Coppin, Esq., in the *Atlantic Monthly*:—
"There was no committee of reception, no guard of honour, no grand display of troops, no assembling of an eager multitude to welcome him. He entered the city unheralded. Six sailors, armed with carabines, stepped upon the shore, followed by the President, who held his little son by the hand, and Admiral Porter; the officers followed, and six more sailors brought up the rear. There were forty or fifty freed-men, who had been sole possessors of themselves for twenty-four hours, at work on the bank of the Canal, securing some floating timber, under the direction of a lieutenant. Somehow they obtained the information that the man who was head and shoulders taller than all others around him, with features large and irregular, with a mild eye and pleasant countenance, was President Lincoln.

"'God bless you, sah!' said one, taking off his cap, and bowing very low.

"'Hurrah! Hurrah! President Linkum hab come!' was the shout which rang through the streets.

"The lieutenant found himself without command. What cared those freed-men, fresh from the house of bondage, for floating timber and military commands? Their deliverer had come—he who next to the Lord Jesus was their best friend. It was not a hurrah that they gave, but a wild, jubilant cry of inexpressible joy.

"They gathered round the President, ran ahead, hovered upon the flanks of the little company, and hung like a dark cloud upon the rear. Men, women, and children joined the constantly-increasing throng. They came from all the by-streets, running in breathless haste, shouting, hallooing, and dancing with delight. The men threw up their hats; the women waved their bonnets and handkerchiefs, clapped their hands, and sang—'Glory be to God! glory, glory, glory!' rendering all the praise to God who had heard their wailings in the past, their moaning for wives, husbands, children, and friends sold out of their sight, had given them freedom, and, after long years of waiting, had permitted them thus unexpectedly to behold the face of their great benefactor.

"'I thank you, dear Jesus, that I behold President Linkum!' was the exclamation of a woman who stood upon the threshold of her humble home; and with streaming eyes and clasped hands gave thanks aloud to the Saviour of men.

"Another, more demonstrative in her joy, was jumping and striking her hands with all her might, crying, 'Bless de Lord, bless de Lord, bless de Lord!' as if there could be no end of her thanksgiving.

"The air rang with a tumultuous chorus of voices. The streets became almost impassable on account of the increasing multitude. Soldiers were summoned to clear the way.

How strange the event! The President of the United States—he who had been hated, despised, maligned above all other men living—to whom the vilest epithets had been applied by the people of Richmond—was walking their streets, receiving their thanksgiving, blessings, and prayers from thousands who hailed him as an ally of the Messiah.

. . . "Abraham Lincoln was walking in their streets; and, worst of all, that plain, honest-hearted man was recognising the 'niggers' as human beings by returning their salutations! The walk was long, and the President halted a moment to rest. 'May de good Lord bless you, President Linkum!' said an old negro, removing his hat, and bowing, with tears of joy rolling down his cheeks. The President removed his own hat and bowed in silence; but it was a bow that upset the forms, laws, customs, and ceremonies of centuries. It was a death-shock to chivalry, and a mortal wound to caste. Recognise a nigger! Faugh! A woman in an adjoining house beheld it, and turned from the scene in unspeakable disgust. There were men in the crowd who had daggers in their eyes, but the chosen assassin was not there, the hour for the damning work had not come, and that great-hearted man passed on to the Executive Mansion of the Confederacy.

"Want of space compels us to pass over other scenes—the visit of the President to the State House; the jubilant shouts of the crowd; the rush of freed-men into the Capitol grounds, where, till the appearance of their deliverer, they had never been permitted to enter; the ride of the President through the streets; his visit to Libby Prison; the distribution of bread to the destitute, etc."

Mrs. Lincoln went the next day to see the city, and Lincoln held important interviews with Judge Campbell and others. He also had a drive round the city, and visited General Weitzel's headquarters. But he was anxious to get back to Washington, because during his absence Mr. Seward, the Secretary of State, had met with a serious accident, and was confined to his bed. Mr. Lincoln went to him, and after kind words of sympathy, he threw himself across the bed, and rehearsed the story of Grant's wonderful generalship, the bravery of the soldiers, their success, Richmond's fall, and the vigorous pursuit of Lee, which was then going on. At the close of his narration he said, "Now for a day of National Thanksgiving!"

CHAPTER XIV.

PEACE AND VICTORY.

"Hushed to-day are sounds of gladness,
 From the mountains to the sea;
And the plaintive voice of sadness
 Rises, mighty God, to Thee.

Freedom claimed another martyr,
 Heaven received another saint;
Who are we Thy will to question?
 Lord, we weep without complaint."
—Phebe A. Hanaford.

ON the morning of the 14th of April 1865 a Cabinet Council was held, and no one thought that the President had awoke to spend his last day on earth. The whole nation was given up to rejoicing. On the eleventh there had been an impromptu gathering of the masses before the White House, and every face seemed lighted with hope and happiness. But the fourteenth was Good Friday, and the peace rejoicings were to be on a large scale. Four years ago that day the war had commenced, and now it was virtually at an end.

At the Cabinet meeting rather a singular incident occurred.

PEACE AND VICTORY. 125

"Have you heard from General Sherman?" asked the President of General Grant.

"No, but I am hourly expecting to hear, and I hope he will tell me that Johnston has surrendered."

"Well," said the President, "you will hear very soon now, and the news will be important."

"Why do you think so?" inquired Grant.

"Because I had a dream last night, and ever since the war began I have invariably had the same dream before any important military event occurred."

He turned to Secretary Welles, and said, "It is in your line too, Mr. Welles. The dream is, that I saw a ship sailing very rapidly, and I am sure that it portends some important national event."

Later in the day the carriage was ordered for a drive.

"Would you like any one to go with us?" asked Mrs. Lincoln.

"No; let us go alone. I prefer to ride by ourselves to-day," said the President.

During the drive he was full of fun, making his wife laugh at his jokes and gaiety.

"Dear husband, you almost startle me by your great cheerfulness," she said.

"And well I may feel so, Mary," he replied, "for I consider this day the war has come to a close."

"That is indeed reason for rejoicing."

"Yes; and, Mary, we must be more cheerful in the future. Between the war and the loss of our darling Willie we have been very miserable."

Alas! that was the last drive they had together.

In the evening there was to be a grand performance at the theatre. The Washington papers announced that "Lieutenant-General Grant, President Lincoln, Mrs. Lincoln and Ladies will occupy the State box at Ford's Theatre to-night." General Grant declined to attend, and Mr. Lincoln did not wish to go, but he thought the people would be disappointed if neither he nor Grant was present; and so, as he was "fixed upon having some relaxation," he went. He and Mrs. Lincoln and their friends were greeted as soon as they entered the box with prolonged cheering. The President bowed his acknowledgments, and was soon quietly watching the transactions upon the stage.

Many people were feeling anxious as to the safety of the President, for there were rumours of an intended assassination. He greatly objected to be always guarded, and liked freedom and movement too well to submit to the restraint. But he had only that day written to a friend that "he would in future see that all due precautions were taken."

To another friend, who had expressed the fear that the rebels might take his life, he had shown a packet of letters, saying, "There, every one of these contains a threat to assassinate me. I might be nervous if I were to dwell upon the subject, but I have come to the conclusion that there are opportunities to kill me every day of my life, if there are persons disposed to do it. It is not possible to avoid exposure to such a fate, and I shall not trouble myself about it."

He was certainly not troubling himself about it when the deed was done.

He was seated on a cushioned, rocking arm-chair, at the end of the box farthest from the stage, and nearest to the audience, and was already interested. Mrs. Lincoln sat in a chair between the President and the pillar in the centre of the box; Miss Harris and Major Rathbone occupied other chairs. The box was not closed during the evening.

At fifteen minutes after ten a young man passed along the passage behind the dress circle, and showing a card to the President's messenger, stood for a few minutes looking down upon the audience and the stage below. He then entered the vestibule of the President's box, and softly closed the door behind him, so that it could not be opened from the outside. Every one in the President's box was intently watching the play; and no one there noticed the new comer, as he drew from his pocket a silver-mounted Derringer pistol, which he held in his right hand, while in his left he held a long, double-edged dagger.

He stepped within the inner door of the President's box, and stood immediately over the chair of the President.

The next moment he pulled the trigger, and Abraham Lincoln leaned slightly forward, and closed his eyes. He had been shot through the back of the head.

The flash, the report, and the puff of smoke roused the inmates in the box, and Major Rathbone at once seized the intruder. He dropped the pistol, and struck at Rathbone with a dagger. The Major tried still to grapple with the assassin, but he wrenched himself away. He went to the front of the box, and shouted the insulting words, *Sic semper tyrannis.* He then sprang from the box to the stage below. As he did so his spur caught in the flag hung below the State box, and he fell; but quickly recovering himself, he faced the audience, and cried, as he brandished his dagger, "The South is avenged."

It all happened so quickly that no one had any idea of what had really occurred. The people thought the shot was part of the play. A man named Hawke was the only person on the stage when Booth leaped down, and he, seeing the dagger, thought the man meant to do him some mischief, and he ran away. But Mrs. Lincoln screamed, and Miss Harris called for water. As Booth rushed off the stage, some one said, "That is John Wilkes Booth;" and Major Rathbone cried, "Stop that man." The confusion of the moment was so great that no one attempted to follow the murderer but one man, Mr. J. B. Stewart of the Washington Bar. But Booth lost not a moment. He was an actor, and knew the ways of exit from the theatre, and as Mr. Stewart reached the door he saw the assassin spring upon a horse that a boy was holding, and ride away. In the theatre all was excitement. The people answered their own question, "What is it?" with "The President has been shot;" for all feared it must be so. Laura Keene's clear voice was the first to ring through the theatre, "Keep quiet in your seats, give him air;" and she herself, with water and cordials, went into the President's box.

He neither spoke nor moved after the shot was fired. Several surgeons at once came forward; and as soon as they found the wound, they carefully carried Mr. Lincoln out of the theatre to the house of Mr. Peterson. Surgeon-General Barnes at once said that the President had not many hours to live. He was immediately surrounded by the members of his Government, who remained with him through the night. Mrs. Lincoln had fainted after the scream which had first given intimation of that which had occurred; but when she had returned to consciousness she was led to the house where her husband was dying; and there she sat in another room, crushed and stunned by grief. Her son Robert was there supporting her, and Mrs. Senator Dixon was by her side. No one could realise the blow that had fallen. Every one felt as Secretary Stanton did, when Surgeon-General Barnes announced the wound to be a mortal one—"Oh, no, General, no, no," he said, as he burst into tears. The Hon. M. B. Field, Assistant Secretary of the Treasury, thus writes:—

"For several hours the breathing continued, and apparently without pain or consciousness. But about seven o'clock a change occurred, and the breathing, which had been continuous, was interrupted at intervals. These intervals became more frequent, and of longer duration, and the breathing more feeble. Several times the interval was so long that we thought him dead, and the surgeon applied his finger to the pulse, evidently to ascertain if such were the fact. But it was not until twenty-two minutes past seven o'clock in the morning that the flame flickered out. There was no apparent suffering, no convulsive action, no rattling of the throat, none of the ordinary premonitory symptoms of death. Death in this case was a mere cessation of breathing.

"The fact had not been ascertained one minute when Dr. Gurley offered up a prayer. The few persons in the room were all profoundly affected. The President's eyes after death were not, particularly the right one, entirely closed. I closed them myself with my fingers. The expression immediately after death was purely negative; but in fifteen minutes there came over the mouth, the nostrils, and the chin, a smile that seemed almost an effort of life. I had never seen upon the President's face an expression more genial and pleasing.

"About fifteen minutes before the decease, Mrs. Lincoln came into the room, and threw herself upon her dying husband's body. She was allowed to remain there only a few minutes, when she was removed in a sobbing condition, in which, indeed, she had been during all the time she was present."

It was some time before any one had the presence of mind to turn out the lights in the theatre, and tell the frightened people to go home. When they went out into the streets they were met by a crowd equally excited with themselves.

"The President has been shot!" they said; and were confronted with the appalling news, "Mr. Seward has been assassinated."

The dreadful story was all too soon confirmed.

A little after ten on that fatal evening a man called at the residence of the Secretary of State, who was still very ill, and under surgical treatment.

"I come from Dr. Verdi, Mr. Seward's physician," he said, "and I have brought some medicine which it is necessary for me to give to the Secretary myself." "No one is allowed to see the Secretary," said the servant. The man then pushed him aside, and mounted the stairs.

He was about to enter the Secretary's room, when Mr. Frederick Seward appeared, and demanded to know his business.

"I have some medicine for the Secretary," he said.

"But you will not be allowed to enter my father's room," was the reply. The villain at once struck Mr. F. Seward with the butt end of a pistol, and pushing him aside, went into the Secretary's room, and mounting the bed, stabbed the Secretary several times, aiming at his throat. But he did not succeed in killing him, for his nurse and a soldier rushed in and pulled the man away. Mr. Seward managed to roll off the bed, and the assassin began to stab Robinson, the soldier. Presently he rushed downstairs, meeting on the way Major Augustus Seward and another of the Secretary's attendants. He stabbed them both; altogether he stabbed five persons, and then escaped into the street.

He was afterwards discovered to be Lewis Payne Powell.

The Secretary did not die; but he was very ill, and his friends dared not tell him of the President's death. He found it out for himself at last. "Is Lincoln dead?" he said. "Was he stabbed too? I think he must be, or he would have come to see me." When he was well enough to be moved nearer the window, he saw the flags half-mast high, and said, with tears, "The President is dead; I knew it."

Raymond says:—"When the news of this appalling tragedy spread through the city, it carried consternation to every heart. Treading close on the heels of the President's murder—perpetrated, indeed, at the same instant—it was instinctively felt to be the work of a conspiracy—secret, remorseless, and terrible. The Secretary of War, Mr. Stanton, had left Mr. Seward's bedside not twenty minutes before the assault, and was in his private chamber, preparing to retire, when a messenger brought tidings of the tragedy, and summoned his instant attendance. On his way to Mr. Seward's house Mr. Stanton heard of the simultaneous murder of the President, and instantly felt that the Government was enveloped in the meshes of a conspiracy, whose agents were unknown, and which was all the more terrible for the darkness and mystery in which it moved. Orders were instantly given to close all drinking-shops, and all places of public resort in the city; guards were stationed at every point, and all possible precautions were taken for the safety of the Vice-President and other prominent Government officials. A vague terror brooded over the population of the town. Men whispered to each other as they met in the gloom of midnight, and the deeper gloom of the shadowy crime which surrounded them. Presently, passionate indignation replaced this paralysis of the public heart, and but for the precautions adopted on the instant by the Government, the public vengeance would have been wreaked upon the rebels confined in the Old Capitol Prison. All those feelings, however, gradually subsided, and gave way to a feeling of intense anxiety for the life of the President. Crowds of people assembled in the neighbourhood of the house where the dying martyr lay, eager for tidings of his condition throughout the night; and when, early in the morning, it was announced that he was dead, a feeling of solemn awe filled every heart, and sat, a brooding grief, upon every face.

"And so it was through all the length and breadth of the land. In every State, in every town, in every household there was a dull and bitter agony as the telegraph bore tidings of the awful deed. Everywhere throughout the Union, the public heart, bounding with exultation at the triumphant close of the great war, and ready to celebrate with a mighty joy the return of peace, stood still with a sacred terror as it was smitten by the terrible tidings from the capital of the nation. In the great cities of the land all business instantly stopped—no man had the heart to think of gain—flags drooped half-mast from every winged messenger of the sea, from every church spire, from every tree of liberty, and from every public building. Masses of the people came together by a spontaneous impulse to look in each other's faces, as if they could read there some hint of the meaning of these dreadful deeds—some omen of the country's fate. Thousands upon thousands, drawn by a common feeling, crowded around every place of public resort, and listened eagerly to whatever any public speaker chose to say. Wall Street in New York was thronged by a vast multitude of men, to whom eminent public officials addressed words of sympathy and hope. Gradually, as the day wore on, emblems of mourning were hung from the windows of every house throughout the town; and before the sun had set every city throughout the length and breadth of the land, to which tidings of the great calamity had been borne by the telegraph, was enshrouded in the shadow of the national grief. On the next day, which was Sunday, every pulpit resounded with eloquent eulogies of the murdered President, and with such comments on his death as faith in an over-ruling Providence alone could prompt. The whole country was plunged into profound grief, and none deplored the crime which deprived the nation of its head with more sincerity than those who had been involved in the guilt of the rebellion, and who had just begun to appreciate those merciful and forgiving elements in Mr. Lincoln's character, whose exercise they themselves would need so soon."

In the meantime all the world was filled with horror at the event, and the condolences of other nations began to flow in. The Queen of England, herself a widow, sent a kind autograph letter to the widow of the President.

Mrs. Stowe, who was moved by the fact of death following so soon after victory, said, "This our joy has been ordained to be changed into a wail of sorrow. The kind hand that held the helm so steadily in the desperate tossings of the storm has been stricken down just as we entered port; the fatherly heart that bore all our sorrows can take no earthly part in our joys. His were the cares, the watchings, the toils, the agonies of a nation in mortal struggle; and God, looking down, was so well pleased with his humble faithfulness, his patient continuance in well-doing, that earthly rewards and honours seemed all too poor for him, so He reached down and took him to immortal glories. 'Well done, good and faithful servant! enter into the joy of thy Lord.'"

The body of the President was embalmed, and it was thought that not less than 25,000 persons went to look at the face that was so dear to them. The rich and the poor came alike, and hundreds brought flowers as little offerings of love. The following Wednesday was the day of the funeral ceremony. Service was first held in the east-room of the Executive Mansion, and then the remains were removed to the Rotunda of the capital. There was an enormous procession, and vast crowds thronged to see it. There were funeral services in all the churches of Washington, and in most of the churches throughout the United States, and indeed throughout the world. Dr. Gurley preached the funeral sermon at Washington. He said, "As we stand here to-day, mourners around this coffin, and around the lifeless remains of our beloved Chief Magistrate, we recognise and we adore the sovereignty of God. . . . It was a cruel, cruel hand, that dark hand of the assassin, which smote our honoured, wise, and noble President, and filled the land with sorrow. But above and beyond that hand there is another which we must see and acknowledge— it is the chastising hand of a wise and a faithful Father."

But the body of the good President was not to rest in Washington, but near the old home at Springfield.

CHAPTER XV.

AFTERWARDS.

"He went about his work—such work as few
    Ever had laid on head and heart and hand—
As one who knows, where there's a task to do,
    Man's honest will must heaven's good grace command:

The Old World and the New, from sea to sea,
    Utter one voice of sympathy and shame!
Sore heart, so stopped when it at last beat high;
    Sad life, cut short just as its triumph came."
                            —*Punch.*

THERE was something exceedingly pathetic in the long funeral procession which bore the dead body of President Lincoln from the palace at Washington, where he had lived his life of exaltation, back to Springfield, among whose quiet scenes the foundation of his future greatness had been laid.

On the morning of the 21st of April, at six o'clock, the members of the Cabinet, Lieutenant-General Grant and his staff, several senators, the Illinois delegation, and a large number of army officers, took their last farewell of their President. Dr. Gurley offered a solemn prayer, and the coffin, accompanied by that of Willie Lincoln, was taken to the railway station. The engine bell tolled, and the train slowly moved away from the depôt; "and thus Abraham Lincoln slowly moved away from Washington, the scene of his life's work and his glory."

The funeral *cortége* was conveyed by special train over almost the same route as that which he had taken on his journey to Washington after his election. The car, too, was the same, only now it had been appropriately draped in mourning. The rate of speed was limited; but the train did not stop until it arrived at Baltimore. In out-of-the-way places, people came from their cottages or farms, and stood bareheaded as it went past. Mourners waited along the whole line, wearing badges of sorrow, to catch a view of the train that bore the dead body of him whom they loved so well.

Baltimore, through which he had hurried *incognito* four years before to escape threatened assassination, was anxious now to render every tribute of respect. The body was placed on a splendid catafalque in the Exchange, and thousands looked, through tears, on the dead face of the man whom they honoured. On the route from Baltimore to Philadelphia six ladies came into the car, and placed upon the coffin an exquisite wreath of flowers. At Harrisburg the obsequies commenced in the evening, and until midnight the catafalque was surrounded by groups of mourners. At Philadelphia the body rested in the old Independent Hall, above which, half-mast high, waved the American flag which Lincoln had hoisted as he passed through the city before. The bier was close to the old bell which in 1776 had first rung out the tidings of independence. The lines of persons passing in to see the remains "extended to at least three miles." At Newark it seemed that the whole city came out. At Jersey City solemn strains of funeral music from choirs of singers mingled with the cannon and tolling bells. In the metropolis of New York the scene was so imposing as to baffle description. The fronts of the houses were draped in mourning, and the streets and windows were full of people; "while from distant batteries the cannon belched each minute their thunder-tones of woe, from all the steeples came forth the wailing of bells, and from old Trinity's lofty spire floated upon the breeze the tuneful chimings of 'Old Hundred.'" The coffin was taken into the City Hall amid the solemn chantings of eight hundred choristers: and there it rested amid emblems of military display and floral tokens of affection, while all day and night the people passed through to take a look at the features of the deceased. At the solemn hour of midnight a funeral chant was performed in the Rotunda by the German musical societies of the town, with an effect that was said to be harmoniously grand and sublime. On the 25th of April the remains were borne away in a procession that was altogether grand and imposing. The military pageant was very fine: there was a force of at least ten thousand men. The procession was closed by the coloured population of New York. They had not been invited to join in the pageant, but they were permitted to do so, and gladly availed themselves of the opportunity to testify their love and gratitude for their great benefactor. They numbered at least two thousand persons, and they were preceded by a banner, which bore on one side the inscription—

"Abraham Lincoln, our Emancipator,"

and on the other,

"To Millions of Bondsmen he Liberty gave."

The coloured people in the procession were vehemently applauded. Everything went to show that the feeling of love and sorrow was unanimous. The *New York Tribune*

Abraham Lincoln's Tomb in Oak Bridge Cemetery.—*Page* 138.

said, "A funeral in each house in Central New York would hardly have added solemnity to the day;" and the *New York Herald* said, "Such an occasion, such a crowd, and such a day New York may never see again." A magnificent address was delivered in Union Square by the Hon. George Bancroft, the historian, and an ode was recited by William Cullen Bryant.

The funeral train reached Buffalo on the morning of the twenty-seventh; men and women had spent wakeful nights in watching for it. It reached Cleveland on Friday, "the most imposing pageant that this beautiful city on the lake had ever created or witnessed. Bishop M'Ilvaine of the Diocese of Ohio read the Episcopal burial service on the opening of the coffin, and offered prayer; after which the long procession filed through the pavilion, and caught a last glimpse of the honoured dead." At Colombus, Indianapolis, and Chicago, the people did all they could to honour the man who had died for them. Holland says, "It seemed almost like profanation of the sleeping President's rest, to bear him so far, and expose him to so much; but the people demanded it, and would take no denial. All parties, all sects—friends and foes alike—mingled in their affectionate tributes of honour and sorrow." In Chicago the remains of the President were at home, in the State in which he had spent most of his life; "and the people grasped him with almost a selfish sense of ownership. He was theirs. Only a short distance from the spot lay his old antagonist, Douglas, in his last sleep. The party champions were once more near each other upon their favourite soil; but their eloquent lips were silent—silent with an eloquence surpassing sound, in the proclamation of mighty changes in the nation, and the suggestions of mutability and mortality among men."

The long journey was ended on the 3rd of May, when the remains reached Springfield, where the chief mourners lived.

A tomb had been prepared in Oak Ridge cemetery, a beautiful spot outside the city; and there he was buried —Little Willie by his side; while those who could, sang "Children of the heavenly King," and "Peace, Troubled Soul," and those who could not sing wept. A beautiful hymn, written for the occasion, was also sung; and Bishop Simpson, a friend of Mr. Lincoln, gave an address. The address was very eloquent; and one of its finest passages contained the memorable words of the dead President on the slave-power in the land:—

"Broken by it, I, too, may be—bow to it, I never will. The probability that we may fail in the struggle ought not to deter us from the support of a cause which we deem to be just; and it shall not deter me. If ever I feel the soul within me elevate and expand to those dimensions not wholly unworthy of its Almighty Architect, it is when I contemplate the cause of my country, deserted by all the world besides, and I, standing up boldly and alone, and hurling defiance at her victorious oppressors. Here, without contemplating consequences, before high Heaven and in the face of the world, I swear eternal fidelity to the just cause, as I deem it, of the land of my life, my liberty, and my love."

There they left the body of the good, great man, in the little cemetery at Springfield, among the sweet scenes of nature, and the silences of rest—left him, "after life's fitful fever," to "sleep well," until he should awake to a greater day at the well-beloved sound of his Master's voice, and the joy of His "Well done, good and faithful servant."

Andrew Johnson, the Vice-President, had, under the provisions of the Constitution, taken the oath of office, and become President of the United States.

And what of the murderer? He was shot on the 26th of April, twelve days after the murder. He was traced to a barn belonging to William Garrett, on the other side of the Potomac. With him was his accomplice, David C. Harold. The barn was surrounded, and the villains ordered to surrender. Booth refused, and the barn was set on fire. The murderer of the President stood with a pistol in each hand, but Sergeant Corbett, by a sudden impulse, shot him through the neck, and he died three hours after. John Wilkes Booth was the son of a famous tragedian, and also himself an actor of more than ordinary ability. He was of good appearance, but led a profligate life; and seems to have committed the deed more from a morbid desire of notoriety than anything else, though he was known to have strong Southern sympathies. Harold was arrested, and he, with Payne, who had attacked the Chief Secretary, Mr. Seward, and other conspirators were hanged for their crime. And the country soon settled down to peace and prosperity again.

Some of the English papers had been very hard upon the President, *Punch* and *The Times* especially; but they hastened to bear their tribute to his worth afterwards. *Punch* had a poem, which exhibited real goodness under that which, being comic, was often severe.

"*You* lay a wreath on murdered Lincoln's bier,
  You, who with mocking pencil won't to trace,
Broad for the self-complacent British sneer,
  His length of shambling limb, his furrowed face.

His gaunt, gnarled hands, his unkempt, bristling hair,
  His garb uncouth, his bearing ill at ease,
His lack of all we prize as *debonair*,
  Of power or will to shine, of art to please!

You, whose smart pen backed up the pencil's laugh,
  Judging each step as though the way were plain;
Reckless, so it could point each paragraph,
  Of chief's perplexity, or people's pain?

> Beside this corpse, that bears for winding-sheet
>   The stars and stripes he lived to rear anew;
> Between the mourners at his head and feet,
>   Say, scurrile jester, is there room for you?
>
> Yes; he had lived to shame me for my sneer,
>   To lame my pencil and confute my pen—
> To make me own this hind of princes peer,
>   This rail-splitter a true-born king of men.
>
> My shallow judgment I had learnt to rue,
>   Noting how to occasion's height he rose,
> How his quaint wit made home-truth seem more true,
>   How, iron-like, his temper grew by blows."

"The assassination of President Lincoln," said a chronicle of the time, "and of the attempt to assassinate Mr. Seward, caused an extraordinary sensation in the city on Wednesday. Towards noon it became known, and spread rapidly from mouth to mouth in all directions. At first many were incredulous as to the truth of the rumour, and some believed it to have been set afloat for purposes in connection with the Stock Exchange. The house of Peabody and Co., American bankers in Broad Street, had received early intelligence of the assassination, and from there the news was carried to the Bank of England, whence it quickly radiated in a thousand directions. Meanwhile it was being wafted far and wide by the second editions of the morning papers, and was supplemented later in the day by the publication of additional particulars. Shortly after twelve o'clock it was communicated to the Lord Mayor, while he was sitting in the justice-room of the Mansion House; and about the same time the 'star-spangled banner' was hoisted half-mast high over the American Consulate at the corner of Gracechurch Street. The same flag had but a few days before floated in triumph from the same place, on the entry of the Federals into Richmond, and still later, on the surrender of General Lee. Between one and two o'clock the third edition of *The Times*, containing a circumstantial narrative of the affair, made its appearance in the city, and became immediately in extraordinary demand. A news-vendor in the Royal Exchange was selling it at half-a-crown a copy, and by half-past three it could not be had for money. The excitement caused by the intelligence was everywhere manifest, and in the streets, on the rail, on the river, and in the law courts, the terrible event was the theme of conversation. Throughout the remainder of the day the evening papers were sold in unexampled numbers, and often at double and treble the ordinary price, all evincing the universal interest felt at the astounding news. On the receipt of the melancholy intelligence in the House of Commons, about sixty members of all parties immediately assembled, and signed the following address of sympathy to the American Minister :—

" ' We, the undersigned Members of the British House of Commons, have learnt, with the deepest horror and regret, that the President of the United States of America has been deprived of life by an act of violence, and we desire to express our sympathy on the sad event with the American Minister, now in London, as well as to declare our hope and confidence in the future of that great country, which we trust will continue to be associated with enlightened freedom and peaceful relations with this and every other country.—London, April 29th, 1865.' "

A London paper said, with reference to Liverpool :— " The scene on the Exchange was such as will not be forgotten for a long time. At half-past eleven it was announced that the secretary and treasurer of the Liverpool Exchange News Rooms was in possession of the news. A terrible rush took place from the 'flags' into the news room ; and, after a few minutes, it was announced that the secretary would read aloud the despatch from the bar of the news room. All was now silent. The passage wherein it was stated that President Lincoln had been shot at caused no great dismay; but when the master of the rooms read, 'The President never rallied, and died this morning,' there was a general expression of horror. Certainly there was one dissentient voice, which had the temerity to exclaim, 'Hurrah!' His presence in the news room was of short duration, for being seized by the collar by as good a Southerner as there is in Liverpool, he was summarily ejected from the room, the gentleman who first seized him exclaiming, 'Be off, you incarnate fiend! You are an assassin at heart.'"

We subjoin a few stories illustrative of Abraham Lincoln from the pen of Carpenter, who, in his six months at the White House, had many opportunities of hearing them:—

"Lincoln was often waylaid by soldiers, importunate to get their back pay, or a furlough, or a discharge; and if the case was not too complicated, would attend to it there and then. Going out of the main door of the White House one morning he met an old lady, who was pulling vigorously at the door bell, and asked her what she wanted. She said she wanted to see 'Abraham the Second!' The President, amused, asked her who Abraham the First might be, if there was a second? The old lady replied, 'Why, Lor' bless you, we read about the first Abraham in the Bible, and Abraham the Second is our President.' She was told that the President was not in his office then, and when she asked where he was, she was told, 'Here he is!' Nearly petrified with surprise, the old lady managed to tell her errand, and was told to come next morning at nine o'clock, when she was received, and kindly cared for by the President. At another time, hearing of a young man who was determined to enter the navy as a landsman, after three years of service in the army, he said to the writer, 'Now, do you go over to the Navy Department, and mouse out what he is fit for, and he shall have it, if it's to be had, for that's the kind of men I like to hear of.' The place was duly 'moused out,' with the assistance of the kind-hearted Assistant Secretary of the Navy; and the young officer, who may read these lines on his solitary post at the mouth of the Yazoo river, was appointed upon the recommendation of the President of the United States.

"Of an application for office by an old friend, not fit for the place he sought, he said, 'I had rather resign my place, and go away from here, than refuse him, if I consulted only my personal feelings; but refuse him I must.' And he did."

But such things added to the burden of sorrow which the President carried. After his death, some one comforted his son by telling him his father had gone to heaven.

"Will he be happy in heaven?" asked Tad.

"Oh, yes; every one is happy there."

"Then," said the boy, "I am very glad he is dead, for he was never happy here."

"One example of his exercise of pardoning power may excite a smile, as well as a tear; but it may be relied upon as a veritable relation of what actually transpired. A distinguished citizen of Ohio had an appointment with the President one evening at six o'clock. As he entered the vestibule of the White House, his attention was attracted by a poorly-clad young woman who was violently sobbing. He asked her the cause of her distress. She said that she had been ordered away by the servants, after vainly waiting many hours to see the President about her only brother, who had been condemned to death. Her story was this:— She and her brother were foreigners and orphans. They had been in this country several years. Her brother enlisted in the army, but through bad influences was induced to desert. He was captured, tried, and sentenced to be shot—the old story. The poor girl had obtained the signatures of some persons who had formerly known him, to a petition for a pardon, and, alone, had come to Washington to lay the case before the President. Thronged as the waiting-rooms always were, she had passed the long hours of two days trying in vain to get an audience, and had at length been ordered away.

"The gentleman's feelings were touched. He said to her that he had come to see the President—but he did not know that *he* should succeed. He told her, however, to follow him upstairs and he would see what could be done for her. Just before reaching the door, Mr. Lincoln came out, and meeting his friend, said, good-humouredly, 'Are you not ahead of your time?' The gentleman showed him his watch with the hand upon the hour of six. 'Well,' returned Mr. Lincoln, 'I have been so busy to-day that I have not had time to get a lunch. Go in and sit down; I will be back directly.'

"The gentleman made the young woman accompany him into the office, and when they were seated, said to her— 'Now, my good girl, I want you to muster all the courage you have in the world. When the President comes back he will sit down in that arm-chair. I shall get up to speak to him, and as I do so you must force yourself between us, and insist upon his examination of your papers, telling him it is a case of life and death, and admits of no delay.' These instructions were carried out to the letter. Mr. Lincoln was at first somewhat surprised at the apparent forwardness of the young woman, but observing her distressed appearance, he ceased conversation with his friend, and commenced an examination of the document she had placed in his hands. Glancing from it to the face of the petitioner, whose tears had broken forth afresh, he studied its expression for a moment, and then his eye fell upon her scanty but neat dress. Instantly his face lighted up. 'My poor girl,' said he, 'you have come here with no Governor, or

Senator, or Member of Congress, to plead your cause. You seem honest and truthful; *and you don't wear hoops*—and I will be whipped, but I will pardon your brother!'"

One of the most eloquent testimonies to Lincoln's life and work was borne by the Rev. Henry Ward Beecher, in a sermon preached at Plymouth Church, Brooklyn, on the Sunday after his death. It contained the following words:—
"Even he that now sleeps has, by this event, been clothed with new influence. Dead, he speaks to men who now willingly hear what before they shut their ears to. Like the words of Washington will his simple, mighty words be pondered on by your children, and children's children. Men will receive a new accession to their love of patriotism, and will for his sake guard with more zeal the welfare of the whole country. On the altar of this martyred patriot I swear you to be more faithful to your country. They will, as they follow his hearse, swear a new hatred to that slavery which has made him a martyr. By this solemn spectacle I swear you to renewed hostility to slavery, and to a never ending pursuit of it to its grave. They will admire and imitate his firmness in justice, his inflexible conscience for the right, his gentleness and moderation of spirit; and I swear you to a faithful copy of his justice, his mercy, and his gentleness. You I can comfort, but how can I speak to the twilight millions who revere his name as the name of God. Oh, there will be wailing for him in hamlet and cottage, in woods and wilds, and the fields of the South. Her dusky children looked on him as on a Moses come to lead them out from the land of bondage. To whom can we direct them but to the Shepherd of Israel, and to His care commit them for help, for comfort, and protection? And now the martyr is moving in triumphal march, mightier than when alive. Cities and States are his pall-bearers, and cannon beat the hours with solemn procession. Dead! dead! dead! yet he speaketh! Is Washington dead? Is

Hampden dead? Is David dead? Now, disenthralled of flesh, and risen to the unobstructed sphere where passion never comes, he begins his illimitable work. His life is grafted upon the Infinite, and will be fruitful now as no earthly life can be. Pass on, thou that hast overcome? Your sorrows, O people, are his pæan. Your bells, and bands, and muffled drum sound in his ear a triumph. You wail and weep here. God makes it triumph there. Four years ago, O Illinois, we took him from your midst, an untried man from among the people. Behold, we return him a mighty conqueror. Not thine, but the nation's; not ours, but the world's! Give him place, ye prairies! In the midst of this great continent his dust shall rest a sacred treasure to millions who shall pilgrim to that shrine, to kindle anew their zeal and patriotism. Ye winds that move over the mighty spaces of the West, chant his requiem! Ye people, behold a martyr, whose blood, as articulate words, pleads for fidelity, for law, for liberty!"

News had reached New York that President Lincoln had been shot and was dead; further tidings came that Secretary Seward had also been assassinated. The people were in the state of mind which urges to violence. Loud cries of vengeance were raised by the crowd, and ten thousand faces, angry and white, were turned in the direction of the office of *The World* newspaper. At that moment a man appeared on the balcony, waving a small flag. "Another telegram from Washington!" said some one, and the mass of people grew quiet. Then a clear voice rang through the air—"Fellow citizens! clouds and darkness are round about Him! His pavilion is dark waters, and thick clouds of the skies! Justice and judgment are the establishment of His throne! Mercy and truth shall go before His face! *Fellow citizens, God reigns, and the Government of Washington still lives!*" A great awe fell upon the crowd. It seemed as if a voice from heaven had spoken, and over the surging sea of human hearts a divine "Peace, be still" had fallen. Then some asked, as in a whisper, "Who is he?" and the answer was, "GENERAL GARFIELD OF OHIO."

JAMES A. GARFIELD.

JAMES A. GARFIELD

NEW WORLD HEROES.

CHAPTER I

A FOREST FUNERAL.

"This is the forest primeval. The murmuring pines and the hemlocks,
Bearded with moss, and in garments green, indistinct in the twilight,
Stand like Druids of old, with voices sad and prophetic."
—LONGFELLOW.

T was July, and the sun shone down upon the forest with great strength; but whether the weather was hot or cold, the people living in Orange Cuyahoga County were going to a funeral. They were all settlers, living their lives of solitary toil, but "a fellow-feeling made them wondrous kind;" and on all great occasions, such as weddings and funerals, they paid visits of congratulation or condolence to their neighbours. There were only about six families within a radius of ten miles; and there would not be a very large gathering: but those who could go willingly gave up the day and walked the distance, to say

a comforting word or two to the mourners. So a few stalwart men and pitiful women, strong lads and thoughtful girls, made their way from their different farms, and travelled through the pathless forest to meet together in the log-cabin of Abram Garfield.

The widow spoke quietly to them as they came, one by one, through the plank door, and they took their seats on the three-legged stools, which formed the chief furniture of the house, and looked the sorrow which they could not speak. On the bed, made in the side of the cabin, was stretched the long, straight figure of the hardy pioneer, whom every one knew and all respected.

"Ah, poor fellow! You have had a fire in the forest hereabouts, I see," said one; "had that anything to do with it?"

"Yes," said the young widow, bending her head down to the little boy of eighteen months who was nestling in her arms, "the forest fire had all to do with it."

"The fires are dreadful things, and no one seems to know how they begin. But with such heaps of dry dead leaves lying about, it is no wonder that when they do once begin they should keep on."

"The fire did not begin on our farm," said the widow, "but we saw it raging, and were afraid it would reach our corn and our home; so Abram set to work to make a wall of earth between his fields and the fire. There was no time to lose, and he had no one to help him, but he worked for home and life. We must be starved if the fields were destroyed, and we should be homeless if the cabin got burnt; so the man worked like a hero to save his own."

"He was a hero," said a woman; and the little company assented.

"And he got his barrier up in time?"

"Oh, yes. We watched the fire creeping nearer and

nearer; but Abram was quicker than the flames, and before they reached our farm he had finished his work."

"That was a good thing."

"Oh, I don't know," said the woman through her tears. "Perhaps it would have been better if we had all perished together."

But here little James put his hand up to his mother's face, and the childish touch at the same time rebuked and comforted her.

"It was too much for him," she said presently. "He got very warm and tired, and then he sat down to rest. Although the sun was hot, there was a cold wind, and I suppose he took a chill. He could not sleep when he got to bed; his limbs ached, and he was very feverish, and towards morning his throat got very sore. If there had been a doctor he might have been saved. We did what we could, and he was not long ill. He sat here, with his head leaning on the bed, and he looked out on his little farm, and in on his four children. 'Eliza,' he said, 'I have planted four saplings; you will have to see that they grow straight.' He could not talk much, his throat was so bad, and at last he was choked."

There was a little silent weeping after that; and then one of the men said gently, "We had better see about making a coffin."

Who does not know what is meant by the bringing in of a coffin to an English home? But even the undertakers are careful to do it in the evening, and as privately as possible, so that the feelings of the mourners may not be harrowed by the sight of it. In the very poorest homes there is almost always a room sacred for the time to the dead; but this was not possible here. The corpse lay in the only room there was, except a rude loft above, and no reticence was possible.

The neighbours soon made a rough box, and the dead

man, with his strong limbs composed into quietness, and his weather-beaten face looking calm in the majesty of death, was laid down in it. Little James looked wonderingly on, prattling in his baby-unconsciousness about "Pap-pap," and rather pleased than not—in baby-fashion—at the unusual commotion in his log-cabin home.

"Where would you like the grave to be ?" asked the nearest neighbour, Mr. Boynton, her husband's half brother, whose kindness and sympathy had often been shown already.

"I should like it yonder in the corner of the wheat-field," she said; "I can see it then from the house, and perhaps I shall feel comforted sometimes."

So the sturdy men dug a grave on the little farm, and then they carried the coffin to the place, and lowered it in the hole that had been made.

It was a strange funeral. It was altogether a silent one, for no words were spoken, no prayer uttered, no hymn sung. The hush was but broken by the sobs of Mehetable, the eldest girl, the sighs of Thomas, the eldest boy, the tears of Mary, who did not know what it all meant, and the strange little noises of baby James; and it seemed as if a wail went up from the forest trees as the wind moved among them. But Mrs. Garfield and her neighbours bore their grief in quietness, and the widow's tears went up to God for funeral dirge and prayer. She stood a little while by the open grave, and then straining her child to her heart, she went back to the log-home. One thing sustained her. She sorrowed not as those who have no hope. Her husband had been a Christian: and if there were no ordained minister to pronounce words of comfort, the still small voice of the Spirit of God set to solemn music, that thrilled the woman's heart, the grand triumphant words:—"*It is sown in dishonour: it is raised in glory. It is sown in weakness: it is raised in power. O death, where is thy sting? O*

A FOREST FUNERAL.   155

grave, where is thy victory? Thanks be to God, who giveth US the victory through our Lord Jesus Christ."

There was a considerable walk before most of the neighbours, and they might not stay long even to offer what consolations they could to the widow and the children. Their own hearts were sad enough, because there was one neighbour the less. In the life which the pioneers live, the social intercourse with each other forms a very considerable compensation for the isolation and loneliness which must be endured. All who were present at the funeral felt that the dead man would be greatly missed from among them.

"It is hard work to bear it all," they said one to another.

"But God's will be done," suggested one who knew that the hearts of the others would add "Amen."

"The years bring changes to all parts of the world."

"Yes, but they mean more to us here in the forest than to most people, because we are obliged to depend on each other for comfort."

The widow sighed. It seemed that all the comfort and joy of her existence had been buried that afternoon in the grave in the wheat-field.

"Is there anything we can do for you?" they asked.

"No, thank you."

"It is not very far to Zanesville. As soon as you can you had better go home to your friends," remarked Mr. Boynton.

But Mrs. Garfield shook her head. "My home is here with my children, near the grave of their father."

"But you will never be able to manage alone, with none to help you. The children are all so young."

"Yes; but they will be growing older every day. I must do the best that I can."

They saw there was nothing for it but to let her try. She would soon find out that the burden was too heavy.

"At all events," said Mr. Boynton, "you know where I live. You can send one of the children to fetch me any time you want a little neighbourly advice or help, and I will come at once. Thomas here looks as if he means to be a good, brave boy, and help his mother; and you will see in a little while what is best to do."

"Oh, yes; I am not afraid—at least, not very much afraid. Thomas is ten, and he is a strong boy, and knows how to do many things."

"And God will help you."

"Yes; if it was not for that I should sink altogether."

So presently the friends departed as they had come, in little groups, to their forest homes, and the woman and her orphaned ones were left alone with God.

Night came on. The children were put to bed in the little loft above, and the baby James fell asleep on the fresh straw bed that had been spread in the house-room. The woman dried her tears, and a steady light came into her eyes. Not yet must she let herself think of the happy years that had gone; not yet must she even admit to herself that she missed the protection of the kind arms in which she had found rest, or the tender smile that had made the log-hut a palace, or the cheery words that had been like a song of hope. She must sternly put all such memories from her. They belonged to the past, and she had a future. God had taken away her husband, but she had her children. Nothing should part her from them. She was strong, and she would herself do the man's work that there was no one else to do. What she did not know she would learn. She was not afraid of work, no matter what the kind or the quantity; and she would labour, and keep her children with her. No poverty nor want should drive her from them, or from her home. It was a good home, not small, and cramped, and cold, as some log-cabins were. It had been built by a clever man, a man who loved his work, and had taken pride in laying the logs one upon another, and filling up the spaces with clay. From first to last it was her husband's work; it belonged to her, and she would die rather than give it up. So much she was determined upon, so much was plain. She would keep her house and her children, come what would.

And what might come?

She knew that though she had lived in hard times, the hardest were to follow. There was a debt on the farm: that was the worst of it, and there was no money with which to pay it. This was the weight which, next to that caused by her widowhood, pressed the most heavily upon the poor woman's desolate heart. The debt must be paid, but how, she did not know: she could only wait and pray that God would show her the way. At present the prospect was altogether dreary. Then the winter would soon come, with its cold and loneliness, its dreary long nights and its hard days. But the woman resolved that nothing should rob her of her courage and her resolution to maintain the old home, and keep her children with her. She could not see how it was to be done; but that was no matter. She would certainly do it somehow. And after all there was God! He would never leave her nor forsake her. He had not shielded her from the heaviest blow that could have fallen: but He would surely help her now. So, with a mute appeal to that divine tenderness which is ever the solace of the sorrowful, the widow crept into her hard bed, and took little James in her arms, and wearied out as she was with sorrow and care, soon fell asleep.

But a "Good night" had been spoken in the log-hut, and the place was not too poor for the angels to come into it with a message: "*Leave thy fatherless children, I will preserve them alive, and let thy widows trust in Me.*"

CHAPTER II.

HARD TIMES.

> "Be strong to bear, oh heart,
>   Nothing is vain;
> Strive not, for life is care,
>   And God sends pain;
> Heaven is above, and there
>   Rest will remain."
>   —ADELAIDE PROCTER.

AMONG the heroines of these times the name of Mrs. Eliza Garfield, the mother of James, must never be forgotten. The courage with which —her heart aching all the while for the loss of her beloved husband—she faced her life was truly remarkable. Difficulties were pressing and almost insurmountable; but she was quietly resolved on overcoming them, and she did not flinch from the rough and stormy path through which she had been called to walk. It has been said already that there was a debt upon the farm, and this was at first the heaviest part of the burden. It kept her as full of care and thought as of work, and made her wonder how she could possibly maintain the position in which she had been left. The stock was not paid for; and creditors, if patient, cannot wait too long. The farm was not fenced either; and that was a work that was absolutely necessary to attend to. The fruit-trees on the farm looked promising; but poor Mrs. Garfield needed something more than promises, and it was not yet time for the fruit to be ripe. The anxious expression on the widow's face grew deeper as the weeks went on, and some of her friends feared that the struggle would prove too severe for her strength.

"Eliza," said Amos Boynton to her one day, "I was your husband's friend and brother, and I am yours. You have undertaken more than you can do. Give it up."

"No; I have no intention of giving it up."

"There are several ways in which you might find relief."

"Tell me what they are, then?"

"You might go home to your friends. They would find you a place, and when your children are older you might get a house of your own again."

"But this is our very own; I can never give it up. Don't you know the place which the children call 'Mother's Retreat?' It was there that Alpha told me how good it was to have one's own land, and I have since discovered for myself what it is. I could not bear to part with it. It ought to be made to pay; and it can be in time! I will not go away from Abram's land."

"Then why not let some of your children go from home? There are good people to be easily found, who would be willing to take Jimmy, and bring him up carefully and comfortably. If you were free to work you could do so much more than is possible now. Supposing you gave him up for a few years only."

"Brother Amos, how you talk! If anyone had my James for a few years, do you think he would ever want to let him go again? I do not want it. I am his mother, and I will keep him. I could not be parted from my bonny baby."

"Let the others go, then!"

"No, indeed; which could I spare? I can let neither be away from me in my struggle. I should quite lose hope and courage without my children."

"Then what will you do?"

"I will tell you what I have thought we might do. We could sell a part of the farm. That would not be like parting with all of it. I could manage to live on the rest of the land, and we need not be parted."

"Perhaps that could be done," said Mr. Boynton, doubtfully. "You would not have much to live on then."

"No, but we should have the home."

"True. I will see if I can find any purchaser to suit you."

In time one was found. A man bought fifty acres of the little farm of eighty acres; and the Garfield family had the house, and thirty acres of land on which to thrive.

"It will be hard work for you, Thomas," said the mother to the eldest son.

"I don't mind, mother; I am glad to work for you and the children."

"You are but a child yourself, my poor son."

"Oh, no, mother. Don't say that. I am almost a man, and you will find that I can and will do a man's work."

"We must fence the farm in."

"Yes, that must be done, and this is the time to set about it."

"Have courage, my boy, and we will do what we can. I will split the rails."

"You? Oh, mother!"

But the woman, slim and weak as she was, actually did make an effort to split the rails—the woman whom James Garfield turned to kiss when, long years afterward, he was elected President of the United States. Never did mother more thoroughly earn the honour and the right! She could

MOTHER OF PRESIDENT GARFIELD. —*Page* 158.

not have worked more resolutely than she did had she known what was before her.

Thomas was ten years old, and he it was who ploughed the land and became farmer-in-chief. They had no longer a horse of their own, but they were able to hire one, and that did the work. When the next harvest came all would be well; and so the boy toiled away, as heartily as the mother, and neither complained.

But the harvest was long in coming. A terrible fear entered the widow's heart that their stock of corn would not last until the next ingathering. The fear grew upon her until it was too awful to bear.

"I must satisfy myself on that point before I can go further," she said; and one morning she arose a little earlier than usual, and measured out the corn that was left. She then made a calculation; and found that at the present rate of consumption it would all have been consumed before the new corn was ready.

The mother smiled tenderly as she arrived at her conclusion. The children were not yet awake, and she looked upon them in their quiet sleep with the love and pity that only mothers feel.

"Dear little mouths, they shall not hunger! They need food to help them to grow and to thrive. Very little will suffice to keep me alive. I will take only one meal a day, or at the most two, and see if we can make the corn suffice."

She did not tell the children of the sacrifice upon which she had resolved: they would have wished to share it with her. It was only afterwards, when better times had come, that Mrs. Garfield could bring herself to talk about such hardships. In the meantime she worked and struggled on. When she was not working out of doors she was busy within the house. She spun the cloth, and made the clothes of herself and her children. She also did sewing for the neighbours, and did not in the least care what she did so long as the children were warmly clad and sufficiently fed. She must have understood very well the meaning of the modern term "over-work" but she did not let her work crowd out the higher interests from her life. She read four chapters of the Bible every day, and never let any evening pass without finding time for the instruction of her children.

James was not precocious, but he was intelligent, and from the first his mother was anxious that he should be a scholar. By the time he was five years old his mother had taught him to read, and she was very delighted that he not only read the words, but understood the meaning of them. On one occasion he was reading, "The rain came pattering on the roof," when he exclaimed, "Why, mother, I know what that means. I have heard the rain do that myself many a time."

From that day he took a greater delight in books, and read them with more vivid interest than before; indeed, he generally took a book to bed with him, that he might read it in the morning when he awoke.

One of Garfield's biographers says that his first attempt to go to school was before he was old enough to walk, and that his sister Mehetable carried him. After that, in the true settler's fashion, a teacher came to the neighbourhood and boarded with the people, and kept school in any accessible cabin. He took an especial liking to little James Garfield from the first.

"James, you must be a good boy and learn," he said, "and then when you grow up you shall be a general."

And the little fellow answered merrily, "Oh, yes, sir, I'll learn, and I'll be a general."

When he went to school he found it impossible to obey the rule which ordered him to sit still. He tried, and he failed, and the teacher wondered what to do with him again and again. At last the mother was appealed to.

"I don't want to grieve you, ma'am," said the teacher, "but James won't sit still, and I am afraid I shall never make anything of him. He won't learn his lessons, and it is no use for him to come to school. It is only waste of time, and waste is bad anyhow."

"Oh, James!" said the mother, looking at the child with a sad, grieved expression, "your father wanted you to be a scholar, and so do I."

The little boy made a great resolve: and from that time, although he could not sit still any better than before, he did learn his lessons. When the teacher went away he gave James a New Testament in token of his approval and pleasure in regard to the progress which he had made. James was proud, but his mother was prouder still of this reward.

In the meantime his brother Thomas was proving himself a boy of more than ordinary strength of body and character. He gathered in the harvest, and became almost a man in his thoughtfulness and industry. He could not go to school, but he worked that his brother might; and when the first ingathering took place, he said with joy, "Now, mother, the shoemaker can come and make James some shoes."

"Do you not want a pair for yourself, Thomas?" asked the mother.

"No; it does not matter in the least about me, but James must be shod."

"Do you love James?"

"Yes, mother, nearly as much as you do. But isn't he lively? Since we have slept together he kicks the bed-clothes off every night. I am sure to hear him some time say, 'Thomas, cover me over.' I think he says it in his sleep."

Many years after, when he was at the war, James Garfield dreamed that he was again a boy, sleeping with his brother; and an officer relates how he cried out in the night, when they were camping out, " Thomas, cover me up."

It will be seen that the Garfields, poor as they were, had that love for each other which does more than riches to brighten a home, and make the lives of children glad. The years passed away pleasantly and brightly to them all the same for their poverty. The children loved their mother, and took care of her as far as they were able, and she devoted herself entirely to them. As they grew older they were able to render more efficient help, and every year made them all more fond of little James. They shared their mother's faith that he would prove the clever one of the family.

James was known at school as a fighting boy. It is said that he never began an attack, but when big boys bullied or beat him he turned on them like a young lion; and his big brother always took his part.

In regard to the religious training of the Garfields, Ogilvie says: "The children lived in an atmosphere of religious thought and discussion. Uncle Boynton, who was a second father to the Garfield family, flavoured all his talk with Bible quotations. He carried a Testament in his pocket wherever he went, and would sit on the plough-team at the end of a furrow to take it out and read a chapter. It was a time of religious ferment in Northern Ohio. New sects filled the air with their doctrinal cries. The Disciples, a sect founded by the preaching of Alexander Campbell, a devout man of Scotch descent, who ranged over Kentucky, Ohio, Virginia, and Pennsylvania, from his home at Bethany in the 'Pan Handle,' had made great progress. They assailed all creeds as made by man, and declared the Bible to be the only rule of life. Attacking all the other denominations, they were vigorously attacked in return. James's mind was filled at an early day with the controversies this new sect excited. The guests at his mother's house were mostly travelling preachers; and the talk of the neighbourhood, when not about the crops and farm labours, was usually on religious topics."

One pleasing incident is related of James, which proves that his love of truth was exceedingly strong. He had gone to visit an uncle who lived three miles away. It was night before he began the return journey; and a shower, which developed into a storm, came on. It grew so dark that the boy was evidently frightened. "Stay all night, James," said his aunt and cousins.

"No, I must not do that," said James. "Mother will be wondering what has become of me, and would be angry with me if I stayed."

"If you go, you had better start at once, then."

"So I will. Good night;" and the boy boldly walked away. But the road led through a lonely district, thickly wooded, and altogether unguarded. The maples groaned, and the beeches cracked, as the winds beat upon them and bent them. The night was very cold, very wet, and very dark. The boy manfully trudged along for about half a mile, and then his courage failed him; fear took possession of him, and he ran back to his uncle's house as fast as his legs would take him. He arrived out of breath, looking pale and excited.

But no sooner was he there than he felt ashamed of his fears.

"What a coward I am," he said.

"Oh, no; it is such a bad night; it is not fit for you to go home," said his aunt.

"But I will try again," said the boy. "I was foolish to come back; it has made me another mile."

"Don't attempt it again, James. Your mother need not know that it was because you were frightened. You can tell her that the mud was too deep for you to get home."

That settled the matter. The boy's face flushed, and his eyes flashed.

"I will never tell my mother a lie," he said; "and I should not like her to know I was afraid. I will go home. She is too good a mother to have a falsehood told her by her son."

And away he started, and kept bravely on until he had reached home.

Mr. Russell Connell says of this incident:—"That tradition is in accord with many others, and shows truthfulness, a brave spirit, and a self-sacrificing life. The *truth* was his good angel. It kept him from everything which he would be afraid to confess. It overcame his indisposition to labour. It guided him safely over the dangerous bar of a petted boyhood. Inasmuch as he was more true in his speech and actions than other boys, just that much was his boyhood nobler and more promising than theirs, and no more. In all other things he was like the multitude. The determination and habit of speaking the simple truth was a badge of honour more honourable and more respected than the kingly ermine on the heraldic shield of his ancestors.

"Wild and rough oftentimes, rude in his sports, and awkward in the presence of visitors, often in rags and dust he had carelessly made, with no other title or claim to respect, and no other capital to begin life upon, he found in his truth-telling an infallible guide to nobility and human greatness. This was the only very remarkable thing about his young life, and very curiously and surely it guided him upwards."

The same writer says—"James was favoured with opportunities for reading which the other members of that industrious family did not get. It was usually accidental, however. He was a careless, awkward boy in the use of tools in his work, and was often laid up by self-inflicted wounds. He cut his feet with his axe or scythe. He wrenched his back by the fall of a fence rail upon him. He fell from the barn upon a pile of wood. So that while he was, perhaps, not more careless or awkward than boys of his age usually are, yet he was more often confined to the house as a result of accidents, and the hours of his retirement he most earnestly employed in studying all the books they had in the house, and all he could borrow of the neighbours. It was to his credit that he used his books with care, and any of his neighbours were willing to entrust their volumes to him. His neighbours say that he learned much more in his early days by studying history, and reading stories of scientific discovery out of school, than he ever gained from teachers. He was greatly interested in the debates and literary exercises which were often held on winter evenings at the school-house; and it is said that as a critic he was dreaded by some of the old men before he was ten years of age."

From this it will be seen that James was getting some very important lessons early. A good foundation was being laid on which to build a future character. The hand of God was in it all. Had his mother been able to choose, she would have elected happier conditions, with less of hardship and penury for her boy. But God puts His heroes into schools where the training is severe. David the King was the more illustrious because he had once been David the shepherd boy. It is quite possible that the world would never have heard the name of James Garfield if he had not been the poor son of a poor widow.

CHAPTER III.

A TOW-PATH BOY.

> "What, and if thy lot be hard?
> Do not grumble;
> Though the path be steep and rough,
> Do not stumble:
> Oaks by sunbeams only nourished,
> Were but weak, and never flourished."

THOMAS GARFIELD was still hard at work for his mother and the rest of the family. He greatly desired to see them in a better house than the log-cabin which they occupied.

"Jamie," he said one day, "I have got the timber and the boards ready for a new home, will you help me build it?"

"Yes, I should like to do that. Uncle Amos says he thinks I was born to be a carpenter."

"But you cannot use the tools without hurting yourself."

"Oh, yes, I will. If you let me try I will take care and keep my thoughts upon the work. But do you think you have got enough stuff to build with?"

"I guess so. And I have the money too. We will get a man to help us. Our mother shall have a framed house."

So they set to work to pull the old house down and put up a new one, of which, when it was completed, they were more than a little proud. It had three rooms below and two above ; and it was painted red outside.

James was so delighted with his success as a carpenter, that he thought of adopting it as his future trade.

His first situation was at Cleveland, above ten miles from his mother's house, with a man who was a black-salter. This man had a large establishment ; and as it was growing, he needed a wood shed added to the log shanties. James Garfield helped in building it ; and the owner, watching him at his work, thought he was a likely lad whom it would be wise to secure.

"You had better stay 'long o' me," said the man ; "you kin read, and you kin write, and you are death on figgers. I'll find you, and give you fourteen dollars a-month, if you'll stay with me and keep my accounts, and 'tend to the saltery."

James thought he would do anything to get fourteen dollars a-month. So he went home to talk it over with his mother.

"Fourteen dollars a-month, my son ! It is a lot of money, and the man must think highly of you or he would not have offered so large a sum. But I don't know if you would like it, or if it would be well for you. This is a wicked world, my boy, and there will be temptations to try you. I don't know what to say."

"Say 'Go,' mother. You aren't afraid to trust me, are you ?"

"No, my boy, not quite that ; but a mother cannot help being anxious about her children when they are away from her."

"But I will come back, mother ; and I will take care and remember your lessons. I know what is right, and I'll try to do it."

So his mother let him go, with some fear, and he was not very long before he came back to her; and then a more terrible anxiety still began to grow in her heart.

"Mother," said James, "I should like to go to sea."

"Oh, my boy, don't think of that."

"It is such a splendid life they live upon ships, mother. No one is so jolly as a sailor. I have read books about sea-life—*Sinbad the Sailor*, *The Pirate's Own Book*, and some capital tales by Marryat."

"I am sorry to hear it, if reading them has made you wish to go to sea."

"I wish you would consent, mother."

"My dear boy, I think I shall never do that. The sailors may be what you call jolly, but I am afraid they are not what I call good."

James was silenced, but not convinced. He undertook to cut twenty-five cords of wood for a farmer, for which he was to receive seven dollars. From where he worked he could see, looking to the north, the slaty-blue of Lake Erie, and in his imagination it was magnified into the ocean. The consequence was, that while he was at work he was dreaming of the sea. When the wood-chopping was finished he went harvesting, but when the harvest had been all gathered in he again spoke to his mother. Her heart ached at the persistent desire of the lad; but she thought no good would come of her refusal, and so she reluctantly consented that he should go to Cleveland, but made him promise to try to find some respectable occupation there. He walked all the way —seventeen miles—and tried to discover someone who wanted a lad who was able to write and cipher. But when he did not succeed he went to the docks among the shipping. A schooner was lying at the wharf, and James went on board.

"Where is the captain?" he asked, and was shown to the room where he would be found.

Presently he saw a drunken, violent-looking man, whom he fearlessly addressed.

"Are you the captain? I want to hire myself out as a sailor."

But the wretch turned upon him with such oaths and curses that James beat a retreat.

He found, soon after, that a cousin had a boat on the Ohio and Pennsylvanian Canal, in which he carried coals from the mines to Cleveland. James went to him, and was engaged as a canal boy, whose duty it was to lead the horses as they dragged the barge along. Here he was often in the worst company. The boys and men were frequently fighting and swearing, and sometimes they were positively cruel to him. Once a bully attacked him so fiercely that James was roused to a fury of self-defence, and sent the fellow rolling to the bottom of the boat. He was anything but happy. He felt that his mother would be grieved if she knew the kind of life he was living, and he felt, too, that his father would have been disappointed if he could have known.

"They wanted me to be a scholar," he said to himself. "This is not much like that! I ought to be too good for such a life as I am living now!"

He was losing his health as well as his refinement. He often had to wade in the water, and afterwards walk in his wet clothes. He met at this time a physician and a preacher—Dr. J. F. Robinson—who talked kindly and seriously to the youth, and advised him to endeavour to do something better with his life.

"Go to school, Garfield," he said. "You can work for your board; and if you get an education you will be fit for anything."

But James could not at once make up his mind; and besides, he had engaged to remain on the boat at advanced wages as steersman for three months. But, as the end of the time drew near he became very weak and ill. At last in attempting to fasten a rope at the stern of the boat, he found that he had scarcely strength to draw it in. It had caught somewhere, and he gave it an impatient jerk. The rope yielded, but the lad fell headlong into the water.

He could not swim, and as the dark waters closed over him he felt as if he would die. Must he drown? Or would he be saved? Would God have mercy? The next moment he felt the rope, and managed by its aid to draw himself out of the water and into the boat. But he was very ill.

"I must go home. I have ague," he said; and his friends saw that it was so.

"We will help you as far as we can," they said; and did accompany him to Newberg.

"I can do the rest of the journey myself," said Garfield; and sick and dizzy, burning with fever, and weak though he was, he walked on.

It was night when he reached home, and stumbled up to the window. There was no lamp, but the firelight made the room visible. His mother was there kneeling in front of an open book. Was she praying? It seemed so. James heard her say, "Oh, turn unto me, and have mercy upon me! Give Thy strength unto Thy servant, and save the son of Thine handmaid!"

He opened the door, and feebly went in. "Mother!" was all he had strength to say; but the next moment his head was upon her bosom, and she was showering gentle kisses upon his hot forehead.

God had brought the widow's son back to her. It was evident that he was very ill, but he had come to the right place to be nursed back to health again. It took longer to do it than she expected. He was ill for three months, and during the whole of the time his mother tended and nursed him as only loving mothers can.

But she was distressed to find that his desire to go to sea

had not left him. He was still dreaming of blue waters, and gliding ships, and foreign lands.

"You will have to let me go, mother," he said one day. "I shall never rest if you do not."

"We will see about that when you are well enough," she said gently. "You must not go at present, for what would you do if you had another attack of ague, and no mother to nurse you?"

"That would be rather bad," said James.

"I have thought it all over," said Mrs. Garfield. "I think it would be a good plan for you to go to school this spring; and then, with another term in the Fall, you may be able to teach next winter. Would you not like to teach in the winters, and work on the canal or the lake in the summers? You would have occupation all the year round, and the change would be pleasant."

James smiled.

"You have set your heart on making me a scholar, mother," he said; "but I am afraid you will never do it."

"Indeed I hope you will be, James."

"But it would cost money, mother."

"I have saved a little, which I would gladly give you for that purpose."

"It would be too bad to take your money, mother; and, besides, I am so big to go to school. All the rest would laugh at me."

"My dear boy, supposing they did! It would not hurt you. If you were honestly trying to do your duty, and prepare yourself for a distinguished future, you would be far more noble than those who sneered, if there were any mean enough to do it; but I do not think there would be."

"I am so very ignorant, mother."

"But you like books. And, James, before your father died, he said he wanted his little one to be a scholar. I have longed for it all your life, and prayed for it too."

Such words as these could not but affect the young man; and their power was deepened by another influence which at that time was brought to bear upon him. His uncle Amos added his words to Mrs. Garfield's; and Mr. Samuel Bates, a Baptist preacher, visited the house and talked most earnestly to James.

"Boys as old and as ignorant as you, James, have become good and great by perseverance and industry. The first thing for you to do is to get an education. I will help you while you are too weak to go away; and then I hope you will set your mind on a college education. It will be difficult, but it is not impossible."

"I WILL TRY," said James at last; and he meant it.

There was in the town of Chester, about twelve miles from Orange (the village which had come into existence where the Garfields lived), a school of higher grade than most, called the "Geauga Seminary;" and it was towards this that James's heart began to turn. Mr. Bates had been a student there; and he talked of the advantages of attending it with so much enthusiasm, that James quite longed to become a scholar at Geauga.

"You must go," said Thomas, his brother; and his sisters, Mehetable and Mary, echoed the words. But it was not easy to see how it could be managed, though they were resolved that if possible it should be done.

"When you have settled how to do it," said Uncle Amos, "I shall see what I can do for my son Henry. He will have to work and earn the money to pay for it as well as James."

After a time James had an unusually profitable job of carpentering; and having by this means obtained a few dollars to begin with, he resolved to start on his search for an education.

Conwell, who had the account from one who was in the Geauga Seminary, thus describes their style of living:—

"There were three of them in one room—James, his cousin Henry Boynton, and Orren Judd. The room was about ten feet wide and twelve feet long, and was in a farm house near the academy. They selected that room because it was cheaper than those which were let in the academy building, and for that same reason the three boys occupied one room. With the two narrow beds, their cook-stoves, boxes, and three chairs, there was but little room for themselves. They divided up the work, and each alternately prepared the meals for the day. When the fire was burning in the old box stove, which had but one cover, the heat frequently drove out all but the cook.

"Their meals, however, were often cold, and for many weeks their only diet consisted of mush and milk. When the bread from home gave out, the supply being renewed nearly every week, they returned invariably to hasty pudding, or corn-cakes and molasses. They were at the academy to study and not to cook. To keep alive was the only object in eating at all; and whenever they were compelled to eat, they did it with despatch, and returned to their books. Near the end of their second term the boys became very much dissatisfied with their board, and made up their minds that boarding themselves was not a successful enterprise. James is said to have thrown down his spoon one day as he finished his dish of molasses and pudding, saying, 'I won't eat any more of that stuff if I starve.'"

Kirke says—"When the summer vacation came, he took a job of chopping one hundred cords of wood for twenty-five dollars, and with the fund thus realised he was in the Fall able to board with one of the neighbouring families, and so dispense with the drudgery of housekeeping. The price he paid for board, lodging, and washing, was one dollar and six cents per week. His landlady was a Mrs. Stiles; and after Garfield had become somewhat distinguished she was fond of relating an incident connected with his residence in her family. The young man was without overcoat or underclothing, and had only one suit of clothes, and those were of cheap Kentucky jean. Towards the close of the term his trousers had worn exceedingly thin at the knees, and on one occasion, when he was bending forward, they tore half way round the leg, exposing his bare knees to view. The mortified young man pinned the rent garment together as well as he could, and to the family that night bewailed his poverty, and his inability to remedy the misfortune to his only pair of trousers. "Why, that is easy enough," said the good Mrs. Stiles. "You go to bed, and one of the boys will bring down your trousers, and I will darn the hole so that it will be better than new. You shouldn't care for such small matters. You will forget all about them when you get to be President."

The author adds, "The good lady is still alive to see her prediction verified."

One great thing in James Garfield's favour was, that he was strong and in excellent health. Nothing hurt the frame, made vigorous by hard fare and constant exercise. And that which he had undergone had prepared him for his future position and work. It is a mistake to suppose that a youth spent in indigent circumstances is necessarily bad for any one. Those who have to "rough it" in their boyhood are frequently receiving the exact training necessary for the demands of their manhood. How many of the great men, both of England and America, were poor boys we can scarcely estimate; but one thing that poverty helps to secure, is health; and health is the best qualification for a good start in life that any one can have.

CHAPTER IV.

"THE DISCIPLES OF CHRIST."

"Awake to the call, and prepare for the strife
  That all men must face on the great field of life;
  The armour to wear is the armour of light,
And the King to be served is the Lord in His might."

IT has been said that James Garfield owed more than a little to the splendid health which he enjoyed. An amusing story, which throws some light upon the character and habits of thought of the young man, is told in Kirke's life of him. Hearing that Dr. Robison was in the neighbourhood, he went to consult him.

"Doctor," he said, "I want to go in for a college education—but first I want to be sure that I have the necessary strength of body. It would be useless to begin the work and then find that my strength failed. Will you examine me, and tell me candidly what you think?"

"Certainly," said the doctor. "What is your name?"

"James Garfield."

"I knew your mother. I am glad you mean to be a scholar."

The doctor then examined the young man, and afterwards gave this account of the affair:—

"I felt as if I was on my sacred honour, and the young man looked as if he felt himself on trial. I had had considerable experience as a physician, but here was a case much different from any other I had ever had. I felt that it must be handled with great care. I examined his head, and saw that there was a magnificent brain there. I sounded his lungs, and found that they were strong, and capable of making good blood. I felt his pulse, and saw that there was an engine capable of sending the blood up to the head to feed the brain. I had seen many strong physical systems with warm feet, but cold, sluggish brain; and those who possessed such systems would simply sit around and doze. Therefore, I was anxious to know about the kind of an engine to run that delicate machine, the brain. At the end of a careful examination of this kind, which lasted fifteen minutes, we rose, and I said, 'Go on, follow the leadings of your ambition, and ever after I am your friend. You have the brain of a Webster, and you have the physical proportions that will back you in the most herculean efforts. All you need to do is to work, work hard—do not be afraid of over-working—and you will make your mark.'"

Thus fortified and encouraged, James Garfield did work as few before have done, with avidity, perseverance, and success.

He was all the time under the necessity of providing for his own livelihood as well as gaining an education—and the result of this was that he had sometimes to leave his studies and betake himself to manual labour. The spirit in which he did his work, and the kind of work he did, was thus described by an old American who knew him:—

"His conscience kinder went ahead on him inter his work, and ye could allers trust him to do any job, hocin', rakin', hewin', planin', teachin', or any other thing, fur he'd feel much the wuss ef he left any on't as it hadn't dorter be. He didn't cover up nothin' he'd spiled, and he'd work just as fast if the man who paid him warn't around. He was right-up-and-down squar!'"

At one time he arranged to live with a carpenter in the village, and earn enough by working at the bench on Saturdays, and every possible leisure hour in the week, to pay for his board and lodging. This he did, and so hard did he work that one day he planed fifty-one boards.

After that he tried to get an engagement as a teacher, but failed. The persons to whom he applied all thought him too young. He was very much cast down by this failure, and was wondering what he should do next, when early one morning he heard a man calling to his mother—

"Widow Garfield, where's your boy Jem?"

"He is here, at home; do you want him?"

"Yes, I do. I wonder if he wouldn't like to teach our school at the Ledge?"

The Ledge was a mile away, and James knew it well. He appeared on the scene with a new light in his eyes.

"You haven't had a school at the Ledge for two winters, have you?" he asked the neighbour, who had kindly made the offer.

"No, and I guess you know the reason. The big boys at the school are awful to manage. They have mastered the masters twice, so we've had to shut up the school."

"It does not sound very promising for a youngster."

"No. It is not of the least use for you to come unless you mean to make up your mind beforehand to lick them. Can you lick them?"

"I guess I could, if I tried."

"Will you try, then?"

"Do you think I am old enough? Will the boys take advantage of my age?"

"Oh, yes, they are sure to do that, if you let them. But

I suppose you can take your own part; if not, you know they will lick you."

"I will talk to my Uncle Amos about it. If he advises me to take it, I will do so."

"Very good; and I hope you will. The boys have been more than a match for the old men; perhaps they will treat you with more respect."

When the neighbour had gone, James turned to his mother.

"What do you think of it, mother?"

"I think you could do it, but you would find it very hard work."

"I would not mind how hard it was, if I could only do it."

"Here comes Uncle Amos; ask him."

Mr. Boynton took a little time to consider the proposition, but finally came to this conclusion—

"You may as well go and try it. You will go into the school as the boy 'Jim Garfield;' but I hope you will come out of it as Mr. Garfield the schoolmaster."

So James decided to accept the post. He was to have twelve dollars a-month, and to board around among the parents. He found the duties trying enough; and he had a hard struggle with the boys before he became master. They thought at first that it would be an easy matter to dispose of the young teacher, whom they all knew, and who had been brought up among them; but they gradually discovered their mistake. There were several fights, but Garfield always won the victory. One young bully, who had been rather severely flogged, tried to brain the young teacher by striking him with a billet of wood; but he was immediately afterwards felled to the floor by the strong hand of his conqueror.

Conwell says, in regard to this experience—"That school was a difficult one to control, and was noted for its unruly boys. James was an enthusiast then on the subject of learning, and took the most eager interest in all the lessons of the school. He was also a believer in good order, and in his ability to maintain it. It is told of him that several of the boys, led by a stubborn young giant, attempted to conduct themselves unseemly during the school hours, and engaged in open rebellion. When the rebellion was crushed, which was not long after the teacher set about it, there were several sore heads, a giant with a lame back, and the most perfect decorum throughout the school-room."

It was about this time that James Garfield joined the "Church of the Disciples," of which his mother was a member. She had often before urged him to do so, but the young man would not be hurried. He knew that the impulse should come, not from without, but from within.

"When I quite see my way, mother, I will be only too glad to do it."

At last, with his whole soul on the side of righteousness and truth, he was baptised.

The "Church of the Disciples" professed to have no creed, to be fettered by no traditions, and trammelled by no laws save those of the Bible. One of their doctrines was, that any one who could preach, might, and ought to do so. All were supposed to have an equal share in this religious community; and every member was supposed to have perfect freedom of opinion and action, so long as both were in accordance with the revealed Christ. This church, therefore, exactly suited the independent character of James Garfield, who speedily became the outspoken champion of religious freedom in its utter reality. He was courageous in discussion; and the fact of the persecution which other sects exercised towards the Disciples only made him the stronger and more resolute in the defence of that which he held to be taught in the Bible. The opposition was carried to great length, and all the more determined was James Garfield to uphold the right. He was at this time about twenty years old. One who often heard him speak thus described him:—

"As a popular speaker he has few equals; even his scholarly and thoughtful manner is forgiven him in view of his earnestness, directness, and honesty of speech. He does not stab his opponents whenever he detects a weak place in their armour, and then play with the wounds he has succeeded in making. He indulges in no fantastic or over-strained flights of exaggerated rhetoric; and he wants also the nervous energy, the word-and-a-blow manner, which sometimes makes other speakers so effective. But he is none the less a very successful orator, and wins his way to the favour and conscience of his audience when all his rivals fail."

It was sometimes said of Garfield that he became a minister of the gospel. This is not the case. He did occasionally preach, as many other young men connected with the Disciples' Church did, but he never intended to become a preacher.

All this time he was poor. Some years afterwards, when he had entered the political field, old stories to his discredit were told; and among the rest the *Troy Press* published an assertion that he had gone into debt for his clothes, and been dunned for the money. It mentioned the name of the creditor, Mr. Peter S. Haskell—who, however, hastened to deny its truth in the following letter, published in the *Troy Times*:—

"It is true I made a suit of clothes for Mr. Garfield when he was preaching and teaching in Poestenkill, in this county. He was then a poor young man, struggling to obtain an education. One of my customers came to me and said, 'There is a young man in the village who wants a suit of clothes. He cannot pay for them now, but you will get your money. Will you make them for him?' I replied that I would. In a day or two Mr. Garfield came in, told me his circumstances and the amount of time he would require to pay for the clothes. In exact accordance with his agreement he paid me, and I did not have to jog his memory in order to get my money. I regard James A. Garfield as an honest, truthful man."

It was at this time that James Garfield became acquainted with a young lady, the daughter of a farmer in the neighbourhood, whose name was Lucretia Rudolph, and this acquaintanceship ripened into love. She is described as "a quiet, thoughtful girl, of singularly sweet and refined disposition, fond of study and reading, and possessing a warm heart, and a mind capable of steady growth."

This young lady brought the poetry into the life of James Garfield that it needed: henceforth there was another inducement added to the rest in the heart of the young man, who meant to make his way in the world, and especially to become a scholar.

CHAPTER V.

AT HIRAM AS A STUDENT.

"And first, with nicest skill and art,
Perfect and finished in every part,
A little model the master wrought,
Which should be to the larger plan
What the child is to the man—
Its counterpart in miniature."

—LONGFELLOW.

EVERY one in England who in future hears of Hiram Academy will at once associate it with James Garfield. Hiram is a small town, lying close to that elevated line where the waters divide, one part flowing southward to the Ohio river, and the other northward to Lake Erie. It was here, where the Disciples had a large and influential church, that they resolved to locate their own seminary. It was beautifully situated. "The spectator looks down upon fields of grain and tracks of woodland, and away to hills and forests, with glimpses of the neatest farm-houses in the country, and of clustered dwellings in the distant villages, adding the romance of art to the attractions of nature. So varied is the landscape, and so serenely quiet seems everything in sight, that the beholders stand and gaze, and gaze again, with inexhaustible satisfaction. It is one of those sweet and quiet retreats, whose embowered walks and shady lawns seem most consistent with a thoughtful mood and a virtuous mind. Strikingly suggestive of the sylvan shades of antiquity, in the shape of the hills and the verdure of the trees, the college seems to be a part of the natural landscape."

Mr. Zeb Rudolph, the father of Miss Lucretia, already mentioned, was one of the founders of the college, and the young lady herself was a student in the institution.

James Garfield first presented himself before the Board of Trustees at a time when the members of the Board were holding a session with closed doors. The door-keeper entered the room, and said, "A young man at the door is very desirous to see the Board without delay."

"Let him come in."

James Garfield entered, and announced his business.

"Gentlemen, I want an education, and should like the privilege of making the fires and sweeping the floors of the building to pay part of my expenses."

The gentlemen looked at the tall, plainly dressed youth, and noted his shock of yellow hair, his good-natured countenance, and his plainly made clothes.

Mr. Williams, one of the number, was pleased with his frankness and earnestness, and he said—"Gentlemen, I think we had better try this young man."

The others, however, were more doubtful.

"How do we know, young man," said one, "that the work may be done as we may want?"

"Try me," said James. "Try me for two weeks, and if the work is not done to your satisfaction I will retire without a word."

So they agreed that they would try him, and the result was satisfactory. He rang the bell to call the teachers and students in the morning, and when it was time for them to begin their work. The floor was always clean that he had swept, and he was never behind with his duties. He became one of the most popular persons in the academy. He had a pleasant word for every one, and every one liked him. He was witty and quick at repartee, and his jokes were often brilliant and striking, but they were never ill-natured. He was always good-natured and kindly. He had excellent conversational powers, and was very entertaining. He had always some poetry to recite, for he was fond of it and had a retentive memory. He seldom spent time in the playground; he was too much in earnest in regard to his studies to care for amusements. A lady, who was at the college with him, said—"He was almost too industrious, and too anxious to make the utmost of his opportunities to study." The same lady says—"At the institute the members were like a band of brothers and sisters, all struggling to advance in knowledge. They all dressed plainly, and there was no attempt or pretence at dressing stylishly or fashionably. Hiram was a little country place, with no fascinations or worldly attractions to draw off the minds of the students from their work. Two churches, the post office, one store, and a blacksmith's shop, with the college buildings, constituted the village."

The aims which the founders had in establishing the school were thus described in the *Centennial History of Education in Ohio* :—

"The aims of the school were both general and special; more narrowly they were these—

"(1.) To provide a sound, scientific, and literary education.

"(2.) To temper and sweeten such education with moral and Scriptural knowledge.

"(3.) To educate young men for the ministry.

"One peculiar tenet of the religious movement in which it originated was impressed upon the Eclectic Institute at its organisation. The Disciples believed that the Bible had

AT HIRAM AS A STUDENT. 187

been in a degree obscurated by the theological and ecclesiastical systems. Hence, their religious movement was a revolt from the theology of the schools, and an overture to men to come face to face with the Scriptures. They believed also, that to the holy writings belonged a larger place in general culture than had yet been accorded to them. Accordingly, in all their educational institutions they have emphasised the Bible and its related branches of knowledge. This may be called the distinctive feature of their schools. The charter of the Eclectic Institute, therefore, declared the purpose of the institution to be—The instruction of youth of both sexes in the various branches of literature and science, especially of moral science, as based on the facts and precepts of the Holy Scriptures.

"The institute rose at once to a high degree of popularity. On the opening day, eighty-four students were in attendance; and soon the number rose to two or three hundred per term. Students came from a wide region of country. Ohio furnished the larger number; but there was a liberal patronage from Canada, New York, and Pennsylvania. A considerable number came from the Southern States, and a still larger from the Western. These students differed widely in age, ability, culture, and wants. Some received grammar school instruction, while others still pushed on far into the regular college course. Classes were organised and taught in the collegiate studies, as they were called, for language, mathematics, literature, science, philosophy, and history. No degrees were conferred, and no students were graduated. After they had mastered the English studies, students were allowed a wide range of choice. The principle of election had free course. A course of study was published in the catalogue after the first year or two; but it was rather a list of studies taught as they were called for than a *curriculum* that students pretended closely to follow."

The writer of this sketch was Professor B. A. Hinsdale, who has since given to the world a beautiful book— *The Hiram College Memorial of President Garfield.* The following occurs in it:—

"An obvious and interesting analogy between the school and the pupil could be readily traced out. Both were in the formative period; both were full of strength and enthusiasm: but both needed growth and ripeness. He was strong-framed, deep-chested, six feet high, with a blue eye, and a massive head surmounted by a shock of tow-coloured hair. Physically he was the Garfield of twenty years later, only he had the pulpy adolescence of twenty. Time had not yet rounded out his figure, browned and thinned his hair, and put into his face the lines of thought. The school was growing, and he was growing. His intellectual and moral qualities had already declared themselves. Having lost his father in his infancy, and having been thrown upon his own resources at an early age, in the midst of the pioneers of Ohio, his sense of responsibility, his judgment, and his self-helpfulness, were developed much beyond the average. He was full of animal spirits and young joviality; but he had had his ear upon the human heart, and had heard its reverberatory murmur in the minor key. Two years or more before he had finished the studies of the Orange District School. At Chester, O., where he had attended Geauga Seminary four terms in 1849 and 1850, he had studied natural philosophy, algebra, and botany, and begun Latin and Greek. He had taught District School two terms, and received a full measure of the benefit which comes from that valuable discipline. He had already put his early longings for the lake and the sea behind him, and had determined to have the best education he could obtain. His coming to Hiram was the next step toward carrying out this resolution."

Soon after he entered the college he became acquainted

with a lady who exercised a strong personal influence upon him, and of whom he always spoke with the greatest veneration and gratitude—Miss Almeda A. Booth, a woman of great ability. "She was only nine years his senior; but she concentrated upon him all the impassioned force of a strong maternal soul, and she led him to intellectual heights seldom trod by any but the highest intellects."

Garfield thus described his first glimpse of her:—

"A few days after the beginning of the term, I saw a class of three reciting in mathematics—geometry, I think. They sat on one of the red benches, in the centre aisle of the lower chapel. I had never seen geometry; and in regarding both teacher and class with a feeling of reverential awe for the intellectual heights to which they had climbed, I studied their faces so closely that I seem to see them now as distinctly as I saw them then."

He afterwards said of her:—

"On my own behalf, I take this occasion to say, that for her generous and powerful aid, so often and so efficiently rendered, for her quick and never-failing sympathy, and for her intelligent, unselfish, and unswerving friendship, I owe her a debt of gratitude and affection, for the payment of which the longest term of life would have been too short."

Miss Booth was one of the teachers in the college; and although James Garfield was not much in her class, she yet helped him very considerably. He once said to Mr. Kirke, "I never met the man whose mind I feared to grapple with; but this woman could lead where I found it hard to follow." Kirke adds—"She not only guided his studies, but she shared in them as a comrade and co-worker; and a friend relates how she sat with him after school one night, taking up a thesis he was preparing for an exhibition day, both so supremely absorbed in the work that neither realised the night had worn away till the morning light came breaking through the window."

The two often talked together of their future. "I intend to go to college," Garfield would say, and Miss Booth was of the same mind. The learning they had made them both wish for more. They longed to climb the heights and delve into the depths of knowledge; and the one helped the other on.

Before Garfield left Hiram for college he was appointed a teacher; and so satisfactorily had both he and his friend done their work, that when they left they received a distinguished mark of the approbation of the college authorities.

Professor Hinsdale thus writes:—

"His early engagement as a teacher may point to a certain rawness in the school. However that may be, the pupil lost nothing, but gained much. That the engagement was of great value to him all will admit, who hold with the ancients and with the founders of the European Universities, that teaching is essential to the progress and perfection of the scholar. In this respect Hiram gave him an advantage that an older school, with a higher standard and more conventionality, could not have given. The two years following he taught arithmetic, grammar, algebra, penmanship, geometry, and classes in classics. He handled large classes in the English studies with conspicuous power. He took captive the members of his classes. He won the students as a body. His pupils and fellow-students had a great deal to say about him, as well as much to write in their letters, and the result was, that he made a deep impression, both directly and indirectly, upon the patrons of the school generally. The managers of the institute saw that his services would be most desirable when he had finished his own studies. He and Miss Booth left college at the same time. As they took their leave—he to return in two years, and she in one—the Board adopted this resolution:—

"In view of the faithfulness and service to the institution

of James A. Garfield and Almeda Booth, we recommend to appropriate to each fifty dollars in addition to their salaries."

The log-cabin boy was winning his way. He was conquering, one by one, the difficulties of his position. He was fighting in a good conflict, and going not only onward, but upward in a straight course. He had made his choice now, and was so living as to fill his mother's heart with joy, and give promise of future greatness.

"How much better is it to get wisdom than gold! Understanding is a well-spring of life unto him that hath it."

CHAPTER VI.

IN COLLEGE, AND PRESIDENT OF HIRAM.

> "Dear Alma Mater, long as stand,
> Like pillars of our native land,
> These everlasting hills,
> Thy grateful children shall proclaim
> In every clime thy growing fame."

THE additional fifty dollars generously presented to James Garfield were exceedingly useful to him; for he hesitated long in regard to his collegiate course for lack of means. In a talk which he had with his mother, he mentioned a plan that had come into his head.

"Uncle Thomas has been getting rich, has he not, mother?" he asked, as one day, during vacation, he and she walked in the apple-orchard, among the one hundred apple trees which his father had planted.

"He has certainly appeared to thrive for the last few years," she answered.

"Then, mother, I think I shall ask him to lend me the necessary money to go to college with. I don't like borrowing; but if I could go now for a couple of years, and graduate, it would be the making of me. Do you think uncle would do it?"

"I cannot tell, my son; but I think it is likely that he would. There would be no harm in asking him."

"I mean to insure my life in a Life Assurance Company, and then give the policy to uncle as security."

"That would be very fair. I hope you will succeed, James. It is wonderful how you have been helped onward and upward, is it not?"

"Yes, it is; and by God's help I will get further yet. Oh, mother, I am very glad and thankful that you talked me out of my foolish desire to go to sea, and persuaded me to try to get an education. It is of greater worth than a fortune to me; only I want to improve myself more and more. Nothing is so pleasant as mounting the steps of learning."

"I knew you would find it so, James; and we cannot tell what position in life you may yet fill. God has been very good to you hitherto, and He may be preparing you for something of which you have never dreamed."

"Nothing can be better than to do the present thing as well as I can, mother."

"No, my son; and then wait to see the development of events."

"That is what I will try to do."

"Go on as you have begun. That you should be so respected at Hiram is a great joy to your mother, who has never forgotten to pray for you."

"And it may be to your prayers that I owe all my success."

The money that was necessary to enable James Garfield to go through his college course was provided by a worthy gentleman who had watched his progress with interest. The life insurance policy was handed to him with the words, "If I live, I shall pay you; and if I die, you will suffer no loss."

The money having been found, the next thing was to decide upon which college to choose. There was a college of his denomination at Bethany; but he decided not to go there, and explained his reasons in a letter to a friend:—

"After thinking it all over, I have made up my mind to go to Williamstown, Massachusetts. There are three reasons why I have decided not to go to Bethany. 1st. The course of study is not so extensive or thorough as in Eastern colleges. 2nd. Bethany leans too heavily towards slavery. 3rd. I am the son of Disciple parents, am one myself, and have had but little acquaintance with people of other views; I having always lived in the West, I think it will make me more liberal, both in my religious and general views and sentiments, to go into a new circle, where I shall be under new influence. These considerations led me to conclude to go to some New England college. I, therefore, wrote to the President of Brown University, Yale, and Williams, setting forth the amount of study I had done, and asking how long it would take me to finish their course. The answers are now before me. All tell me I can graduate in two years. They are all brief, business notes; but President Hopkins concludes with this sentence: 'If you come here, we shall be glad to do what we can for you.' Other things being so nearly equal, this sentence, which seems to be a kind of friendly grasp of the hand, has settled that question for me. I shall start for Williams next week."

He accordingly said good-bye to his mother, and to his friend and former class-companion, Miss Lucretia Rudolph, and went to college.

The students at once dubbed him the "Ohio giant," for he was so tall as to be head and shoulders above most of them. He was the picture of health and strength; and his "broad shoulders, large face, bright blue eyes, and brown hair," made him interesting to them all. But there is some difference of opinion in regard to his appearance.

Edmund Kirke says:—"By those who knew Garfield at this time he is described as a tall, awkward youth, with a great shock of light hair rising nearly erect from a broad, high forehead, and an open, kindly, and thoughtful face, which showed no traces of his long struggle with poverty and privation. His class-mates will speak of his prodigious industry; his cordial, hearty, and social ways; and the great zeal with which he entered into all the physical exercises of the students. He soon became distinguished as the most ready and effective debater in the college; and one occasion on which he displayed these peculiar abilities is specially mentioned. Charles Summer had been stricken down in the Senate Chamber by Brooks of South Carolina, and the news reaching the college, caused great excitement among the students. An indignation meeting was that evening held among them; and mounting the platform, Garfield—so says my informant, who was himself one of the students—delivered 'one of the most eloquent and impassioned speeches that was ever heard in old Williams.'"

Whitelaw Reid, in his *Ohio in the War*, speaks thus of Garfield at Williams College:—"The western carpenter and village school-teacher received many a shock in the new sphere in which he now entered. On every hand he was made to feel the social superiority of his fellow students. Their ways were free from the little awkward habits of the labouring untrained youth. Their speech was free from the uncouth phrases of the provincial circles in which he had moved. Their toilets made the handiwork of his village tailor look sadly shabby. Their freehanded expenditures contrasted strikingly with his enforced parsimony. To some tough-fibred hearts these would have been only petty annoyances; to the warm, social, generous mind of young Garfield they seem, from more than one indication of his college life that we can gather, to have been a source of positive anguish. But he bore bravely up, maintained the advanced standing in the junior class to which he had been admitted on his arrival, and at the end of his two years' course bore off the metaphysical honour of the class, which was reckoned at Williams College among the highest within the gift of the institution to her graduating members."

One of the letters written by Garfield to his friend when in Williams College, and just recovering from an illness, is interesting. It is dated—

"WILLIAMS COLLEGE, 10th August 1854.

"MY DEAR SIR—I have been down near to the gates of the 'Silent City' since last I wrote to you. Perhaps it were better had I entered—God knoweth. But the crisis is passed, and I am slowly returning now. Your kind, good letter was received to-day, and I will respond immediately. I think I told you in my other that I had taken cold nearly every night since I came, and had had a severe headache for about ten days. However, I kept on studying until Friday, the 4th, when the hot water streamed from my eyes so that I could not see, and I was obliged to stop and send for a physician. . . . Oh, how much I have felt the absence of dear friends during these long, dreary hours of pain! I must subjoin some lines that have been ringing through the chambers of my soul; and though I do not know the name of the author, yet they possess the elements of immortality. I know you will love them and feel them :—

'Commend me to the friend that comes
  When I am sad and lone,
And makes the anguish of my heart
  The suffering of his own;
Who coldly shuns the glittering throng,
  And pleasure's gay levee,
And comes to gild a sombre hour,
  And give his heart to me.

'He hears me count my sorrows o'er,
   And when the task is done,
He freely gives me all I ask—
   A sigh for every one.
He cannot wear a smiling face
   When mine is touched with gloom,
But, like the violet, seeks to cheer
   The midnight with perfume.

'Commend me to that generous heart,
   Which, like the pine on high,
Uplifts the same unvarying brow
   To every change of sky;
Whose friendship does not fade away
   When wintry tempests blow,
But like the winter's icy crown,
   Looks greener through the snow.

'He flies not with the flitting stork,
   That seeks a southern sky,
But lingers where the wounded bird
   Hath laid him down to die.
Oh, such a friend! he is in truth,
   Whate'er his lot may be,
A rainbow on the storm of life,
   An anchor on its sea.'

"Thank God, I enjoy such friends as that, though they are not with me. But I must stop. . . . I need not say I am, as ever, your brother,   "JAMES."

A pleasant circumstance occurred during one of the vacations which he spent in college. He had the free use of the college library. He had never read a line of Shakespeare, excepting the extracts which he had seen in school reading-books. Nor was he at all acquainted with the poets. He had voluntarily, at the age of eighteen, resolved to shun novel-reading. The Disciples thought it a wicked waste of time, and not compatible with the serious business of life. But during this holiday he read

Shakespeare "from cover to cover," and then looked to see what the other poets had to say. He decided that he preferred Tennyson to any of them, and he revelled in the beautiful thoughts of the Laureate through all the holidays.

During the second year, James Garfield joined the Philologian Society, and he became a debater of more than ordinary vigour. He studied Latin, and Greek, and German, which last he carried on so successfully that he could read Goethe and Schiller readily. During this year, too, he became one of the editors of *The Williams Quarterly*, a college magazine of high merit.

It was during his last college term that he made his first political speech. Although he was now nearly twenty-five he had never voted; but when the Republican party arose, and a strong feeling against slavery began to grow among them, he became interested in politics.

He graduated in August 1858 with a class honour by President Hopkins, won by his essay on "The Seen and the Unseen." He left college with regret, and always spoke of President Hopkins with gratitude and veneration.

In the meantime, a position in the Troy School, at an excellent salary, had been offered him: but if he had accepted it he could not have finished his college education, and he therefore declined it. But as soon as he was free, Hiram offered him a position as Principal, and though the salary was small, he accepted it. As he went away from the college he said of President Hopkins:—

"Give me a log-hut, with only a simple bench, Mark Hopkins on one end and I on the other, and you may have all the buildings, apparatus, and libraries without him." And on another occasion he said, "I am surprised to meet President Hopkins—some thought or word of his—so often along the path of my life."

President Hopkins closed the session with a sermon, of

which these were the final words:—"Go to your posts; take unto you the whole armour of God; watch the signals and follow the footsteps of your Leader. That Leader is not now in the form of the Man of Sorrows; not now does the sweat of agony rain from him. Him the armies of heaven follow; and He hath on His vesture and on His thigh a name written, 'King of kings and Lord of lords.' The conflict may be long, but its issue is not doubtful. You may fall upon the field before the final peal of victory; but be ye faithful unto death, and ye shall receive a crown of life."

One at least of the earnest listeners who caught and treasured the words of President Hopkins endeavoured to live in the spirit of them.

James Garfield went to his work at Hiram College, firmly resolved that in righteousness and truth should be his strength. Whether or not he knew at that time that the motto of the Garfield coat-of-arms was *Through faith I conquer*, it was certainly the motto of his heart and life.

A year after he became the President of Hiram Academy he was married to Lucretia Rudolph. They had been true to each other for many years, and patient also; but now there was nothing to hinder their union, and accordingly the marriage took place at the home of the bride on the 11th November 1858. Garfield had now two helpers at Hiram, for Miss Booth was there too. Kirke says—"His wife proved herself a most efficient helpmate in his studies and college duties. His life now was a most laborious one, and he has often said that he could not have gone through with his work without her aid and that of his accomplished friend, Miss Almeda Booth. At one time he delivered a course of lectures on geology, held debates on subjects of public interest, spoke frequently on Sundays, and heard the recitations of five or six classes every day, besides attending to all the financial affairs of the college, and studying for admission to the bar. But these glorious women followed him in all his studies, and shared his labours. When he had speeches to make, or lectures to deliver, they would ransack the library by day, collecting facts and marking books for reference, to be at night used in the preparation of his discourses."

Connell says:—"After his marriage he continued to board in a very plain style, his wife being one of those notable young women whose pretty face and social position in no way interfered with her common-sense and her willingness to make her life conform to their financial circumstances. A kind Providence, which for his good had often left him to hardships and toil, most signally blessed his life through his mother and his wife. Both women had a great influence upon his later life. His wife, in her modesty, industry, economy, and intellectual keenness, was a treasure of incalculable value to him in every walk of life; and on the day of their marriage the line can safely be drawn in his history, between the old rough, self-sacrificing struggle with adversity, and the new era of joy, prosperity, and fame."

Hinsdale says—"His obligations to her in the wifely relation he strongly and beautifully recognised on all fitting occasions. Her great strength of character, long before known to private friends, was fully revealed to the world in the long tragedy that closed at Elberon, 19th September 1881. Mr. and Mrs. Garfield's domestic life was eminently happy and beautiful. After the war, Grandma Garfield, now known so pleasantly to the world as 'the little white-haired mother,' was generally a member of the family. They were a happy trio—a fond mother, a dutiful son and husband, a faithful daughter and wife. Both General and Mrs. Garfield were always conspicuous for private and domestic virtues, filial affection, unbroken troth, and parental love."

Every one was glad that the Principal should be so happy

WIDOW OF PRESIDENT GARFIELD. —Page 199.

in his private life. The boys loved him, and found in him a true friend. "Their minds began to open; new aspirations began to stir in their hearts. Often these boys had troubles peculiarly their own. Some were poor; some were tethered to home; some wanted courage and self-reliance; some tended to despondency. Mr. Garfield found them out. He remembered his own experience. He seemed to read by intuition a mind that teemed with new facts, ideas, and impressions, that was stirred by a new spirit and power, that sighed for wider and higher activity. These students he aided with his counsel and encouragement. A boy who wanted to study, and was poor, called out his full interest."

CHAPTER VII.

GARFIELD ON COLLEGE EDUCATION.

"Sail on, nor fear to breast the sea,
Our hearts, our hopes are all with thee."

THE following speech by the man whose life is before us is worth the earnest attention of all Englishmen interested in the great question of the education of the people of the future:—

"Gentlemen of the Literary Society—I congratulate you on the significant fact, that the questions which most vitally concern your personal work are at this time rapidly becoming—indeed, have already become—questions of first importance to the whole nation.

"In ordinary times we could scarcely find two subjects wider apart than the meditations of a school-boy, when he asks what he shall do with himself, and how he shall do it, and the forecastings of a great nation, when it studies the laws of its own life, and endeavours to solve the problem of its destiny. But now there is more than a resemblance between the nation's work and yours. If the two are not identical, they at least bear the relation of the whole to a part.

"The nation, having passed through the childhood of its history, and being about to enter upon a new life, based on a fuller recognition of the rights of manhood, has discovered that liberty can be safe only when the suffrage is illuminated by education. It is now perceived that the life and light of a nation are inseparable. Hence the Federal Government has established a National Department of Education, for the purpose of teaching young men and women how to be good citizens.

"You, young gentlemen, having passed the limits of childhood, and being about to enter the larger world of manhood, with its manifold struggles and aspirations, are now confronted with the question, What must I do to fit myself most completely, not for being a citizen merely, but for being all that doth become a man, living in the full light of the Christian civilisation of America? Your disenthralled and victorious country asks you to be educated for her sake, and the noblest aspirations of your being still more imperatively ask it for your own sake.

"In the hope that I may aid you in solving some of these questions, I have chosen for my theme on this occasion 'The Course of Study in American Colleges, and its Adaptation to the Wants of our Time.' Before examining any course of study, we should clearly apprehend the objects to be obtained by a liberal education.

"In general, it may be said that the purpose of all study is twofold—to discipline our faculties, and to acquire knowledge for the duties of life. It is happily provided in the constitution of the human mind, that the labour by which knowledge is acquired is the only means of disciplining the powers. It may be stated as a general rule, that if we compel ourselves to learn what we ought to know, and use it when learned, our discipline will take care of itself

"Let us, then, inquire what kinds of knowledge should be the objects of a liberal education? Without adopting in full the classification of Herbert Spencer, it will be sufficiently comprehensive for my present purpose to propose the following kinds of knowledge, stated in the order of their importance:—

"*First*, That knowledge which is necessary for the full development of our bodies and the preservation of our health.

"*Second*, The knowledge of those principles by which the useful arts and industries are carried on and improved.

"*Third*, That knowledge which is necessary to a full comprehension of our rights and duties as citizens.

"*Fourth*, A knowledge of the intellectual, moral, religious, and æsthetic nature of man, and his relations to nature and civilisation.

"*Fifth*, That special and thorough knowledge which is requisite for the particular profession or pursuit which a man may choose as his life-work after he has completed his college studies.

"In brief, the student should study himself, his relations to society, to nature, and to art; and, above all, in all, and through all these, he should study the relations of himself, society, nature, and art, to God, the Author of them all. Of course it is not possible, nor is it desirable, to confine the course of development exclusively to this order; for Truth is so related and correlated, that no department of her realm is wholly isolated.

"We cannot learn much that pertains to the industry of society without learning something of the material world and the laws that govern it.

"We cannot study nature profoundly without bringing ourselves into communion with the spirit of art which pervades and fills the universe. But what I suggest is, that we should make the course of study conform generally to the order here indicated; that the student shall first study that which he most needs to know; that the order of his needs shall be the order of his work. Now, it will not be denied, that from the day the child's foot first presses the green turf till the day when, an old man, he is ready to be laid under it, there is not an hour in which he does not need to know a thousand things in relation to his body— 'what he shall eat, what he shall drink, and wherewithal he shall be clothed.' Unprovided with that instinct which enables the lower animals to reject the noxious and select the nutritive, man must learn even the most primary truth that ministers to his self-preservation. If parents were themselves sufficiently educated, most of this knowledge might be acquired at the mother's knee; but, by the strangest perversion and misdirection of the educational forces, these most essential elements of knowledge are more neglected than any other.

"School committees would summarily dismiss the teacher who should have the good sense and courage to spend three days of each week with her pupils in the fields and woods, teaching them the names, peculiarities, and uses of rocks, trees, plants, and flowers, and the beautiful story of the animals, birds, and insects, which fill the world with life and beauty. They will applaud her for continuing to perpetrate that undefended and indefensible outrage upon the laws of physical and intellectual life, which keeps a little child sitting in silence, in a vain attempt to hold his mind to the words of a printed page, for six hours in a day. Herod was merciful, for he finished his slaughter of the innocents in a day; but this practice kills by the savagery of slow torture. And what is the child directed to study? Besides the mass of words and sentences which he is compelled to memorise, not one syllable of which he understands, at eight or ten years of age he is set to work on English grammar—one of the most complex, intricate, and metaphysical of studies, requiring a mind of much muscle and discipline to master it. Thus are squandered—nay, far worse than squandered—those three precious years when the child is all ear and eye, when its eager spirit, with insatiable curiosity, hungers and thirsts to know the what and the why of the world and its wonderful furniture. We silence its sweet clamour by cramming its hungry mind with words—words, empty, meaningless words. It asks for bread and we give it a stone. It is to me a perpetual wonder that any child's love of knowledge survives the outrages of the schoolroom. It would be foreign from my present purpose to consider further the subject of primary education; but it is worthy your profoundest thought, for 'out of it are the issues of life.' That man will be a benefactor of his race who shall teach us how to manage rightly the first years of a child's education. I, for one, declare that no child of mine shall ever be compelled to study one hour, or to learn even the English alphabet, before he has deposited under his skin at least seven years of muscle and bone.

"What are our seminaries and colleges accomplishing in the way of teaching the laws of life and physical well-being? I should scarcely wrong them were I to answer nothing—absolutely nothing. The few recitations which some of the colleges require in anatomy and physiology unfold but the alphabet of those subjects. The emphasis of college culture does not fall there. The graduate has learned the Latin of the old maxim, "*Mens sana in corpore sano;*" but how to strengthen the mind by the preservation of the body he has never learned. He can read you in Xenophon's best Attic Greek that Apollo flayed the unhappy Marsyas, and hanged up his skin as a trophy; but he has never examined the wonderful texture of his own skin, or the laws by which he may preserve it. He would blush to mistake the place of a Greek accent, or put the ictus on the second syllable of

Eolus; but the whole circle, "*liberalium artium*," so pompously referred to in his diploma of graduation, may not have been taught him, as I can testify in an instance personally known to me, whether the jijunum is a bone, or the humerus an intestine. Every hour of study consumes a portion of his muscular and vital force. Every tissue of his body requires its appropriate nourishment, the elements of which are found in abundance in the various products of Nature; but he has never inquired where he shall find the phosphates and carbonates of lime for his bones, albumen and fibrine for his blood, and phosphorus for his brain. His chemistry, mineralogy, botany, anatomy, and physiology, if thoroughly studied, would give all this knowledge; but he has been intent on things remote and foreign, and has given but little heed to those matters which so nearly concern the chief functions of life. But the student should not be blamed. The great men of history have set him the example. Copernicus discovered and announced the true theory of the solar system a hundred years before the circulation of the blood was known. Though from the heart to the surface, and from the surface back to the heart, of every man of the race, some twenty pounds of blood had made the circuit once every three minutes; yet men were looking so steadily away from themselves that they did not observe the wonderful fact. This habit of thought has developed itself in all the course of college study.

"In the next place, I inquire, what kinds of knowledge are necessary for carrying on and improving the useful arts and industries of civilised life? I am well aware of the current notion that those muscular arts should stay in the fields and shops, and not invade the sanctuaries of learning. A finished education is supposed to consist mainly of literary culture. The story of the forges of the Cyclops, where the thunderbolts of Jove were fashioned, is supposed to adorn elegant scholarship more gracefully than those sturdy truths which are preaching to this generation in the wonders of the mine, in the fire of the furnace, in the clang of the iron-mills, and the other innumerable industries, which, more than all other human agencies, have made our civilisation what it is, and are destined to achieve wonders yet undreamed of. This generation is beginning to understand that education should not be for ever divorced from industry, that the highest results can be reached only when science guides the hand of labour. With what eagerness and alacrity is industry seizing every truth of science and putting it in harness! A few years ago Bessemer of England, studying the nice affinities between carbon and the metals, discovered that a slight change of combination would produce a metal possessing the ductility of iron and the compactness of steel, and which would cost but little more than common iron. One rail of this metal will outlast fifteen of the iron rails now in use. Millions of capital are already invested to utilise this thought of Bessemer's, which must soon revolutionise the iron manufacture of the world.

"Another example: The war raised the price of cotton and paper made of cotton rags. It was found that good paper could be manufactured from the fibre of soft wood; but it was expensive and difficult to reduce to a pulp without chopping the fibre in pieces. A Yankee mechanic, who had learned in the science of vegetable anatomy that a billet of wood was composed of millions of hollow cylinders, many of them so small that only the microscope could reveal them, and having learnt also the penetrative and expansive power of steam, wedded these two truths in an experiment, which, if exhibited to Socrates, would have been declared a miracle from the gods.

"The experiment was very simple. Putting his block of wood in a strong box, he forced into it a volume of super-heated steam, which made its way into the minutest pore and cell of the wood. Then, through a trap-door suddenly opened, the block was tossed out. The outside pressure being removed, the expanding steam instantly burst every one of the million tubes; every vegetable flue collapsed, and his block of wood lay before him a mass of fleecy fibre, more delicate than the hand of man could make it.

"Machinery is the chief implement with which civilisation does its work, but the science of mechanics is impossible without mathematics.

"But for her mineral resources, England would be only the hunting-park of Europe, and it is believed that her day of greatness will terminate when her coal-fields are exhausted. Our mineral wealth is a thousand times greater than hers; and yet, without the knowledge of geology, mineralogy, metallurgy, and chemistry, our mines could be but little value. Without a knowledge of astronomy, commerce on the sea is impossible; and now at last it is being discovered that the greatest of all our industries, the agricultural, in which three-fourths of all our population are engaged, must call science to its aid if it would keep up with the demands of civilisation. I need not enumerate the extent and variety of knowledge, scientific and practical, which a farmer needs in order to reach the full height and scope of his noble calling. And what has our American system of education done for this controlling majority of the people? I can best answer that question with a single fact. Notwithstanding that there are in the United States one hundred and twenty thousand common schools, and seven thousand academies and seminaries; notwithstanding there are two hundred and seventy-five colleges, where young men may be graduated as bachelors and masters of the liberal arts—yet in all these the people of the United States have found so little being done, or likely to be done, to educate men for the work of agriculture, that they have demanded, and at last have secured, from their political servants in congress, an appropriation sufficient to build and maintain in each state of the Union a college for the education of farmers. This great outlay would have been totally unnecessary, but for the stupid and criminal neglect of college, academic, and common-school boards of education to furnish that which the wants of the people require. The scholar and the worker must join hands if both would be successful.

"I next ask, What studies are necessary to teach our young men and women the history and spirit of our government, and their rights and duties as citizens? There is not now, and there never was on this earth, a people who have had so many and weighty reasons for loving their country, and thanking God for the blessings of civil and religious liberty, as our own. And yet, seven years ago, there was probably less strong, earnest, open love of country in the United States than in any other nation of christendom. It is true that the gulf of anarchy and ruin into which treason threatened to plunge us, startled the nation as by an electric shock, and galvanised into life its dormant and dying patriotism. But how came it dormant and dying? I do not hesitate to affirm, that one of the chief causes was our defective system of education. Seven years ago there was scarcely an American college in which more than four weeks out of the four years' course were devoted to studying the government and history of the United States. For this defect of our educational system I have neither respect nor toleration. It is far inferior to that of Persia three thousand years ago. The uncultivated tribes of Greece, Rome, Libya, and Germany, surpassed us in this respect. Grecian children were taught to reverence and emulate the virtues of their ancestors. Our educational forces are so wielded as to teach our children to admire most that which is foreign, and fabulous, and dead. I have recently examined the catalogue of a leading New England college, in which the geography and history of Greece and Rome are required to be studied five terms; but neither the history nor the geography of the United States is named in the college course, or required as a condition of admission.

"Our American children must know all the classic rivers from the Scamander to the Yellow Tiber; must tell you the length of the Appian Way, and of the canal over which Horace and Virgil sailed on their journey to Brundusium: but he may be crowned with bacchalaureate honours without having heard, since his first moment of freshman life, one word concerning the one hundred and twenty-two thousand miles of coast and river navigation, the six thousand miles of canal, and the thirty-five thousand miles of railroad, which indicate both the prosperity and the possibilities of his own country.

"It is well to know the history of those magnificent nations whose origin is lost in fable, and whose epitaphs were written a thousand years ago; but, if we cannot know both, it is far better to study the history of our own nation, whose origin we can trace to the freest and noblest aspirations of the human heart—a nation that was formed from the hardiest, the purest, and most enduring elements of European civilisation; a nation that, by its faith and courage, has dared and accomplished more for the human race in a single century than Europe accomplished in the first thousand years of the Christian era. The New England township was the type after which our Federal Government was modelled; yet it would be rare to find a college student who can make a comprehensive and intelligent statement of the municipal organisation of the township in which he was born, and tell you by what officers its legislative, judicial, and executive functions are administered. One half of the time which is now almost wholly wasted in district schools on English grammar, attempted at too early an age, would be sufficient to teach our children to love the Republic, and to become its loyal and life-long supporters. After the bloody baptism from which the nation has arisen to a higher and nobler life, if this shameful defect in our system of education be not speedily remedied, we shall deserve the infinite contempt of future generations. I insist that it should be made an indispensable condition of graduation in every American college, that the student must understand the history of this Continent since its discovery by Europeans; the origin and history of the United States, its constitution of government, the struggles through which it has passed, and the rights and duties of citizens who are to determine its destiny and share its glory.

"Having thus gained the knowledge which is necessary to life, health, industry, and citizenship, the student is prepared to enter a wider and grander field of thought. If he desires that large and liberal culture which will call into activity all his powers, and make the most of the material God has given him, he must study deeply and earnestly the intellectual, the moral, the religious, and the æsthetic nature of man; his relations to nature, to civilisation, past and present; and, above all, his relations to God. These should occupy nearly, if not fully, half the time of his college course. In connection with the philosophy of the mind he should study logic, the pure mathematics, and the general laws of thought. In connection with moral philosophy he should study political and social ethics—a science so little known either in colleges or congresses. Prominent among all the rest should be his study of the wonderful history of the human race, in its slow and toilsome march across the centuries—now buried in ignorance, superstition, and crime; now rising to the sublimity of heroism, and catching a glimpse of a better destiny; now turning remorselessly away from, and leaving to perish, empires and civilisations in which it had invested its faith and courage and boundless energy for a thousand years, and plunging into the forests of Germany, Gaul, and Britain, to build for itself new empires, better fitted for its new aspirations; and, at last, crossing three thousand miles of unknown sea, and building in the wilderness of a new hemisphere its latest and proudest monuments. To know this as it ought to be known requires not only a knowledge of general history, but a thorough understanding of such works as Guizot's *History of Civilisation*, and Draper's *Intellectual Development of Europe*, and also the rich literature of ancient and modern nations.

"Of course, our colleges cannot be expected to lead the student through all the paths of this great field of learning; but they should at least point out its boundaries, and let him taste a few clusters from its richest vines.

"Finally, in rounding up the measure of his work, the student should crown his education with that æsthetic culture which will unfold to him the delights of nature and art, and make his mind and heart a fit temple where the immortal spirit of beauty may dwell for ever.

"While acquiring this kind of knowledge the student is on a perpetual voyage of discovery, searching what he is, and what he may become; how he is related to the universe, and how the harmonies of the outer world respond to the voice within him. It is in this range of study that he learns most fully his own tastes and aptitudes, and generally determines what his work in life shall be.

"The last item in the classification I have suggested—that special knowledge which is necessary to fit a man for the particular profession or calling he may adopt—I cannot discuss here, as it lies outside the field of general education, but I will make one suggestion to any of the young gentlemen before me who may intend to choose, as his life-work, some one of the learned professions. You will find it a fatal mistake if you make only the same preparations which your predecessors made fifty or even ten years ago. Each generation must have a higher cultivation than the preceding one, in order to be equally successful; and each must be educated for his own times. If you become a lawyer, you must remember that the science of law is not fixed like geometry, but is a growth which keeps pace with the progress of society. The developments of the late war will make it necessary to re-write many of the leading chapters of international and maritime law. The destruction of slavery and the enfranchisement of four millions of coloured men will almost revolutionise American jurisprudence. If Webster were now at the bar, in the full glory of his strength, he would be compelled to reconstruct the whole fabric of his legal learning. Similar changes are occurring both in the medical and military professions. Ten years hence the young surgeon will hardly venture to open an office till he has studied thoroughly the medical and surgical history of the late war. Since the experience at Sumter and Wagner, no nation will again build fortifications of costly masonry; for they have learned that earthworks are not only cheaper, but a better defence against artillery. The text-books on military engineering must be re-written. Our Spencer rifle and Prussian needle-gun have revolutionised both the manufacture and the manual of arms; and no great battle will ever again be fought with muzzle-loading muskets. Napoleon, at the head of his Old Guard, could to-day win no Austerlitz till he had read the military history of the last six years.

"It may perhaps be thought that the suggestion I have made concerning the professions will not apply to the work of the Christian minister, whose principal text-book is a divine and perfect revelation; but, in my judgment, the remark applies to the clerical profession with even more force than to any other. There is no department of his duties in which he does not need the fullest and the latest knowledge. He is pledged to the defence of revelation and religion; but it will not avail him to be able to answer the objections of Hume and Voltaire. The arguments of Paley were not written to answer the scepticism of to-day. His *Natural Theology* is now less valuable than Hugh Miller's *Footprints of the Creator*, or Guizot's *Lectures on Earth and Man*. The men and women of to-day know but little, and care less, about the thousand abstract questions of polemic theology which puzzled the heads and wearied the hearts of our Puritan fathers- and mothers. That minister will make, and deserves to make, a miserable failure, who attempts to feed hungry hearts on the dead dogmas of the past. More than that of any other man, it is his duty to march abreast with the thinkers of his time, and be not only a learner, but a teacher, of its science, its literature, and its criticism.

"I beseech you to remember that the genius of success is still the genius of labour. If hard work is not another name for talent, it is the best possible substitute for it. In the long run, the chief difference in men will be found in the amount of work they do. Do not trust to what lazy men call the spur of the occasion. If you wish to wear spurs in the tournament of life, you must buckle them to your own heels before you enter the lists. Men look with admiring wonder upon a great intellectual effort, like Webster's reply to Hayne, and seem to think that it leaped into life by the inspiration of the moment. But if by some intellectual chemistry we could resolve that speech into its several elements of power, and trace each to its source, we should find that every constituent force had been elaborated twenty years before—it may be in some hour of earnest intellectual labour. Occasion may be the bugle-call that summons an army to battle; but the blast of a bugle cannot make soldiers or win victories.

"And finally, young gentlemen, learn to cultivate a wise reliance, based not on what you hope, but on what you perform. It has long been the habit of this institution, if I may so speak, to throw young men overboard, and let them sink or swim. None have yet been drowned who were worth the saving. I hope the practice will be continued, and that you will not rely upon outside help for growth or success. Give crutches to cripples, but go you forth with brave, true hearts, knowing that fortune dwells in your brain and muscle, and that labour is the only symbol of omnipotence."

In point of time we have anticipated events in our reproduction of this speech, one of the most able spoken on the subject by any man in any land.

CHAPTER VIII.

SENATOR GARFIELD AT THE WAR.

"There is a poor, blind Samson in the land,
  Shorn of his strength, and bound in bonds of steel,
Who may, in some grim revel, raise his head,
  And shake the pillars of this commonweal,
Till the vast Temple of our liberties
A shapeless mass of wreck and rubbish lies."
—LONGFELLOW.

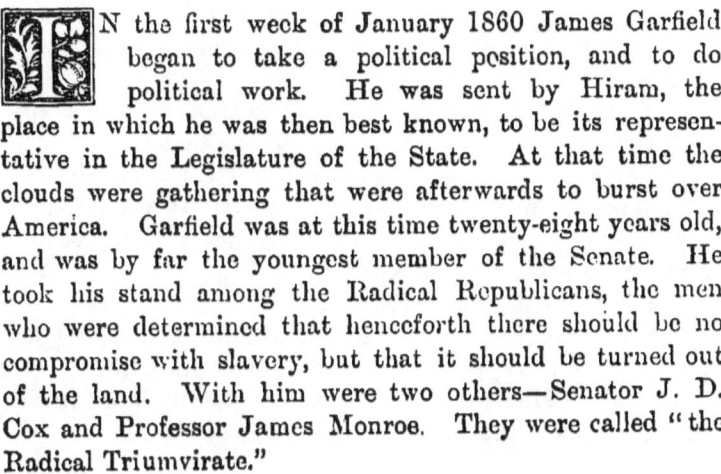IN the first week of January 1860 James Garfield began to take a political position, and to do political work. He was sent by Hiram, the place in which he was then best known, to be its representative in the Legislature of the State. At that time the clouds were gathering that were afterwards to burst over America. Garfield was at this time twenty-eight years old, and was by far the youngest member of the Senate. He took his stand among the Radical Republicans, the men who were determined that henceforth there should be no compromise with slavery, but that it should be turned out of the land. With him were two others—Senator J. D. Cox and Professor James Monroe. They were called "the Radical Triumvirate."

Mr. Garfield was sometimes congratulated upon his success, and sometimes he received the reverse of congratulation from his friends.

"I am sorry," said an old man, shaking his head. "You were in the way to become a successful worker in the Lord's vineyard, and now you have gone into the world."

"But we are all in the world," replied Garfield; "and we all have work to do. I believe that if I lift my voice, as I will do, and my hand too, if necessary, against slavery, I shall be doing the Lord's work as really as if I were preaching."

"But it would have been a more noble thing to have given your life to the ministry. A Christian man has no business meddling with politics."

"There I think you are entirely in the wrong. Who should take up politics if not Christian men? They are the men above all others who ought to rule the world."

His friend did not agree with him; but his wife and mother were both glad that he should have been elected. Woman-like, they believed that it would be more to the State than to him that he was a senator. "The times need wise men," said the good little widow, who had prayed for her boy for so many years; "if all senators were like my James, the world would be better."

But she did not always thus speak to him.

"There are responsibilities, James," she said.

"Yes, mother, I know; but I will not shirk my duties. The appointment will help me many ways. It will increase my income, which will be a good thing, and it will give me a better position in every respect."

"You will not give up Hiram?"

"Not altogether. But I mean to read up law, and in time become a lawyer; so I shall have to work hard."

But his studies were destined to be speedily interrupted by the events of that most eventful year, 1861.

In January he declared in the Ohio Senate that he would oppose slavery altogether. "When the constitutional amendment was submitted to the Ohio legislature which would guarantee to the slave states the perpetuity of slavery, he led the uncompromising minority, and with a remarkable display of ability opposed, with pointed speeches and his vote, every measure or resolution which could be construed into a concession to the party in favour of human bondage. His speeches were eloquent, thoughtful, and sincere. He seemed to care nothing for popularity, and expected only to do his duty there, and retire with a clear conscience to private life, when his term of office had expired."

Speaking of this time some years afterwards he said—

"Long familiarity with the bodies and souls of men had paralysed the consciences of a majority of our people. The baleful doctrines of state sovereignty had shaken and weakened the noblest and most beneficent powers of the national government, and the grasping power of slavery was seizing the virgin territories of the West, and dragging them into the den of eternal bondage. At that crisis the Republican party was born. It had its first inspiration from the fire of liberty which God has lighted in every human heart, and which all the powers of ignorance and tyranny can never wholly extinguish. The Republican party came to deliver and save the Republic. It entered the arena where the beleagured and assailed territories were struggling for freedom, and drew around it the sacred circle of liberty which the demon of slavery has never dared to cross. It made them free for ever."

It will be seen by this, that President Lincoln was a man after Garfield's own heart, and that his election to the Presidency delighted no American more than the young man who, in course of time, would fill the same place—and die the same death as Lincoln.

The "coming events threw their shadows before." The Southern States seceded, knowing that secession must mean war. Garfield uttered the following words on the occasion of the discussion in the Ohio Senate of a bill to provide for the raising and maintaining 6000 militia. Some one had declared the measure would mean coercion, to which objection Garfield replied—

"If by coercion it is meant that the Federal Government shall declare and make war against a State, then I have yet to see any man, Democrat or Republican, who is a coercionist But if by the term it is meant that the general government shall enforce the laws by whomsoever violated, shall protect the property and flag of the Union, shall punish traitors to the constitution, be they ten men or ten thousand, then I am a coercionist. Every member of the Senate, by his vote on the eighth resolution, is a coercionist: nine-tenths of the people of Ohio are coercionists. Every man is a coercionist or a traitor."

Still lovers of peace hoped against hope that differences might be healed without recourse to war, until, only a short time after the election of President Lincoln, the battle of Bull Run settled the matter, and every man felt that it must be war and not peace.

James Garfield's mind was at once made up, and he announced his decision to the little family circle.

"Every man who is a patriot must respond to the call of President Lincoln for volunteers! I shall be one."

It was only natural that the faces of the mother and the wife should grow a little pale as they thought of the possible consequences of this decision on the part of the man who was more to them than all the world beside. But this war awoke as much enthusiasm in the hearts of the women as the men. It was a war upon which grand issues depended; and all noble souls put self out of the question, and only asked to be allowed to do their part. It was wo'se for the women than the men; harder to give up their dearest than go themselves; but they did it. There was scarcely a home that had a man in it which did not yield some one to the call of patriotism. These women would only suffer with the rest.

"It is not what I have hoped and prayed for," said the mother of James Garfield. "Through all my years of poverty and work I used to dream about the future of my boy, but I never dreamed of his filling a soldier's grave."

"Perhaps I shall not do that, mother. We are not all going to be killed, you know. But this is a cause that is worthy of any man's life."

"So it is. If ever there were such a thing as a righteous war, this must be one."

"Yes; and you know we do not begin it. Lincoln would never have fired the first shot; but now a man with any manliness in him must fight; he would be less than a man if he did not."

"Oh, I see, James, what your feeling is. Your life belongs to your country. Go, my son, and may God protect you," said the mother. And her daughter-in-law added, "And may He prosper the right!"

We have seen in our sketch of the life of Lincoln how unprepared for war was the North as compared with the South; and we have also seen how one disaster followed another. But some of the men were heroes, and geniuses too, and among these we must reckon Garfield.

A week after the Bull Run battle James Garfield was made Lieutenant-Colonel of a regiment at Camp Chase. He was to organise and command a new regiment, the Forty-second Ohio Infantry. A hundred students from Hiram College volunteered, and in August the regiment was complete. During the next months, Garfield, its commander, set to work to teach himself and his men the art of war.

"Bringing his saw and jack-plane again into play, he

fashioned companies, officers, and non-commissioned officers, out of maple blocks, and with those wooden-headed troops thoroughly mastered the infantry tactics in his quarters. Then he organised a school for the officers in his regiment, requiring thorough recitation in the tactics, and illustrating the manœuvres by the blocks he had prepared for his own instruction This done, he instituted regimental, company, squad, skirmish, and bayonet drill; and kept his men at these exercises from six to eight hours a-day, until it was universally admitted that no better drilled or disciplined regiment could be found in Ohio."

As soon as this was accomplished, very important work was given him to do. He was sent against the Confederate General, Humphrey Marshall, who had invaded Eastern Kentucky.

General Buell said to him—"If you were in command of Eastern Kentucky, what would you do? Think this question over to-night, and let me have your answer in the morning."

Garfield spent most of the night in drawing plans, and when they were submitted to the General, he ordered Garfield to go and expel Marshall's army in his own way.

The story of the battle has been often told, but in no language more forcible and vigorous than that of the man who wrote for the firm of Harper Brothers, New York— Mr. Edmund Kirke—who relates the conclusion thus:—

"For five hours the contest rages. Now the Union forces are driven back, then charging up the hill they regain the lost ground, and from behind rocks and trees pour in their murderous volleys. Then again they are driven back, and again they charge up the hill, strewing the ground with corpses. So the bloody work goes on; so the battle wavers, till the setting sun, wheeling below the hills, glances along the dense lines of rebel steel moving down to envelop the weary eleven hundred. It is an awful moment, big with the fate of Kentucky. At its very crisis two figures stand out against the fading sky, boldly defined in the background.

"One is in Union blue, with a little band of heroes about him; he is posted on a projecting rock, which is scarred with bullets, and in full view of both armies. His head is uncovered, his hair streaming in the wind, his face upturned in the darkening daylight, and from his soul is going up a prayer—a prayer for Sheldon and his forces. He turns his eyes to the northward, and his lip tightens as he throws off his outer coat, and as it catches in the branch of a tree, says to his hundred men, 'Come on, boys; *we* must give them "Hail, Columbia!"'

"The other is in Confederate grey. Moving on to the brow of the opposite hill, and placing a glass to his eye, he, too, takes a long look to the northward. He starts, for he sees something which the other, on lower ground, does not distinguish. Soon he wheels his horse, and the word 'Retreat!' echoes along the valley between them. It is his last word; for six rifles crack, and the Confederate major lies on the ground.

"The one in blue looks to the north again, and now, floating proudly among the trees, he sees the starry banner. It is Sheldon and reinforcements! On they come like the rushing wind, filling the air with shouting. The weary eleven hundred take up the strain, and then, above the swift pursuit, above the lessening conflict, above the last boom of the wheeling cannon, goes up the wild huzza of victory! The gallant Garfield has won the day, and rolled back the tide of disaster which has been sweeping on ever since Big Bethel.

"As they come back from the short pursuit, the young commander grasps man after man by the hand, and says—'God bless you, boys, you have saved Kentucky!'

"At about eight o'clock that night, at a gathering of his officers, Garfield showed them the intercepted letter of

Marshall, and for the first time they knew that the valiant eleven hundred had routed an intrenched force of 5000, strongly supported with artillery, and that their leader was fully conscious of his enemy's strength when he moved to attack him.

"Thus ended this remarkable battle. It was the first wave in the tide of victory which, with now and then an ebbing flow, swept on to the capture of Richmond. President Lincoln, when he heard of it, said to a distinguished army officer who happened to be with him, 'Why did Garfield in two weeks do what would have taken you regular folks two months to accomplish?'

"'Because he was not educated at West Point,' answered the West Pointer, laughing.

"'No,' replied Mr. Lincoln, 'that wasn't the reason. It was because, when he was a boy, he had to work for a living.'"

An American poet wrote the following in 1880—

"GIVE THEM, 'HAIL, COLUMBIA.'"

"In one hot fight that Garfield won,
    The loyal-souled commander
Sent back a word among his men
    That stirred up all their dander.

He was not quite so fast to cuss
    And swear around as some be,
And all he said was, 'Come on, boys,
    We'll give them "Hail, Columby."'

He led, they followed, spreading wide
    Among the rebels routed,
From rank to rank in liberal gift,
    The self-same thing he shouted.

Year after year, a leader still,
    In camp, and field, and forum,
His feet beside his colours tread
    As when the bullets tore 'em.

> Year after year, upon his lips,
>   Through every contest ringing,
> The men who follow hear, as when
>   The shells were o'er him singing.
>
> The words that harsh to many an ear,
>   But bugle sweet to some be,
> For peace or war a charging-cry—
>   'Boys, give 'em "Hail, Columby!"'
>   —WILLIAM O. STODDARD.

The first battle in which Garfield engaged was by no means his last. It was for his victory at Middle Creek that Colonel Garfield was made a Brigade-General of Volunteers. He several times rendered most important services. He was the first officer who refused to return a fugitive slave.

"I respectfully but positively decline," he said, "to allow my command to search for, or deliver up, any fugitive slaves."

He was told that he would probably be court-martialled, and he replied—"The matter may as well be tested first as last. Right is right, and I do not propose to mince matters at all. My soldiers are here for far other purposes than hunting and returning fugitive slaves. My people on the Western Reserves of Ohio did not send my boys and myself down here to do that kind of business, and they will back me up in my action."

And so they did; for the principle that he had thus asserted was afterwards embodied in a general order.

The last service rendered by Garfield to the army was at the battle of Chickamauga; and for this he was raised to the rank of Major-General. It only took him about eighteen months to rise from a Lieutenant-Colonelcy to be a Major-General. In the famous battle of Chickamauga he fought under General Rosencrans; but those who knew, declared that much of the success was due to Garfield.

CHAPTER IX.

GENERAL GARFIELD IN CONGRESS.

> " So let it be. In God's own might ;
> We gird us for the coming fight,
> And strong in Him whose cause is ours
> In conflict with unholy powers,
> We grasp the weapons he has given—
> The light, and truth, and love of heaven."
> —WHITTIER.

THE Nineteenth District of Ohio had, more than a year before, voted James Garfield to a seat in Congress. He accepted it, feeling sure that the war would be over before the time came for him to take his seat. This, however, was not the case ; and he was greatly perplexed to know to which of the two duties, political or military, he ought to give his attention. He consulted his friends, and received their counsel ; but the words that decided him were those of President Lincoln—

"I want you in Congress," he said ; "the Republican majority is so small, that we have some difficulty in carrying our war measures. There are able generals in the army, but few men of sufficient military experience in the House to regulate the legislation of the army. *It is your duty, therefore, to enter Congress.*"

But before doing so General Garfield took a holiday, and went home to Hiram; and a very sad holiday it proved to be.

His mother met him with a grave face, and his wife with tears.

An addition had been made some time before to the home company; a little babe had come with all its joyous young life, and the interest that circles around it. This little daughter was very dear to her father. She was so very tiny when he saw her last, that he longed to look upon her face again.

"Will she know me? Is she old enough now to take notice of things? Will she be pleased with my uniform?" Such were the questions that he asked himself.

And the news that awaited the brave General on his return, was, "She is dying."

He took the little darling in his arms, and as he did so all the glory faded away from his military career. He glanced with a bitter smile at the signs of his new rank, and cared nothing for the distinction that he had won.

"How vain a thing is life!" he said; and in that hour wondered whether or not it was worth living at all.

But his mother comforted him.

"After all, there is duty," she said.

"Yes, but even that we cannot be sure of. We may easily make mistakes. I am on my way to Washington now to see the President, and I suppose that will mean my resignation as an officer in the army."

"Have you not fought long enough?" asked his mother.

"You must not leave us quite at once," said his wife; "it will not be long before baby's sufferings are ended."

And indeed it was not. The time was sorrowful, but it was short; and Mr. Garfield waited for the funeral. They had no photograph of their little darling, and one was taken after death. Altogether the visit to Hiram was very full of a trouble that stole the brightness from the heart of the General.

But he was thoroughly brave; and he went at the call of duty to the House, in which he retained a seat for the rest of his all too short life.

There were very important questions awaiting consideration. The first measure introduced was a bill for the confiscation of rebel property, and Garfield's first speech in Congress referred to it.

The next bill concerned bounties. Garfield alone opposed it; but on the votes being taken, another, Mr. Grinnell of Massachusetts, voted with him, so that the result stood thus: Yeas, 112; Nays, 2.

Mr. Chase, who was then Secretary of the Treasury, said to him, "I was proud of your vote the other day. You were right. But you have just started in public life, and I want you to bear in mind that it is a very risky thing to vote against your party. It is a good thing to do sometimes, but not very often. Do it sparingly and carefully."

It was good advice, and so was that given by Rosencrans —"When you go to Congress, be careful what you say. Don't talk too much, but when you talk, speak to the point. Be true to yourself, and you will make your mark through the country."

He was true to himself, and he certainly made his mark.

In regard to Garfield's conduct in the House, J. S. Ogilvie thus writes of an incident that created some stir at the time:—" In the summer of 1864 a breach occurred between the President and some of the most radical of the Republican orders in Congress over the question of the reconstruction of the States of Arkansas and Louisiana. Congress passed a bill providing for the organisation of loyal governments within the Union line of these States, but Lincoln vetoed it, and appointed military governors.

Senator Ben Wade, of Ohio, and Representative Henry Winter Davis, of Maryland, united in a letter to the *New York Tribune*, sharply criticising the President for defeating the will of the Congress. This letter became known as the Wade-Davis manifesto, and created a great sensation in political circles. The story got about in the Nineteenth District that General Garfield had expressed sympathy with the position of Wade and Davis. His constituents condemned the document, and were strongly disposed to set him aside and nominate another man for Congress. When the convention met, the feeling against Garfield was so pronounced that he regarded his re-nomination as hopeless. He was called upon to explain his course. He went upon the platform, and everybody expected something in the nature of an apology; but he boldly defended his position, approved the manifesto, justified Wade, and said he had nothing to retract, and could not change his honest convictions for the sake of a seat in Congress. He had great respect, he said, for the opinions of his constituents, but greater for his own. If he could serve them as an independent representative, acting on his own judgment and conscience, he would be glad to do so, but if not, he did not want their nomination; he would prefer to be an independent private citizen. Probably no man ever talked in that way, before or since, to a body of men who held his political fate in their hands. Leaving the platform, he strode out of the hall and down the stairs, supposing he had effectually cut his own throat. Scarcely had he disappeared when one of the youngest delegates sprang up and said, 'The man who has the courage to face a convention like that deserves a nomination. I move that General Garfield be nominated by acclamation.' The motion was carried with a shout that reached the ears of the Congressman, and arrested him on the side-walk as he was returning to the hotel. He was re-elected by a majority of over 12,000."

One of his finest speeches was made in answer to Mr. Long, who proposed a peace at any price:—

"Now, when tens of thousands of brave souls have gone up to God, under the shadow of the flag; when thousands more, maimed and shattered in the contest, are sadly waiting the deliverance of death; now, when three years of terrific warfare have raged over us; when our armies have pushed the rebellion back over mountains and rivers, and crowded it into narrow limits, until a wall of fire girds it; now, when the uplifted hand of a majestic people is about to hurl the bolts of its conquering power upon the rebellion; now, in the quiet of this hall, hatched in the lowest depths of a similar dark treason, there rises a Benedict Arnold, and proposes to surrender all up, body and spirit, the nation and the flag, its genius and its honour, now and for ever, to the accursed traitors of our country! And that proposition comes—God forgive and pity my beloved State—it comes from a citizen of the time-honoured and loyal commonwealth of Ohio.

"I implore you, brethren in this house, to believe that not many births ever gave pangs to my mother State such as she suffered when that traitor was born! I beg you not to believe that on the soil of that State another such growth has ever deformed the face of nature, and darkened the light of God's day."

But we may be sure that when, at last, the fire of battle ceased, when the slaves were free, and the country that so long had mourned lifted up its head to rejoice, no one was more grateful than was Garfield, the Disciple.

And when, in the midst of the peace-rejoicings, the President was smitten down, no one's heart ached with a more tender sorrow than the heart of James Garfield. He had not only known, but he had understood and loved Abraham Lincoln, and he felt that he had lost a friend. The self-control which he manifested, however, was very remarkable, and the way in which his voice stilled the mad crowds in the streets of New York will never be forgotten. They cried for vengeance, but he saw that behind the deed was mercy. He knew that the righteous cannot die too soon, that the swift stroke of the assassin only hurries on the soul that is ready to go to the Father's house. He therefore took comfort when others almost lost hope. His words on the first anniversary of Lincoln's death were descriptive of his real feelings :—

"In all future time, on the recurrence of this day, I doubt not that the citizens of this Republic will meet in solemn assembly to reflect on the life and character of Abraham Lincoln, and the awful tragic event of the 14th of April 1865—an event unparalleled in the history of nations, certainly in our own. It is eminently proper that this House should this day place upon its record a memorial of this event. The last five years have been marked by wonderful developments of individual character. Thousands of your people, before unknown to fame, have taken their places in history, crowned with immortal honours. In thousands of humble homes are dwelling heroes and patriots whose names shall never die. But greatest amongst these developments were the character and fame of Abraham Lincoln. Such a character will be treasured for ever as the sacred possession of the American people and of mankind. In the great drama of the rebellion there were two acts. The first was the war, with its battles and sieges, victories and defeats, its sufferings and its tears. That act was closing one year ago to-night; and just as the curtain was lifting on the second and final act—the restoration of peace and liberty—just as the curtain was rising upon new characters and new events, the evil spirit of the rebellion, in the fury of despair, nerved and directed the assassin to strike down the chief character in both. It was no one man who killed Abraham Lincoln; it was the embodied spirit of treason and slavery, inspired with fearful despairing hate, that struck him down in the moment of the nation's supremest joy.

"Ah! sir, there are times in the history of men and nations, when they stand so near the veil that separates mortals from immortals, time from eternity, and men from their God, that they can almost hear the beatings, and feel the pulsations of the heart of the Infinite. Through such a time has this nation passed. When two hundred and fifty thousand brave spirits passed from the field of honour, through that thin veil, to the presence of God; and when at last its parting folds admitted the martyr President to the company of the dead heroes of the Republic, the nation stood so near the veil, that the whispers of God were heard by the children of men. Awe-stricken by His voice, the American people knelt in tearful reverence, and made a solemn covenant with Him, and with each other, that their nation should be saved from its enemies; that all its glories should be restored, and on the ruins of slavery and treason the temple of freedom and justice should be built, and should survive for ever. It remains for us, consecrated by that great event, and under a covenant with God, to keep that faith, to go forward in the great work until it shall be completed. Following the lead of that great man, and obeying the high behests of God, let us remember that—

"'He hath sounded forth a trumpet that shall never call retreat;
He is sifting out the hearts of men before his judgment-seat;
Be swift, my soul, to answer him; be jubilant, my feet;
For God is marching on.'"

The speech seems almost prophetic, as we remember how appropriate were the words to the speaker himself, when, afterwards, he too had fallen.

One of the matters to which, especially, Garfield gave his attention in Congress were those which related to the finance of his country. He was a great financier, and his opinions were opposed to that of many of his supporters. He believed in "honest money," and not in "greenbacks," and did not hesitate to say so.

One friend cautioned him against this. "The State is swept into the greenback current, and there is no stemming the torrent; so say nothing on the subject, for the feeling is too strong to be resisted."

But Garfield replied, "Much as I value your opinions, I here denounce this theory, that has worked its way into this State, as dishonest, unwise, and unpatriotic; and if I were offered a nomination and election for my natural life, from this district, on this platform, I should spurn it. If you should ever raise the question of re-nominating me, let it be understood you can have my services only on the ground of the honest payment of this debt, and these bonds in coin, according to the letter and spirit of the contract."

The manly spirit thus manifested did not cost him his seat, but, on the contrary, appealed so strongly to his Ohio friends, that when the convention met he was re-nominated by acclamation.

CHAPTER X.

THE NEW HOME AT MENTOR.

" And still the Pilgrim State remains
What she hath been;
Her inland hills, her seaward plains,
Still nurture men."

—WHITTIER.

GENERAL GARFIELD was many years before he had a home of his own. Then, while still at Hiram, he purchased a small frame-cottage facing the college green, which he enlarged by adding to it a wing. The ceiling was low, and the rooms small; but the clever housewife soon made them look pretty and homelike; and this was the only home which the family had for many years. When they went to Washington, they lived in apartments for some time; and it was not until the General had been three times elected that he decided to buy a house there; but then he felt that for the sake of the children it would be well to have a settled home amid wholesome influences. He had in all seven children. Little Mary, whose death has been already mentioned—the first to come and the first to die—Henry, James, Molly, Irwin, Abram, and Edward, the youngest, who also died early. Ogilvie thus described the survivors as they were at the time of their father's death :—" Harry and James are preparing for college at St. Paul's School, in Concord, New Hampshire. Harry is the musician of the family, and plays the piano well. James, who more resembles his father, is the mathematician. Molly, a handsome girl of thirteen, is ruddy, sweet-tempered, vivacious, and blessed with perfect health. The younger boys are still in the period of boisterous animal life. All the children have quick brains, and are strongly individualised. All learned to read young except Abe, who, knowing that his father had years ago said, in a lecture on education, that no child of his should be forced to read until he was seven years old, took refuge behind the parental theory, and declined to learn his letters until he had reached that age."

To house these children, and make a home for them, General Garfield bought a lot on the corner of Thirteenth Street, facing Franklin Square, and with money lent to him by an old army friend, built a plain, square, brick house, substantial enough for a home, and large enough to hold his family and one or two guests besides. The manner of life in the Garfield house was simple and quiet. It was cheerful, and it was pious. There was a hospitable table bountifully supplied; and any friend was welcome. The General was himself an abstainer, and no alcoholic drinks were used in his home. Nothing was artificial; there was no effort visible either in the furniture of the house or the dress of its inmates to be fashionable. But there was a handsome collection of books in the library, which the master never grew weary of studying. He was also fond of a game at chess or whist; and he relieved the tedium of work by reading Tooke's *History of Prices*, the *Biglow Papers*, and *Pickwick*. "I believe Dickens will kill me yet," he used to say after a good laugh at some of the humourist's fancies. Scott and Shakespeare were also favourites; and he delighted in that leader of magazines, *The Atlantic Monthly.*

But after a time, and when he had paid off the mortgage on his house, and had a little money in hand, he was able to gratify a desire he had long felt to go back a little to the old pursuits of his youth, and have a farm. At this time he had proved himself a very remarkable and successful lawyer, and had made his way into the good opinions of many men; but he had worked hard, and needed rest and quiet.

"Where shall the new home be?" was a question often debated in the Washington home.

"Let it be in some pretty locality," was one suggestion.

"And among green fields," was another.

"And near the hills," was a third.

"Are we to be always there?" asked one of the boys.

"Oh, no, we will keep on the Washington home for the winter, and spend the summer in the real country, where the flowers grow and the birds sing, and the waters are blue. The boys can learn the arts of haymaking and harvesting, and we can grow our own corn, make our own butter, and eat our own mutton."

Everybody agreed that it would be delightful, and many excursions were taken while they were occupied in the search for it. At last it was found in the vicinity of the Lake Shore railroad, on a fine hill near Lake Erie. A farm of one hundred and sixty acres was bought. It was sufficiently secluded, for it was a mile from any railway, and half-a-mile from the post office. The land was beautifully fertile, and the summer climate, tempered by the lake breezes, delightful. The buildings were not much to look at; they consisted of a tumble-down barn, and an ancient farm-house only a storey and a half high.

But improvements were rapidly made, and as soon as the house was covered the inmates moved into it, not waiting for it to be all finished. They did not in the least object to the shavings and the new paint, and the music of the hammers. A friend who called said he "found the General's writing table in the front hall surrounded by boxes, furniture, papers, letters, books, children, and callers. Yet how happy they all seemed!"

Before they went into their new home, the General had felt the need of rest and change. His studies as a lawyer, and especially his great thought and labour in regard to finance had told very strongly upon his health, and in the summer of 1867 he took a holiday.

General and Mrs. Garfield actually came to England together, and moved about in our land with few to recognise or offer them hospitality. How different would it have been later on! They were absent from New York seventeen weeks in all. They landed in Liverpool, and after looking about the city, they went on to Chester. The General was particularly interested in this city, for the home of his ancestors had been near it; and we can imagine with what feelings of delight he would walk by the side of the river, or kneel with the worshippers in the grand old cathedral.

From Chester they went to London, the city which all his life James Garfield had wished to see—the wonderful city so rich and so poor, so generous to guests, so cold to strangers, so wicked and yet so good. He went to the House of Commons and there listened to one of the fine debates which resulted in the giving of the ballot to seven hundred thousand Englishmen. It may be safely presumed that nothing, during his holiday, gave the General greater pleasure.

He went to Westminster Abbey, and declared that he liked the Poets' Corner better than the chapel of Henry VII. In the British museum he was especially delighted with the old autographs, particularly that of Milton.

He went to Hampton Court, walking through Bushy Park, admiring the fine horse-chestnuts, and elms, and oaks that grow there, and being greatly interested in the noble old palace, so long a residence of our kings and queens. The paintings pleased him, especially those of Benjamin West, of Philadelphia. He noted the celebrated Black Homberg vine, which was at the date of his visit a hundred and one years old, and bore fifteen hundred clusters. On another occasion he visited the Tower of London. In the diary which he kept at the time, and which was produced in *The Century Magazine* for January 1884, he wrote :—
"This Tower seemed a monster, tearing down men and families, and crunching them in its merciless jaws, as the dinotherium crushed and devoured the fern-trees dateless ages ago. Both are passed away. The fern-trees burn in the grates, and glow in the chandeliers of thousands of happy homes, and the broken hearts and crushed hopes of a thousand martyrs, who sleep under the shadows of this terrible Tower, have given civil and religious liberty ; and their memories and brave words live and glow in the hearts of many millions of Englishmen, and will bless coming generations. May the Tower stand there many centuries, as a mark to show how high the red deluge rose, and how happy is this England of Victoria compared with that of her ancestors!"

Billingsgate Market, Madam Tussaud's exhibition of wax figures, and South Kensington Museum, were all visited in turn. One Sunday he went to Newington to hear Spurgeon, "to try to discover what manner of man he was, and what was the secret of his power." He was moved by the singing; five thousand voices, without any instrument to lead them, joined in singing the hymn, "There is a land of pure delight."

"The whole building was filled and overflowed with the strong volume of song. The music made itself felt as a living, throbbing presence that entered your nerve, brain, heart, and filled and swept you away in its resistless current." He was altogether pleased with Spurgeon, with his manner and pronunciation, and with the clear, logical and perfectly comprehensible arrangement of his sermons. "His manner is exceedingly simple and unaffected. He does not appear to be aware that he is doing a great thing, and I could see no indication that success had turned his head. . . . God bless Spurgeon! He is helping to work out the problem of religious and civil freedom for England in a way that he knows not of!"

General Garfield stayed a week in London, and then he visited Scotland, and did what all Americans who visit our country like to do, and what every British adult ought to endeavour to do—he made the tour of the Scottish Lakes.

Very good times he and Mrs. Garfield must have had together—for he loved Scott and knew his writings well, and could verify the places mentioned by him, and compare them with the poet's descriptions of them. Those tourists who met the two strangers on coaches or in hotels, and knew their names, must have been very glad afterwards to call up all reminiscences of the holiday.

From Scotland they crossed the North Sea, and landed at Rotterdam. Then they went on to Brussels, and up the Rhine to Switzerland. After a glorious stay among the sublime scenery of the lakes, they crossed the Alps, and went into Italy. They passed some happy days at Milan and Venice, but made their longest stay in Rome, where, among its ruins and monuments, Garfield was carried back to those classic times with which his studies at college had made him familiar. Here he revelled in delight, finding the days pass all too quickly. They went to Paris, and had a joyous time there, and then returned to London, as if loth to leave it altogether. But there was yet one other country which he wished to see, and towards the end of his holiday he went over to Ireland, where he remained until it was time to set sail for home.

His health was thus thoroughly re-established, and he felt strong for work, and courageous for all that was right. His mind had been enlarged, and his knowledge of men and things considerably widened by his travels.

It was then that he made his famous speeches and wrote his famous documents on Banking and Currency, and Public Expenditure and similar subjects.

It was while he was spending a happy time at Mentor with his family that he was chosen to be a delegate to the Republican Convention of 1880, which was afterwards held at Chicago. He was very busy at the time ploughing the land, repairing the fences, and making the house more pleasant.

The little home-circle received the news with dismay. They knew what that would possibly lead to; and they did not want to spare the father to the State.

"We see so little, far too little of you now," they said, "we shall have you less then. It is too bad, now that we are going to have this happy life in the country, for you to be burdened with fresh cares."

But his friends urged his acceptance of the responsibility. It seemed that he could do what no other man could just then. He was well known in the country, and he had more than a little influence. He thought that Mr. Sherman, the successful Secretary of the Treasury, ought to be the next President, and he threw all his power into the scale for his friend. The Hon. James Blaine and General Grant were the leading aspirants; but at the meeting at Chicago Garfield nominated Mr. Sherman, and made the following speech:—

"Mr. President—I have witnessed the extraordinary scenes of this Convention with deep solicitude. No emotion touches my heart more quickly than sentiment in honour of a great and noble character; but as I sat on those seats and witnessed these demonstrations it seemed to me that you were a human ocean in a tempest. I have seen the sea lashed into fury and tossed into spray, and its grandeur moves the soul of the dullest man. But I remember that it is not the billows, but the calm level of the sea, from which all heights and depths are measured! When the storm has passed, and the hour of calm settles on the ocean, when the sunlight bathes its smooth surface, then the astronomer and surveyor take the level from which they measure all terrestrial heights and depths.

"Gentlemen of the Convention, your present temper may not mark the healthful pulse of our people. When our enthusiasm has passed, when the emotions of this hour have subsided, we shall feel that calm level of public opinion below the storm from which the thoughts of a mighty people must be measured, and by which their final action will be determined.

"Not here, in this brilliant circle, where fifteen thousand men and women are assembled, is the destiny of the Republican party to be decreed. Not here, where I see the enthusiastic faces of seven hundred and fifty delegates waiting to cast their votes into the urn, and determine the choice of the Republic, but by four million Republican firesides there are thoughtful voters, with wives and children about them, with the calm thoughts inspired by love of home and country, with the history of the past, the hopes of the future, and the knowledge of the great men who have adorned and blessed our nation in days gone by. There God prepares the verdict that shall determine the wisdom of our work to-night. Not in Chicago in the heats of June, but in the sober quiet that comes to them between now and November, in the silence of deliberate judgment, will this great question be settled."

He little thought that before the end of the Convention

it would be his own name which should be spoken not only with applause but with deep-seated determination and approval.

It was not all strife and not all of political whirlwind at the Convention. A pleasant incident is related in regard to the second day. There had been a temporary adjournment for dinner, and as the delegates were returning to the hall where the Convention was held, a young man, a member of the Chicago Young Men's Christian Association, respectfully presented each delegate as he entered with a slip of paper, on which was printed a verse from the Bible. General Garfield took his, read it, and pinned it on the inside of his straw hat. The words on it were these:—"This is the stone which was set at nought of you builders, which is become the head of the corner. Neither is there salvation in any other."

CHAPTER XI.

ELECTED PRESIDENT.

> "Through wish, resolve, and act, our will
> Is moved by unseen forces still;
> And no man measures in advance
> His strength with untried circumstance."
> —Whittier.

GENERAL GARFIELD had no expectations in regard to the Presidency. He supposed that Grant would be re-elected, or Blaine decided upon, or, as he himself wished, that Sherman should be the chosen of the people. But these things were not to be. Before the Convention came to an end it was his own name that was shouted far and near, his own name that went flashing along the electric wires, and that was found in all the newspapers of the land; and on the 8th of June 1880 he received from the chairman of the Convention a formal and official invitation.

It was very startling news for him to take home; and it was not received with special manifestations of joy. It is said that the youngest son was bare-footed, and sitting in a cherry tree on the Mentor farm, when the news was brought to him.

"President?" he said. "Tell dad not to accept it. There are no such cherry trees, and no such cherries as these, to be found at the White House."

"What do you think of it, mother?" asked the President, as he stooped to kiss the white-haired woman whose early lessons had brought forth such good fruit. But she could only reply, "It is the Lord's doings, and is marvellous in our eyes."

As for the wife, she felt almost as if a calamity had befallen her. "We have been so happy in our simple life," she said, "I do not want to change it for the distinctions and responsibilities of life at the White House."

"But you would grace that or any other position," said a loving voice, and Mrs. Garfield felt that she would not stand in her husband's way to honour for any love of her own ease.

His letter of acceptance was dated—

"MENTOR, OHIO, 10th July 1880.

DEAR SIR—On the evening of the 8th of June last I had the honour to receive from you, in the presence of the committee of which you were chairman, the official announcement that the Republican Convention at Chicago had that day nominated me as their candidate for President of the United States. I accept the nomination with gratitude for the confidence it implies, and with a deep sense of the responsibility it imposes. I cordially endorse the principles set forth in the platform adopted by the Convention. On nearly all the subjects of which it treats, my opinions are on record among the published proceedings of Congress. I venture, however, to make special mention of some of the principal topics which are likely to become subjects of discussion."

He goes on to speak of these, and says among other things :—

"Next in importance to freedom and justice is popular

education, without which neither justice nor freedom can be permanently maintained. Whatever help the nation can justly afford should be generously given to aid the States in supporting common schools ; but it would be unjust to our people, and dangerous to our institutions, to apply any portion of the revenues of the nation, or of the States, to the support of Sectarian schools."

The letter closed thus :—

"The doctrines announced by the Chicago Convention are not the temporary devices of a party to attract votes and carry an election ; they are deliberate convictions, resulting from the careful study of our institutions, the events of our history, and the best impulses of our people. In my judgment these principles should control the legislation and administration of the Government. In any event, they will guide my conduct until experience points out a better way.

"If elected, it will be my purpose to enforce strict obedience to the constitution and the laws, and to promote, as best I may, the interests and honour of the whole country, relying for support upon the wisdom of Congress, the intelligence and patriotism of the people, and the favour of God."

Russell H. Conwell says :—" His speeches during the trying interval between his nomination and election were models of modesty and statesmanship. He possessed a character which would bear study. He was a man of whom the more was known the greater would be the respect for his ability and intentions. The Republican cause thrived through the great impulse which General Garfield's domestic and public life, and self-sacrificing spirit, gave to canvass.

"It was a bitter thing, however, to his affectionate wife and faithful relatives, to see again and again revived the most slanderous statements concerning his life. Stories that were conceived in the purest malice, and enlarged upon by the campaign orators and writers, would not die with repeated killing. It is probable, however, that his repeated candidacy, like every other good cause, prospered by persecution. The more hateful the slanders, the more active were his friends. The more untruthful the statements of the press, the more numerous his adherents. It was a period when General Garfield was compelled to stand silently and immovably before all detractors, enemies, and scandal-mongers, and receive without retaliation all the poisonous darts they incessantly hurled at him. No event of his life was so much used and abused as his acquaintance with Honourable Oakes Ames, during the great Credit Mobilier excitement. Now that both men are seen through the funereal halo which their death have placed about their memories, we only look and wonder that to either of those honourable men such a martyrdom should come, among an intelligent, civilised, and Christian people. The lesson it teaches is very important, but seldom made practical; that is, that we should so regard and so treat the living men that when they are gone we shall not regret it. It is silly, unmanly, unchristian, to vilify a man while he lives, and then exalt his name as a saint or an angel when he is dead—both positions being false and despicable."

The Credit Mobilier scandal referred to certainly threatened at one time to ruin General Garfield altogether. He met it, however, with his own straightforward candour, and his unstained reputation was in itself a denial of the allegation made against him. It was alleged that he and others had sold themselves for sundry amounts of stock of the Credit Mobilier Company, and bonds of the Pacific Railway Company. But so clearly did he show that his dealings in regard to the matter had been perfectly innocent and free from taint, that a reaction in his favour soon set in. He had come out of his time of unpopularity, and was now honoured and trusted by all but his political enemies.

Of course General Garfield had to make what they call in America *stump speeches*. We give some extracts from one :—

"Fellow-citizens—What is the central thought in American life? What is the germ out of which all our institutions were born and have been developed? Let me give it to you in a word. When the *Mayflower* was about to land her precious freight upon the shores of Plymouth, the Pilgrim Fathers gathered in the cabin of that little ship on a stormy November day, and after praying to Almighty God for the success of their great enterprise, drew up and signed what is known in history, and what will be known to the last syllable of recorded time, as "The Pilgrim Covenant." In that covenant is one sentence which I ask you to take home with you to-night. It is this :—'We agree, before God and each other, that the freely expressed will of the majority shall be the law of all, which we will all obey.' (Applause.) Ah, fellow-citizens, it does honour to the heads and to the hearts of a great New England audience here, on this Western Reserve, to applaud the grand and simple sentiment of the Pilgrim Fathers. They said, 'No standing army shall be needed to make us obey. We will erect here in America a substitute for monarchy, a substitute for despotism, and that substitute shall be the will of the majority as the law of all.' And that germ, planted on the rocky shores of New England, has sprung up, and all the trees of our liberty have grown from it, into the beauty and glory of this year of our life. (Applause.)

. . . .

"Is there any death here in our camp? Yes! Yes! Three hundred and fifty thousand soldiers, the noblest band that ever trod the earth, died to make this camp a camp of glory and of liberty for ever. (Tremendous applause.)

"But there are no dead issues here. There are no dead

issues here. Hang out our banner from under the blue sky this night, until it shall sweep the green turf under your feet! It hangs over our camp! Read away up under the stars the inscription we have written on it, lo! these twenty-five years.

"Twenty-five years ago the Republican party was married to liberty, and this is our silver wedding, fellow-citizens. (Great applause.) A worthily married pair love each other better on the day of their silver wedding than on the day of their first espousals; and we are truer to liberty to-day, and dearer to God, than we were when we spoke our first word of liberty. Read away up under the sky across our starry banner that first word we uttered twenty-five years ago! What was it? 'Slavery shall never extend over another foot of the territories of the great West!' (Applause.) Is that dead or alive? Alive, thank God, for evermore! (Applause.) And truer to-night than it was the hour it was written! (Applause.) Then it was a hope, a promise, a purpose. To-night it is equal with the stars—immortal history and immortal truth! (Applause.)

"Come down the glorious steps of our banner. Every great record we have made we have vindicated with our blood and with our truth. It sweeps the ground, and it touches the stars. Come then, young man, and put it in your life, where all is living, and where nothing is dead but the nerves that defended it! (Applause.) I think these young men will do that. (Of course they will!)

"Gentlemen, we are closing this memorable campaign. We have got our enemies on the run everywhere. (Laughter.) And all you need to do in this noble old city, this capital of the Western reserve, is to follow them up and finish it by snowing the rebellion under once more. We stand on an isthmus. This year and next is the narrow isthmus between us and perpetual victory. If you can win now and win in 1880, then the very stars in their courses will fight for us. (Applause.) The census will do the work, and will give us thirty more freemen of the North in our Congress that will make up for the rebellion of the South. (Great applause.) We are posted here, as the Greeks were posted at Thermopylæ, to meet this one great barbarian Terxes of the isthmus. Stand in your places, men of Ohio! Fight this battle, win this victory, and then one more puts you in safety for ever!"

It was wonderful how soon all sorts of names were given to him. In the press he was called "Hero," "Statesman," "Scholar," "Coward," "Bribe-taker," "Charlatan," "Lobbyist," and "Renegade Preacher." But the names neither hurt nor helped him. The opposition did not dishearten him, and it certainly made his friends all the more staunch and true.

One incident that occurred immediately before the election was taken caused a riot that might have led to serious consequences. Some one forged a letter, which purported to have been written by General Garfield to Mr. H. L. Morey on Chinese Labour. It was a cruel electioneering "dodge," and made Garfield to express sentiments which were not his. In denying its authorship, he said—"The lithographic copy shows a clumsy attempt to imitate my penmanship and signature. Anyone who is familiar with my handwriting will instantly see that the letter is spurious."

The election took place on Tuesday, 2nd November. The State of New York voted for the Republican party by a majority of 20,000. The popular majority in favour of General Garfield was 8,235 votes.

The Republican victory gave satisfaction in Great Britain as well as throughout the United States; and the people felt that a time of peace and prosperity had arrived.

The change that had come upon the General and his family was thus described:—"From an early hour on the morning after his election, until his death at Elberon, his time was taken up, his footsteps dogged, or his sick-bed disturbed with the ceaselessly importuning office-seekers. Such a state of affairs is a great disgrace to our nation, and one which General Garfield was determined to remedy if possible.

"The behaviour of many aspirants for official position was but little better than that of the assassin himself. They invaded his private house in swarms. They stopped his carriage in the street; they called him out of bed; they bored him in the railroad carriages and stations; they wrote to his wife and his sons; they courted fawningly all his old neighbours and relatives; they covered him with flattery more contemptible than slander; they filled his office with piles of letters it was impossible to read or answer; they sent him presents to tempt him; they wrote most silly laudations of his life, and published them to his great disgust; and teasing, coaxing, threatening, they made anxious and unhappy nearly every hour of his life after his election. More than six hundred applications were made for one office, before he had the right to make the appointment. He could give it to but one, and thus innocently made more than six hundred enemies.

"As Mrs. Garfield had predicted, their home life was gone. No more domestic quiet; no more social family gatherings; no more rest. Naught came to them but pressing cares and almost disheartening responsibilities. Even the little boys felt the wear of ceaseless visiting, and sought an asylum in the barn or at a neighbour's house. Nothing they possessed was longer their own. They and theirs were treated as public property, and the ceaseless vigils of the press told to the whole world their slightest movements, even to an extended account of the youngest boy's truancy at school, and of the daughter's different dresses."

All this was exceedingly disagreeable; but Garfield knew

that he must be prepared to sacrifice much, and he made up his mind to do it willingly. He gave a great deal of thought in order to endeavour to remedy the evil of partisan appointments in the civil service, and laboured to bring about altogether a better state of things than existed previously.

As the time of the inauguration drew near, the nation resolved to make it one of the most magnificent displays ever witnessed. "With vast throngs of enthusiastic visitors; with long lines of military organisations in their gay trappings; with miles of bunting and clouds of flags and streamers; with trumpets, drums, bands, and singing; with feasts, collations, speeches, and a grand ball; with huzzahs, congratulations, and all kinds of demonstrations of joy, the people hailed him as their chief magistrate."

The Inaugural Address was a splendid one, and the whole ceremony imposing. But what added to the interest of the scene more than all else was the presence of his mother, now eighty years old, and his faithful and beloved wife. At the close of the address, which concluded most solemnly, the oath was administered, and Mr. Garfield bent low and kissed the Bible. He was then declared President of the United States—and the vast throng cheered as only people full of joy can do. Great men pressed forward to greet and congratulate their new chief; but before he spoke to any of them he turned to the two women, who with moved faces had listened to his address, and respectfully and significantly kissed, first his mother, and then his wife.

> "With sudden praise, a mighty voice
> Sweeps all the continent;
> Helpless, before the people's choice,
> The statesmen's wills have bent;
> It honours first, before all other,
> A patient little 'white-haired mother.'

> The day has come—the hour draws near;
>   Look on, the listening land;
> Who brings this ruler, peer with peer?
>   Who stays him, hand in hand?
> Honoured by him above all other,
> He brings his little 'white-haired mother.'
>
> The glittering embassies of kings
>   Are standing in their state;
> Their tributes rank as lesser things,
>   They and their kingdoms wait;
> While reverently, before all other,
> The ruler greets his 'white-haired mother.'
>
> Ah! States may grow, and men may gain,
>   And power and riches swift increase;
> The brunt of every country's strain,
>   Its fights for purity and peace,
> Comes through its husbands, daughters, brothers,
> At last on patient 'white-haired mothers.'

Instead of his Inaugural Address we give the last speech he ever made in Hiram College. The occasion was that of a funeral, and the address was given on 4th February:—

"To-day is a sort of burial-day in many ways. I have often been in Hiram and often left it; but, with the exception of when I went to the war, I have never felt that I was leaving it in quite so definite a way as I do to-day. It was so long a workshop, so long a home, that all absences have been temporary, and involved always a return. I cannot speak of all the ties that bind me to this place. There are other things buried beneath this snow besides dead people. The trees, the rocks, the fences, and the grass, are all reminders of things connected with my Hiram life.

"It is a revival of youth to me to be in this place to see its bright young life. I see before me just such a set of students as I saw here twenty-four, twenty-six—yes, twenty-eight years ago—just as young, just as bright, just as hopeful of the future. It is pleasing to know that Hiram life is ever the same. A few days ago I saw a girl in the full bloom of early womanhood, who is the daughter of a woman who was my pupil here twenty-four years ago. She was the picture of her mother, whom I have never seen since, but I am told she has become a grey-haired matron. As the daughter stood before me, the likeness of what the mother was then, what thoughts and feelings came over me of the years that are gone! There is an idea of immortality in this—life is reproduced in things that follow. A fountain of perpetual youth is this old chapel; there are no wrinkles in its walls. It is a very comforting thought that though the ancients sought the fountain of perpetual youth, and found it not, it can be found in the associations of a place like this.

"It is pitiful that we often do not appreciate good things until they are gone. Emerson has said, 'To-day is a king in disguise.' He passes among us; and, if we heed not, he leaves us, and we are none the wiser. Get acquainted with what there is in to-day; take what it contains and appropriate it to yourself. The strong friendships and deep impressions that you are forming now will live in time to come. The other day a man came to me whom I had known here twenty-five years ago, but he was changed; he was fat and whiskered and half bald; and when I took him by the hand, and called him by name, with 'W. D.' for his initials, he cried like a man to be remembered. I believe he is richer, fuller, more of a man, for what he gained here in Hiram. If I thought the time would ever come when I should live the Hiram life out of me, I should hope to die just before it came.

"Never despise the days of Hiram life and childhood. The associations that you are now forming, your lessons, your thoughts, and your deeds from day to day, are what go to make up your life here; and this is the foundation of your after-life. Be wise now; and when you live over again the life you lived here, may it be such as you could wish!

"I cannot see what lies beyond. I may be going on an Arctic voyage, but, be that as it may, I know that years ago I builded upon this promontory a cairn, from which, wherever my wanderings may lead me, I can draw some sustenance for life and strength. May the time never come when I cannot find some food for mind and heart on Hiram Hill!"

CHAPTER XII.

SMITTEN DOWN.

"Old memories cluster about us to-night,
  Whispering ever of scenes that were all blessing-crowned,
Leading out of the darkness and into the light;
  Yet the sins of the world that so thickly abound,
      Produce sorrow profound."
                    —FARNINGHAM.

THE first thing the new President had to do was to select his Cabinet. And this was a matter of no little difficulty.

He had at once to put his thoughts to his work, and try to forget all that had been and all that might be. He could not help thinking a little of the changes which life had brought him. How far away was the log-cabin of his boyhood, the piles of wood he had chopped, the old books which he had first learned to read! God had been with the fatherless boy, and was with him now that new responsibilities and duties were about him, and that he had harder work to do than any to which he had before put his hands. "He was still a son, a husband, a father, a brother, a friend, a citizen; and yet he was in the seat of a king. To fill the duties of these widely-separated positions, as he nobly filled them, was one of his greatest claims to human greatness."

The position he was in, and the dangers he had to encounter, were these:—He wanted to preserve peace and tranquillity, and he was most anxious not to continue the office-seeking tendencies of the men of the United States. He owed something to those who had supported him, and would have been glad to prove his gratitude; but if he gave them all the offices, the other party would be aggrieved. If he gave the places to those who had opposed him, many would be ready to call it bribery, and declare that he sought to conciliate them in view of a second term. "If he appointed Hon. James G. Blaine, then he should offend Hon. Roscoe Conkling, who was the leading opponent of Mr. Blaine at the Chicago Convention. If he appointed Mr. Conkling, then Mr. Blaine or his friends would accuse the President of partisanship. If he appointed both, there would be a dangerous lack of harmony in the Cabinet. If he omitted them all, and their supporters, there was but a small class from which to choose his councillors. So, endeavouring to look at the question from a citizen's standpoint, but knowing that he could not please all, he selected those who, while they represented each prominent political movement of the day, would be willing to hide their partisan and personal differences for the sake of the public good."

His Cabinet was presently announced as follows:—Secretary of State, James G. Blaine of Maine; Secretary of the Treasury, William Windom of Minnesota; Attorney-General, Wayne MacVeagh of Pennsylvania; Secretary of War, Robert T. Lincoln of Illinois; Secretary of the Navy, William H. Hunt of Louisiana; Secretary of the Interior, Samuel J. Kirkwood of Iowa, and General James, Postmaster-General of New York.

That the President had not pleased every one was soon apparent. Senator Conkling was especially angry that he had not been consulted in regard to the appointment of Judge Robertson to be the Collector of the Port of New York. The President, over-worked and burdened as he was, did not bear the Senator's attacks as patiently as he otherwise might have done; and, in his anger, withdrew several of the friends of Senator Conkling from their appointments. The quarrel was very bitter and disastrous. Sentor Conkling was a man of great influence in the Senate, and was very much honoured and respected throughout the country. People began to choose sides. "It stirred up the whole nation," said an American writer; "created antagonisms, encouraged enmities, injured the public business, created a distrust of our institutions, tending to hinder prosperity, and all on account of petty personal spite, and unconsidered wilfulness!"

Among the rest of the disappointed party-seekers was Charles J. Guiteau, an immoral, licentious, dishonest man, by profession a lawyer. He was clever and unscrupulous. He could not succeed as a lawyer, and was imprisoned in the New York jail for swindling. He then turned his attention to literature, and having been connected with certain religious bodies, he thought that he could make religious literature a success. He wrote a book called *Truth*, and published it. He had a plausible manner, and managed to ingratiate himself with clergymen and churches, and then practised his dishonesty upon them.

He was one of the first to apply to President Garfield for an appointment. The President said he would see him again; and this he took, or pretended to take, as a promise. He called at the White House the day after the inauguration, and then wrote to the President. Next, he followed him about, waiting for him when he was calling at other houses, and in all possible ways intruding himself upon Garfield's notice. At last he received a very decided reply. "I tell you frankly that I do not consider you a suitable man to send to Marseilles as consul, or to fill any office under the State whatever."

This aroused the cruel hatred of the unscrupulous office-seeker, who at once vowed to himself to be revenged.

"Nothing less than murder," he said; and the affair of Senator Conkling made him believe that the President had many enemies, who would not only rejoice in the fact of his assassination, but would shield the murderer.

In the midst of his troubles President Garfield had yet another : Mrs. Garfield fell ill.

"I have never been well in Washington," she said, piteously, "and the excitement of the time has been more than I can endure."

"You must have a change as soon as you are able to bear the journey," said her husband.

"I suppose you could not go also ? You, too, are looking worn and ill."

"Not at present; soon I may be able." But Mrs. Garfield grew worse, and the illness developed into a malady from which the gravest consequences were feared. The shadow on the face of the President grew deeper then. He could not forget his sick wife, no matter how many and great his public duties were. He hurried into the sick-room many times during the day, and sought to cheer her by his merry words and tender caresses, though he was himself full of care and trouble.

But his wife grew worse instead of better, and several whole nights were passed by the devoted husband by the sick bed.

"What avails human honours in the case of such suffering and anxiety?" he frequently thought; and many a prayer went up to God that He would not take from him the dear companion of his life. And the prayer was heard. Gradually the invalid came back to strength after the crisis had been passed and at last there came a time when the doctor counselled removal to a more healthy neighbourhood. It was decided that she was to go to Long Branch, a beautiful little place of resort on the coast of New Jersey. Her daughter Molly went with her, and the fine sea breezes soon restored her to perfect health.

It was then that the President decided to take holiday, and go to New England. His two eldest sons were to go too, and several members of his Cabinet. Mrs. Garfield and Molly were to leave Long Branch and travel to New York, and there join her husband. Together they would all, including Molly, go from New York up the beautiful river Hudson, in a little steamer which the President had chartered. They would go as far as a fine mansion that stood on the banks of the Hudson, and there they would spend a peaceful, happy Sabbath of rest. Afterwards the President had promised to visit Williamstown, and take part in the commencement ceremony at Williams College, where he hoped to meet many of his old friends and class-mates, and have a pleasant reunion. And as soon as that was over—hurrah for New England and the White Mountains!

It was no wonder that it was a very cheerful party that left the White House on that eventful Saturday morning. The President felt as if he were coming safely out of all his troubles. Things appeared to be settling down into quiet. The disappointed seekers were learning to submit to the inevitable. The country was looking forward hopefully. Good harvests were in the fields, and plenty of trade in the towns. It was the time of sunshine and of cheer. The trees and flowers, the waters and hills, were looking their best in the summer robes of gladness, and the faithful heart of the hardly-pressed man had grown quiet within him. He had earned a rest, and the time had come.

Yes, indeed, it had, in a sense of which he did not dream. Charles Guiteau had bided his opportunity, but he had not swerved from his murderous intention. He had several times hidden in dark places with his cocked pistol, but his heart had failed him when the time came for his pulling the trigger.

He nearly did the deed on the occasion when the President went to the railway station to see his wife off on her journey to Long Branch. The loving pair, engrossed in one another, did not notice the presence of the assassin, as he stood scowlingly looking on.

The President lifted his wife tenderly from the carriage, and there was a fine opportunity for shooting him down then. But some feeling of pity prevented. The sight of the thin hands and pale sweet face of the suffering wife touched even his heart, and he put the revolver back into his pocket.

"I will wait until she is better," he said.

And he took more time to consider. He knew, of course, that his deed would at once arouse the mob, and that he might be lynched. This he did not desire. He wanted all the world to be talking of him, and the papers to be filled with his name. He had on his person a letter, asking that a military escort might conduct him to prison in safety.

When he read in the papers the account of the anticipated journey of the President, he thought that would be a good time and opportunity to do the deed. There would be no pale-faced woman to hinder him this time, and he might not only kill one man but two. Secretary Blaine had been as deaf to his requests for office as the President himself. He might as well be shot at the same time.

So he went down to the railway station, and waited for his victim, or victims, as the case might be.

He reached the depôt half-an-hour before the Presidential party, and waited. Policeman Kearney was one of the men stationed there, and he noticed the evil expression on the man's face, and the restless nervousness of his manner.

The President's carriage was seen coming down the street; and Guiteau went to a cabman, and asked, "Can you drive me off in a hurry if I should need you?"

"Oh, yes, sir," was the reply.

The next moment the carriage drove up. The President and Secretary Blaine were in it, alone together. The President stepped out, and spoke to the policeman—

"How much time have we before the train will start?"

The policeman looked at his watch, and replied, "You have ten minutes, President."

"Thank you," was the reply; and the President turned at once to pass through the reception room.

Immediately a shot was fired. The President did not appear to hear it, and the policeman thought some boy had let off a cracker in honour of the occasion.

But then a second shot was heard, and the policeman, looking up, saw Guiteau with a revolver, and saw the President turn and stumble.

Secretary Blaine at once cried out, "My God, he's been murdered! What is the meaning of this?"

The policeman tried to seize the assassin, shouting, "In God's name, man, what did you shoot the President for?"

Instantly there was wild commotion. The first to realise the true state of affairs was Mr. Lincoln. He was the son of a murdered President, and could well guess the meaning of what had happened. He at once gave orders for the troops to hold themselves in readiness, and a strong force of policemen, summoned by telephone, soon appeared. So also did Surgeon-General Barnes, and Drs. Norris, Lincoln, and Woodward.

The President's son could not quite understand what had happened. He looked at his father, but as there was only a little blood to be seen, he did not realise that the wound might be fatal. It is said that he doubled up his fist and looked as if he would like to fight some one.

There were several persons who saw it all, just as it happened, and who afterwards reduced to writing that which they knew. Of course, the intense excitement of the time would stamp the least incident indelibly on the memory of every one who witnessed it.

One of these was Mrs. White, the woman in charge of the ladies' room. She was the first to reach the President when he had been shot down. This is her account:—

"I was standing in the ladies' room, and saw the President as he entered in company with Secretary Blaine. The latter had stepped a little in advance as they entered the door, as if to give the President more room. I had noticed this man Guiteau lounging about the ladies' room for a half-hour before the arrival of the President. I did not like his appearance from the first time I saw him. It is my business to see that such characters do not loaf around the ladies' room, and I thought seriously of having him pointed out to our watchman, Mr. Scott, so that he should be made to stay in the gentlemen's room. When the President and Secretary Blaine entered he was standing near the door. He wheeled to the left and fired, evidently aiming for the heart. It was a quick shot, and struck the President in the left arm. The President did not at first seem to realise that he had been struck, although Secretary Blaine at once stepped to one side as though dazed at this unexpected movement. The President then partly turned round, and the assassin, advancing two steps, fired the second time—the whole thing being the work of a few moments. The President advanced one step, then fell upon the floor. I ran to him at once and raised his head, and held it in that position until some gentlemen came; and we remained until his son came from the car where he was seated, with the rest of the Presidential party awaiting the arrival of his father. The entire party followed in to the scene, and a large crowd gathered about the prostrate form very quickly. When I had a chance to look about me, I saw Guiteau trying to wrench himself from those who held him. When the President fell it was about twenty-five minutes past nine A.M. A mattress was brought in, and the President was removed to the upper floor of the depôt. The President had on a light drab travelling suit and a silk hat, which latter was badly battered in the fall. When I ran to him he was deathly pale, but perfectly conscious. His son was kneeling beside him at the time. He asked me if I knew who shot his father, and I replied, 'Yes, and he is caught.' He said somebody would have to pay for this. The young man and I thought the President was dying, so pale was he. He tried to raise his head, and get his hand on the wound near the thigh, but he was too weak to do so."

Mr. James R. Young, of the Philadelphia *Star*, says of the occurrence :—" I reached the depôt of the Baltimore and Potomac Railroad at about nine o'clock, intending to take the limited express train for New York. It leaves at half-past nine. I found the depôt full of people ; some going south, some west, and others on the train. I was to take north. I passed through the ladies' reception room, where the shooting took place, to the main or general reception room, where the ticket-office is located. After purchasing my ticket, I proceeded immediately to the train, which was standing on the track, south of the main building of the depôt, say about a hundred yards from the ladies' reception room. After locating my seat in the car, I descended to the depôt platform. There I met Mr. Barclay, the old journal clerk of the house, and Messrs. Kilburn and Adams, of the newspaper press of the city, who were about to leave with their families for the north. We stood just opposite the special train, which was waiting for the President. In it were some dozen people, more than half of whom were ladies—the wives, sons, and daughters of Secretaries Windom and Hunt, Postmaster-General James, Colonel

Rockwell, and others of the Presidential party. They were a merry party, laughing and joking with the numerous friends who had come down to see them off for a fortnight's holiday and frolic. Soon Secretaries Windom and Hunt came out of the car, and began promenading up and down the platform, quietly smoking their cigars. Later, Postmaster-General James alighted from the car, and joined our party.

"We began congratulating him and ourselves that we were to escape the fearfully hot weather, and were trying to joke him about the Administration leaving business for pleasure, when a young man stepped up to Mr. James, and said to him, excitedly, that the President had been shot.

"Mr. James turned and said, 'What! There is no joke in a thing like that.'

"His informant, almost scared to death, replied, 'I assure you it is true.'

"Without another word Mr. James turned and ran to the depôt building, and we all naturally followed him. When I reached the ladies' reception rooms the doors were being closed. There were at least two hundred people in and around the building, and I began to inquire if the news I had heard was true. It took only a moment to find out that it was. I could not gain admission at the inside door of the room where the President was, so I ran out into the street, hoping to be more successful at the street entrance. There I found a big crowd already gathered, and a policeman and some others hurriedly hustling a man outside. This was the assassin. I did not follow, as my desire was to learn the extent of the President's wound. Not being able to gain admittance at the door, I saw an open window, say about ten feet from the ground. A coloured news-boy was climbing in, and I concluded to follow suit. It was not more than half-a-minute's work before I got inside. The first person I saw was Secretary Windom. He was standing alone, as pale as death, and the tears were trickling down his cheeks. Knowing him well, I said—

"'Mr. Secretary, where is the President, and what does this mean?'"

"He replied, 'There he lies, in yonder corner, in that group. It is as much of a mystery to me as it is to you!'

"I moved over about two yards, and there I saw the President lying on a mattress, which had been hastily brought from the sleeping apartment by one of the depôt employees. There were probably thirty people around him, many of whom were women, who had been waiting for the southern trains.

"Secretary Blaine had hold of one of the President's hands, and Postmaster-General James was assisting to get him into a sitting posture. His face showed a deathly paleness, and he had a look of surprise, as if caused by pain and despair. He was vomiting, and seemed to have no control of himself. His coat and vest had been ripped from him, and his trousers loosened. The matter he had vomited had fallen on his shirt below the bosom, which made it seem as if the ball of the assassin had penetrated the intestines. Near him was his son, a lad of sixteen. Poor boy, he was almost beside himself. He wrung his hands, and cried in a piteous manner. With him were the son of Colonel Rockwell, and Secretary Hunt, who, in every way natural to human beings, were trying to comfort him. In less than ten minutes Secretary Blaine gave orders to have the President removed to the upper floor of the depôt, to the officer's room, where there were plenty of air, and a freedom from the mob which was rapidly gathering. Colonel Rockwell and Adjutant-General Corbin soon made a passage-way, and the President was borne by a number of the coloured porters of the depôt to the upper floor. I immediately left the depôt, and hurriedly went up Pennsylvania Avenue. Although it was not an hour since the shooting took place, I found the Avenue crowded with people—some standing in groups, regardless of the broiling hot sun, discussing the event; others hurrying towards the depôt; others pushing, and rushing, and wending their way no one knows where."

The first thing to do was to try to get the President back to the White House. A police ambulance was provided, and the President was carefully carried down on the mattress, and placed upon it. The ambulance, surrounded by mounted police, was then driven slowly back over the route along which, in such excellent spirits, he had driven in the state carriage only an hour before. He was taken to the large room on the south side of the White House, and there watched by agonised friends, while the gateways were all closed, and armed sentries kept the place clear of all but those who held the right to enter.

The day was exceedingly hot, but people stood in the sun, asking, with white lips, "Will he die?" "What do the doctors say?" They said they feared he would die. He seemed to be weak and faint; but he was conscious.

Dr. Smith Townsend was the first to examine him.

"What do you think, doctor?" the President asked of the medical man.

"I do not consider it very serious," was the reply.

"I thank you, doctor, but I am a dead man," said the President.

He said afterwards to Dr. Ford, "I am very glad to know my condition. I can bear it."

He spoke very calmly, as if he were not afraid to die. Indeed, the piety which, through all his life, he had manifested was beautifully exhibited now. He had found that faith in God, and the desire to please Him, had enabled him to bear quietly the ups and downs of existence; and he found now that it could keep him steady and tranquil when the crisis had come. He had the blessedness of knowing that he was safe, whether he would live or die.

CHAPTER XIII.

THE WIFE AND MOTHER.

> "The vision of a Christian man,
>   In virtue, as in stature, great,
>   Embodied in a Christian state;
> And thou, amidst thy sisterhood,
>   Forbearing long, yet standing fast,
>   Shall win our grateful thanks at last."
> —WHITTIER.

MRS. GARFIELD and Miss Molly had arisen that morning in the joyous expectation of meeting their beloved one. A shock scarcely less violent than that caused by the bullet of the assassin was in store for them when they heard the evil news.

It did not tarry long.

General Swain was fortunately with them, and to him the first telegram was sent. It was as follows:—

"The President has been shot, and I am afraid is seriously wounded. Keep it from Mrs. Garfield till you hear further."

The General was deeply distressed; but he resolved to do as he had been told, and say nothing about it. So he put the telegram in his pocket, and went to the drawing-room to talk about anything but that which was uppermost in his mind.

"This is one of the hottest days we have had, Mrs. Garfield."

"Yes. It will be all the more delightful to get away to the White Mountains because of the heat we have experienced here. It has no doubt been still less endurable at Washington. I am glad my husband is going for a real holiday."

The General endeavoured to conceal his emotions, and look as cool and unconcerned as if nothing had happened; but he waited anxiously for the next message. It was not long in coming.

"We have the President safely and comfortably settled in the Executive Mansion, and his pulse is strong and nearly normal. So far as I can determine, and from what the surgeons say, and from his general condition, we feel very hopeful. Come on as soon as you can get a special train. Advise us of the movements of your train, and when you can be expected. As the President said on a similar occasion sixteen years ago, 'God reigns, and the Government in Washington still lives.'"

It was necessary now to break the news to Mrs. Garfield. General Swain tried to speak quietly, but his face and the tones of his voice declared that something was amiss.

"Mrs. Garfield," he said, "it may be necessary for us to go direct to Washington. An accident has happened to the President."

Mrs. Garfield and Molly both turned very pale.

"Oh, General, tell me the truth at once," said the agonised wife.

"So far as I am informed," said the General, "the accident is not so serious as was at first supposed."

"But what was the accident? Do not deceive me; I cannot bear the suspense."

Then the General, as gently as he could, told her exactly what had happened.

"We must go at once," said Mrs. Garfield, rising, but she could scarcely stand.

"Mr. Swain and I will make all preparations, mother," said Molly. "Do you keep quiet for a little time."

Presently a telegram came for her. The President had thought of his wife with a great longing to see her, and a great fear that in her present state of health the trouble would prove more than she could bear.

"Send this message to her," he said; "say that I have been seriously hurt, but at present I do not know how seriously. Tell her that I am myself, and hope she will come to me soon. And give my love to her."

This was accordingly despatched at once. Mrs. Garfield received it and two others: one signed J. S. Brown, and another Alonzo B. Cornell:—

"Don't believe sensational despatches about the President. Will keep you constantly advised."

"Please accept my earnest sympathy and sincere hope for the early and complete restoration of the President. Intense feeling of indignation prevails throughout Albany."

At a few minutes before twelve o'clock a carriage was at the door, and Mrs. Garfield was on her journey. A special parlour car was waiting for her at the station, which went away at express speed, and reached Washington at seven.

A few minutes after the carriage rolled up to the door of the White House, and Mrs. Garfield alighted.

The most respectful sympathy was shown to her by all parties; and tears came into the eyes of some who looked at her anxious face. She strove to keep calm, and hurried at once to the side of her husband. He looked up and met her gaze with a sad smile. She began to speak to him in low whispers, and he answered her quietly. Her conduct provoked the admiration of the physicians, for she was absolutely controlled, and exhibited not the least emotion. But it was thought unwise to allow the interview to be a long one, and one of the doctors told her so.

"I must leave you for a few minutes," she said to her husband. "I will come again soon."

She was escorted to the door by two of the doctors, and as soon as she was out of her husband's sight, she broke down completely and bitterly sobbed aloud.

After a time she begged for another interview with her husband, asking that she might see him alone. This was granted, and the room was cleared of all but the family. This time Mrs. Garfield remained with her husband for half an hour, and at the end of the time the physicians pronounced him no worse, but slightly better; although a little time before Dr. Bliss had said, "There is no hope for him; he will not probably live three hours, and may die in half an hour."

His son James was with him at one time, and broke out into sobs of distress at witnessing the sufferings of his father.

"Jimmy, my son, hope for the best," said the President.

Next to the members of the President's own family, Secretary Lincoln seemed to be the most smitten with sorrow. When the doctors told him that the President's case was almost hopeless, he said, "My God, what hours of sorrow I have passed in this town!"

Postmaster-General James said, "Do you remember how often General Garfield has referred to your father during the past few days?"

"Yes," said Mr. Lincoln; "and it was only the night before last that I entered into a detailed recital of the events of that awful night."

Bulletins were issued every half-hour all the evening, and hope alternated with fear.

"The President's condition is not perceptibly changed

either for the better or the worse. His voice is strong, his mind unimpaired, and he talks freely with those about him."

"The President is again sinking, and there is little, if any, hope."

"The President has rallied a little within the last three-quarters of an hour, and his symptoms are a little more favourable. He continues brave and cheerful. About the time he began to rally he said to Dr. Bliss, 'Doctor, what are the indications?' 'There is a chance of recovery.' 'Well, then, we will take that chance.' The President is still sleeping."

"Mrs. Garfield, although weak from her recent illness, and shocked by the suddenness of the grief that has come upon her, has behaved since her arrival with a courage and self-control equal to that of her husband. Not only has she not given way to the terror and grief which she necessarily feels, but she has been constantly by the President's side, encouraging him with her presence and sympathy, and giving efficient aid, so far as has been in her power, to the attending physicians."

Two telegrams came from England, signed by Earl Granville—

"Is it true that President Garfield has been shot at? If so, express at once great concern of Her Majesty's Government, and our hope that report that he has sustained serious injury is not true."

"The Queen desires that you will at once express the horror with which she has learned of the attempt upon the President's life, and her earnest hope for his recovery. Her Majesty wishes for full and immediate reports as to his condition."

There was an old lady in the meantime staying at Solon to whom many thoughts turned.

"The President's mother! What of her? Poor old lady,

it will kill her," said many who knew her. She was staying with her daughters, Mrs. Mary Larabee and Mrs. Mehetable Troubridge, upon their farms. A reporter went to see them in the morning after the occurrence.

"What have you heard from Washington?" was the anxious question put to him by one of the sisters of the President.

"The last news is better," was the reply.

"How does Mrs. Garfield bear the news?" he asked.

"She has not heard a word of what has happened," replied Mrs. Larabee. "We are afraid to tell her."

"She has already had great sorrow, for she has lately lost a brother."

"Mother is so wrapped up in James that we think it will be more than she can bear," said Mehetable.

"Have you received tidings from Mrs. Garfield herself?" inquired the reporter.

"A telegram came to mother a little while ago from Harry Garfield, the President's son."

"May I see it?"

"Certainly."

"EXECUTIVE MANSION, 2nd July.

"To Mrs. ELIZA GARFIELD, Solon, Ohio.

"Don't be alarmed by sensational rumours. Doctor thinks it will not be fatal. Don't think of coming until you hear further. HARRY A. GARFIELD."

"I suppose you had heard of the attempted assassination before you had this message?" asked the reporter of the President's sisters.

"We had not heard until the extra special editions of the papers came in," said Mrs. Troubridge. "My daughter from Brooklyn Village came over from Cleveland this morning, and brought us a copy containing the terrible news. We could not at first believe it. But as we read the bulletins we felt that they were only too true. Harry's telegram came later, and gave us a little hope."

"When will you break the news to Mrs. Garfield?"

"Not yet; we will wait till to-morrow."

But the next morning she was better, and seemed more talkative.

"Last Sunday, Thomas was buried; to-day, Cornelia. I wonder who it will be next Sunday, said his mother."

Mrs. Larabee came in.

"Are you going to Mrs. Arnold's funeral?" asked the old lady of her daughter Mary.

"No, mother; something has happened. I'm afraid I cannot go."

"What has happened?"

"We have heard that James is hurt."

"How? By the cars?"

"No; he has been shot."

"Shot by an accident?"

"No; by an assassin. But he was not killed."

"The Lord help me!"

"I think he will get through. The last news was more favourable. I guess he is resting and getting better."

"When did you hear this?" asked Mrs. Garfield, presently.

"Yesterday noon. But we thought it better not to tell you."

"Thank you. I am glad you did not tell me. It was very thoughtful of you. I was afraid something had happened yesterday. I saw a strange look on your face, but I had not the courage to ask what it meant. Let me see all the despatches as they come."

One came soon from Harry Garfield.

"Thank God, he lives this morning, and the doctors are very hopeful. He has been perfectly himself all the time."

Again news came; and the old lady said—"How could anybody be so cold-hearted as to want to kill my baby!"

The next telegram was still hopeful.

"I am glad to hear it," she replied; "but I am afraid we are hoping against fate. It seems terrible."

She herself sent the following telegram to Washington:—

"The news was broken to me this morning, and shocked me very much. Since receiving your telegram I feel more hopeful. Tell James that I hear he is cheerful, and that I am glad of it. Tell him to keep in good spirits, and accept the love and sympathy of a mother, sister, and friend,

"ELIZA GARFIELD."

The following little domestic incident was told by one of the writers on the subject:—"Miss Molly was very brave, and forced herself to assume a calmness which she could not feel.

"Oh, papa, I am so glad to get back to you, but I'm so sorry to see you in this way," she said.

The President put his arm around her. "Molly, you are a brave, good girl," he whispered, and drew her down to kiss her.

"Well, I'm not going to talk to you now; wait till you get well," said the little girl, who walked out of the room, followed by a beaming smile from the President. He soon fell asleep, with one hand in the hand of Mrs. James.

When he awoke he said, "Do you know where Mrs. Garfield is now?"

"Oh, yes," said Mrs. James; "she is close by, waiting and praying for her husband."

He looked up with an anxious face, and said, "I want her to go to bed; will you tell her that I say if she will undress and go to bed I will turn right over, and I feel sure that when I know she is in bed, I can go to sleep, and sleep all night?"

THE WIFE AND MOTHER. 275

"Tell her," he added, with sudden energy, "that I *will* sleep all night if she will only do as I ask."

M s. James took the message, and Mrs. Garfield replied, "Go back and tell him that I am undressing."

She did so, and he almost immediately fell asleep.

That Sunday was a very different one from that which they expected to spend on the banks of the Hudson.

Happily the President seemed to revive. "Doctor," he said at one time, "you have changed my programme a little. I had prepared to meet death philosophically, but you have changed all that."

One of the attendants said, "I believe he has made up his mind that he won't die, and that he will fight it out."

In the evening a despatch came from the President's mother asking if she might come and see her son."

She was told that the symptoms were more favourable, but she was advised not to come.

A writer said of the conduct of the President, when he lay between life and death—"When first wounded, his thought was of his wife and little ones, and how to spare them pain. His mother's anxiety was also uppermost in his mind. He was once told that he had only a single chance of life, and he said, 'I am not afraid to die.' He was very considerate of others. He moved his arm while in a paroxysm of pain and just touched a little rudely one of his kind-hearted watchers. Instantly he lost all thought for himself, and his lips parted with a heartfelt apology. His demeanour towards his noble-hearted wife has been chivalrous in the extreme. He has ever sought her ease and welfare, and to keep her from all anxiety and suspense. When she first entered his room he met her with a smiling face, and he has had a smile and a word of cheer for her ever since, even though his sufferings have been at times very great. With true wifely devotion, too, has Mrs. Garfield borne herself; and her cheerful, hopeful demeanour has done much to free from care her husband's mind. He feared for her; and she, knowing his fear, steeled herself by a mighty effort. To no one has she made a complaint, to no one has her husband uttered aught but words of kindness. They have been a model husband and wife under circumstances most trying to their natures. Each has brought solace to the other, and the wife has ministered at the bedside of her liege with an intelligence none the less powerful and efficient than the love she has shown. Such stories spread. All are only too willing to help embalm in the memory of friends the ministry of love and gentleness, of kindness and devotion which the National Executive Mansion discloses. There is a hero-worship here that is carried out to a surprising extent; but the people know and feel that there is a good basis for much that they believe, and the glamour of devotion adds bright and attractive colours to the picture, and gives it a setting of love."

Throughout that Sunday, prayers were offered for the wounded President in all churches and chapels, not only of America, but all lands. It was no wonder that in his own country people waited with hushed breath and beating heart for news, and that they joined with sincere earnestness in the prayers. From every town came messages expressive of indignation, and in every pulpit references were made to the event. In the Disciples' church at Washington, which General Garfield and his family attended, and which was thronged, an earnest prayer ascended to God. "Oh, save him, God! We know not what is best for Thee to do: but if it be Thy will, oh, for Christ's sake, have mercy. Lord bless the dear sister, his companion, herself but recently escaped from death. May she be consoled in spirit, and may Providence surround her! Lead her children in the path of righteousness, save them from sin, and lead them to honour and glory. May there go up from thousands upon thousands of sorrowing homes to-day throughout all the land an earnest prayer for the stricken President."

The Rev. Henry Ward Beecher said :—" It is not fitting that we should go hence before we remember the stricken family of President Garfield in their exquisite suffering. In England, noble women are educated for public affairs, and when put in places of honour, they demean themselves with peculiar propriety. We are a Democratic-Republican people, and our women are educated particularly for domesticity and seclusion. It is a matter for congratulation, when the President of the nation has reached his high position, that he has a wife and household who know how to become their elevated station, as if born heirs to titles and courts. If we look at the wives of the Presidents, we see almost not a single cloud in the long succession. The succession is not changed. When that model in the family relation, Mrs. Hayes, left the White House, it seemed as though an equal to her distinguished worth, as mother, wife, and woman, that had rejoiced the hearts of the people, could not be found. But Mrs. Garfield, while differing much, is worthy to succeed her, and need not fear to compare with any of her predecessors. She has just come up from the borders of death, only to meet her husband in peril. Then there is the venerable mother, who should have long preceded her son, who now seems likely to come after him. To-day, if there is any woman here with a heart to pray for the stricken family, and who remembers the sanctities of the household, let her seek God's blessing on the smitten ones."

Mr. Beecher then prayed with deep and earnest feeling for the President's mother, and wife, and his children. There was scarcely a dry eye among the women in the church when he had ended, and tears found their way to the eyes of many men. In closing the petition, he said :—
"Wilt Thou sustain the wounded man? And if the way

of darkness shall open for him—which must open some time for all feet to tread—will God be gracious, and enable him to say, 'I fear no evil; Thy rod and Thy staff, they comfort me.' May there come to us a voice of triumph from beyond. Lord God of our fathers!—our God!—comfort the family, the Government, the nation, and the country; and enable all to say earnestly, no matter what the event may be, 'Thy will be done.'"

CHAPTER XIV.

A FIGHT FOR LIFE.

"The dear Lord's best interpreters
Are humble human souls;
The gospel of a life like his
Is more than books or scrolls."

"WILL he live or die?"

This was the question asked by thousands of people every day, not only in America, but in Europe. We have not yet forgotten how, during the struggle for life, which lasted for eighty days, people in England were more eager to read the tidings from the United States than anything else in the newspapers.

In America the fight was watched with the most solemn anxiety. As is usual in such cases, the people discovered that the President was a nobler man than they had thought, and far dearer to them than they had imagined. Every one felt that his own friend lay in that house, "sick nnto death," unless God in His mercy and wisdom should interpose; and many who had before been indifferent became intensely earnest then. The South as well as the North—the affected and the disaffected—became at once loyal and kindly. Many incidents were told of individuals and of companies taking a strong personal interest in that strife between life and death that went on so long at Washington.

"A coloured man stood waiting at the main entrance, just outside the grounds attached to the Executive Mansion. I could not help noticing him this morning as I passed in through the iron gates, and by the sentries who guarded the opening. He was emphatically hatless, shoeless, and shirtless. The few worn garments which invested his spare frame wanted only an apology for going to pieces. His frizzed hair and thin grey beard were dishevelled; but they seemed to gain a glory from the tints of the bright warm sunshine, whose heat was almost overpowering. Like an ancient servitor stood the old man, close to the sentries, and peered through the iron gates, whose portals he could not pass. When anyone came out of the grounds, he would approach, and eagerly listen for tidings. He kept his vigil well. When I told him the doctors had great hopes of saving the President, he said simply, but with fervour, 'I thank God for that!'"

The narrator of this incident added—"And so it is everywhere about the city. Men are tearful, prayerful, and quiet. High and low share in the feelings of sympathy and devotion. The Cabinet officers and their wives—men of mark, who have won renown in battle, in debate, or in the marts of trade—all have the sense of personal bereavement. It stirs one to see old army veterans, some of them battle scarred, to whom wounds were mere child's play in war time, actually cry outright at the present sad calamity."

Medical men in all parts of the world became especially interested. They would like to have been spectators of the struggle that was going on; but the papers kept the public well-informed, not only in regard to the condition of the sufferer, but the medicines and plans adopted for his relief.

As the weeks passed by, and he still lived, it was hoped

that he would surely recover. Many things were in his favour—his temperate life, his great courage and strength of endurance, his vitality and hopefulness. As July wore away, dread gave place to hopefulness. Three weeks after he was shot, however, there came a relapse. He seemed to recover from that, and on the 28th of July he was moved into an adjoining room. On Monday, the 8th of August, an operation was performed, and a new channel for the flow of the pus from the wound was opened. On the 11th of August he wrote a letter to his mother—the last he ever wrote—

"WASHINGTON, 11th August 1881.

"DEAR MOTHER—Don't be disturbed by conflicting reports about my condition. It is true I am still weak and on my back, but I am gaining every day, and need only time and patience to bring me through. Give my love to all the relatives and friends, especially to sisters Hetty and Mary.—Your loving son,
"JAMES A. GARFIELD."

On Sunday, the 14th of August, the case took a new turn; dyspepsia set in. On Tuesday, the 18th, it was feared that there was blood poisoning. On Saturday he seemed better, but Sunday was a bad day. On Wednesday, the 24th August, the glandular swelling was lanced. The following Sunday was a day of terrible suspense; the President seemed to be in the Valley of the Shadow of Death. But he emerged from it, and was again better.

It was thought that if he could only be removed to the sea, it would give him a better chance of life; and he himself was exceedingly anxious to get away from Washington.

"Oh! the sea, the beautiful sea," he said, with longing and hope.

It was resolved to remove him thither, Mentor was too

far, but Long Branch was not impossible. The weather was very sultry, and the physicians thought there would be less risk to the patient in the journey than in remaining. He seemed to be sufficiently comfortable to warrant them in making the attempt on Wednesday, the 7th of September.

The greatest anxiety was felt, for the distance from Washington to Long Branch was two hundred and thirty-eight miles. The General was himself very nervous. But the doctors administered morphine, and, while he was asleep under its influence, he was carried from his room, and placed on the couch in the railway carriage. This was safely and satisfactorily accomplished, and very slowly at first the train went on its way with its precious freight.

Elaborate preparations had been made; all trains were cleared out of the way; and though the stations were thronged with people, every one was quiet and orderly. As far as Philadelphia the President seemed really to enjoy the ride, but then he grew restless and weary. At Seagirt, however, the salt breezes, blowing through the car, revived him, and he exclaimed again, "Oh, the beautiful sea!" The journey lasted from six o'clock in the morning till one in the afternoon. Immediately on the arrival of the train the President was taken to the cottage of Mr. Francklyn, at Elberon, Long Branch, and though there were some unfavourable symptoms, he did not seem really worse. Indeed, he declared next morning that he was positively better.

A day of fasting and prayer was appointed by all the Governors of the various States at the time President Garfield was removed to Long Branch; and a Philadelphia paper related an incident connected with that solemn and universally observed day:—

"Crete," said the President to his brave little wife,

about eleven on Thursday morning, as the ringing strokes from the belfry of the Episcopal church, which was close to the cottage, reached his ears, "What are they ringing that bell for?" "That?" said Mrs. Garfield, who was waiting for the surprise. "That's the church where we were when you first came down. They're all going to pray for you to get well;" and, falling on her knees, she said, "and I'm going to pray too, James, that it may be soon; for I know already that the other prayer has been heard." From where he lay, Garfield could see the carriages draw up, and group after group go in. He could even hear the subdued refrain of "Jesus, lover of my soul," as it was borne by on its heavenward way. Thrilled with emotion, a tear trickled down the President's face. After a while a woman's sweet voice arose, singing one of Sir Michael Costa's oratorios. "Turn thou unto Me," sang the voice, "for I am desolate; I am desolate and afflicted: the troubles of my heart are enlarged. Oh, bring thou me out of my distresses, my God!" The people in the church sat almost spell-bound under the voice. Mrs. George W. Childs, who sang the recitative, was affected deeply, and made it seem to all, what it must have been to her, a prayer of music.

On Saturday, September the 17th, a severe chill set in, which lasted half-an-hour, and was followed by profuse perspirations and high fever. He got better afterwards, but the physicians knew the situation was exceedingly critical. On Sunday he had another attack of chill, and Monday, the 19th, opened ominously with another. He suffered very much during these attacks, which left him fearfully weak and exhausted. It was feared that the end was near, and yet every one hoped as well as feared. He had got through all sorts of attacks so wonderfully, it was hoped that he would even yet recover.

But the hearts of his nearest grew very sick with dread.

On Monday, September the 19th, the symptoms of the President's case were very discouraging, and nearly every one about him abandoned all hope of recovery. But he had held out so long ; the blood-poisoning, caused by the absorption into the system of the discharge from the wound, had been so insidious and slow, that no one looked for his immediate death. Yet the gloomy presentiment was so strong upon the inmates of the cottage, that they involuntarily began to mourn for him as one dead. An eye-witness related an incident which well illustrates the situation that day.

Late in the morning the President expressed a wish to see his daughter Molly. When the child went into the room she kissed her father, and told him that she was glad to see that he was looking so much better. He said—

"You think I do look better, Molly?"

She said, "I do, papa;" and then she took a chair and sat near the foot of the bed.

A moment or two after, Dr. Boynton noticed that she was swaying in her chair. He stepped up to her, but before he could reach her she had fallen over in a dead faint. In falling, her face struck against the bed-post, and when they raised her from the floor, she was not only unconscious, but also bleeding from the contusion she had received. They carried her out, and she speedily recovered .The President, they thought, had not noticed what had happened to his petted child, for he seemed to have sunk into a stupor ; but when Dr. Boynton came back into the room, he was astonished to hear the President say—

"Poor little Molly; she fell over like a log. What was the matter?"

They assured the President that she was quite restored. He again sank into a stupor or sleep, which lasted until the noon examination.

The end came at last unexpectedly. Judge Advocate-

General Swain, who was present, gave the following account of the scene:—

"It was my night to watch with the President. I had been with him a good deal of the time from three o'clock in the afternoon. A few minutes before ten o'clock I left Colonel Rockwell, with whom I had been talking for some minutes in the lower hall, and proceeded upstairs to the President's room. On entering I found Mrs. Garfield sitting by his bedside; there was no one else in the room.

"'How is everything going?' I said.

"'He is sleeping nicely,' she replied.

"'I think you had better go to bed and rest,' I said.

"I asked her what had been prescribed for the night. She replied that she did not know; she had given him milk punch at eight o'clock.

"I said, 'If you will wait a moment, I will go into the doctor's room and see what is to be given during the night. She answered, 'There is beef-tea downstairs. Daniel knows where it is.' Daniel was the coloured servant. I then went into the doctor's room. I found Dr. Bliss there, and asked what was to be given for the night. He answered, 'I think I had better fix up a lift and bring it to you soon.' I went back to Mrs. Garfield, and had further conversation with her. She felt the President's hand, and laid her hand on his forehead. 'He seems to be in good condition,' she said, and passed out of the room. Dr. Boynton came in, and said the President's pulse, though not so strong as in the afternoon, was good. I said, 'He seems to be doing well.' He replied, 'Yes,' and passed out.

"Shortly after this the President awoke. As he turned his head on awaking, I arose and took his hand. I remarked, 'You have had a nice comfortable sleep.' He then said, 'Oh, Swain, this terrible pain!' placing his right hand on his breast, over the region of the heart. I said, 'Can I get you anything?' He said, 'Some water.' I poured some out, and he took the glass in his hand and drank quite naturally. I then handed the glass to the coloured man Daniel. Afterward, I took a napkin and wiped his forehead, as he usually perspired on awaking. He said, 'Oh, Swain, this terrible pain! Press your hand on it.' I laid my hand on his chest, and he threw up his arms to his head, and said, 'Oh, Swain, can't you stop this! Oh, Swain!'

"I then saw that he was looking at me with a staring expression. I spoke to him, but received no answer. I told Daniel to call Dr. Bliss and Mrs. Garfield. I saw that he was dying. Dr. Bliss came in, and I said, 'Doctor, have you any stimulants; I think he is dying:' and the doctor replied, 'Yes, he is dying.' I then said to Daniel, 'Run and rouse the house.' Colonel Rockwell came, and then Mrs. Garfield. She exclaimed, 'Oh, why am I made to suffer this cruel wrong!' She laid her hand gently on her husband's face and breast. Molly Garfield was near the door. The President lay very still, only now and then gasping for breath; and in about thirty minutes he peacefully passed away. It was thought that death resulted from coagulation of the blood in the region of the heart."

Miss Molly Garfield broke down completely, but the widow was firm, though strongly affected.

There was nothing to say at that supreme moment, excepting "All is over," and "He was ready to die."

At six o'clock the next morning Mrs. Larabee had a despatch announcing the death of her brother. Mrs. Garfield was asleep, and did not awake till eight o'clock. Her daughter did not tell her until she had finished breakfast. Then Miss Ellen Larabee said, "Grandma, would you be surprised to hear news this morning?"

"Why, I don't know," said the old lady.

"I should not," said Mrs. Larabee; "I have been fearing and expecting all the morning."

"Grandma," said Ellen, "there is sad news."

"Is he dead?" the little white-haired mother asked, tremulously.

"He is," was the answer, spoken in low tones of sorrow.

The quick tears started to her eyes, and there was a paroxysm of grief.

"Is it true? Then the Lord help me, for if he is dead, what shall I do?" she said.

She sat in her rocking chair waiting for news, and read the morning papers. "It cannot be that James is dead," she murmured; "I cannot understand it. I have no further wish to live, and I cannot live if it is so."

But after, she said, "I can firmly believe that God knows best, and I must not murmur."

Soon afterwards she said to Mr. Ogilvie, who visited her:—"I am starting on my eighty-first year to-day, and it may be my last. This is a terrible sorrow. He was the best son a mother ever had—so good, kind, generous, and brave. If he had to die, why did not God take him without all the terrible suffering he endured? I ought to submit, but I cannot! He had, I know, fulfilled the full measure of his ambition. He had reached the highest place in the regard of his countrymen. That ought to break the fall to me, but it doesn't seem to. I want my boy, and it seems so hard that he should die away from us. It is wonderful how I live upon thoughts of him. I am glad you should see the old home; but he and his brother built a fence house for me there. He loved every field about the place. He had his father's remains taken up from the grave in the wheat-field, and buried in the grave of the Disciples' church. I cannot last long, and the other world will be brighter for his presence."

So the bereaved parent of the President chatted on to sympathetic ears, scarcely realising all that the trouble meant, and yet feeling that the very light of her life had gone out. No one could look at her without shedding tears. It seemed hard indeed, that after all her work for him and her joy in him, he should die by the hand of the base assassin.

The news of President Garfield's death awoke in England feelings of the deepest regret.

The next morning many of the newspapers were in black, and people knew, even before they read the printed words, that the world had lost a hero. Black crape was hung from many of the windows in London; Fleet Street, the Strand, and Cheapside especially showing in this way the sympathy of the Londoners with America. In all the large provincial towns the feeling was the same, especially in Manchester.

It was at once decided to hold memorial services in many of the churches and chapels; and in all the homes of England there was mourning. All corporate bodies voted messages of sympathy and condolence to Mrs. Garfield and the United States. The lessons of the patient, magnanimous life which had just closed seemed at once to be read by all, and to be understood and taken to heart. The highest people in our land took an early opportunity of testifying to their admiration for the deceased man, and their sorrow at his death.

Alfred Tennyson wrote to Mr. Lowell from Haslemere:— " We learned yesterday that the President was gone. We had watched with much admiration his fortitude, and not without hope, the fluctuations of his health these many days. Now we almost seem to have lost a personal friend. He was a good man, and a noble one. Accept from me, and my wife and family, assurances of heartfelt sympathy for Mrs. Garfield, for yourself, and for your country."

Mr. Tennyson, prompt as he was in his expressions of kindness, was not before others. The English people, from the highest to the lowest, united in the most sincere regrets and good wishes. The Queen, by every means in her power, manifested her intense sympathy. The English Court went into mourning, a very unusual mark of respect; and Her Majesty—filled with tender love towards the woman who had now to comprehend, as she had long done, the desolateness of widowhood—touched all American hearts as well as the most sorrowful one among them, by sending the following message, dated from Balmoral :—" Words cannot express the deep sympathy I feel with you. May God support and comfort you as He alone can."

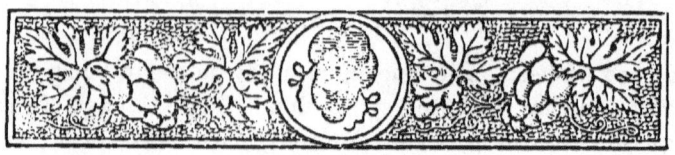

CHAPTER XV.

THE FUNERAL.

> "His will be done
> Who seeth not as man, whose way
> Is not as ours! 'Tis well with thee!
> Nor anxious doubt nor dark dismay
> Disquieted thy closing day;
> But evermore thy soul could say,
> My Father careth still for me."

OVER the cottage at Elberon a deep gloom hung; but General Garfield had belonged to the nation; and now his widow and children must not indulge their grief in solitude. The lawn in front of the cottage was crowded with people; and as soon as they might they poured into the house to look upon the face of the man whom they all mourned. More than three thousand persons passed through and gazed upon the deceased. The coffin was a plain one; and the inscription upon it said as little as it could.

> "James Abram Garfield,
> Born November 19th, 1831,
> Died President of the United States,
> September 19th, 1881."

It was necessary to lose no time in removing the body from Long Branch to Washington, and Mrs. Garfield requested the Rev. Mr. Young to conduct a religious service in the cottage, the first of the many memorial services which were held. At its close the funeral procession set out on the journey to Washington. The same train that had brought the General to Long Branch took him back. Mrs. Garfield, closely veiled, supported by her children, Molly and Harry, and other friends, accompanied the body. In the next car the members of the Cabinet and their wives travelled.

Wherever the train went, manifestations of sorrow and sympathy were abundant. Crowds were everywhere. At Princetown the students from the college strewed the way with flowers. At Philadelphia there was an immense crowd; and not only curiosity and excitement were shown, but traces of deep feeling were upon the faces of the multitude.

Arrived at Washington, the sad procession was re-formed; and every possible token of respect was paid. The United States Marine Band played the beautiful anthem, "Nearer, my God, to Thee," and the people turned it into a prayer. The body was placed on a catafalque in the Rotunda of the Capitol, and during the lying-in-state was visited by hundreds of thousands. The floral contributions excelled anything that had previously been seen. There were globes of immortelles, pillars of roses, and exquisite designs of all kinds. One handsome wreath had a card attached to it, bearing the following inscription :—

"**Queen Victoria,**
To the Memory of the late P<small>RESIDENT</small> G<small>ARFIELD</small>.
An expression of her sorrow and sympathy with Mrs. Garfield and the American Nation. September 22, 1881."

During the time of the lying-in-state, Mrs. Garfield and Harry and Molly went to take a last farewell. The doors were closed and the public excluded. A few personal friends of the General went in, and then Mrs. Garfield entered alone. "Beyond that threshold, rank, nor power, nor curiosity, nor imagination might intrude. The lid of the casket had been removed, and for twenty minutes the widow remained by all that was earthly of her honoured dead. She came out closely veiled, and bearing a few flowers taken from the offerings of affection which had been placed upon the casket. She silently took the arm of General Swain and departed."

She could not bear to remain in the White House, and went away with her children to Mentor. There all the wreaths were sent at her request; all except the palm-leaves and the wreath of the Queen's, which was to go wherever the dead body went. There also remained by its side a scroll with the words—

> "Life's race well run,
> Life's work well done,
> Life's crown well won,
> Now comes rest."

General Garfield was buried at Cleveland. Before the procession set out from Washington a religious service was held at the Rotunda. Prayers were offered by Dr. Errett and the Rev. J. G. Buthin, and Dr. Power pronounced a eulogy.

In the eulogy by Nathaniel P. Banks, given in the "Boston Memorial," occur these words in reference to the funeral obsequies celebrated in the Rotunda of the Capitol at Washington :—

"Simple, brief, and impressive ceremonies heightened the deep and general interest of the occasion. The funeral discourse was of a purely religious character, with scarcely more than a brief allusion to the career of the deceased President, and no mention, I think, of his name. But these omissions intensified the general interest in the life of the President. 'I do believe,' the preacher said, 'that the true strength and beauty of this man's character will be found in his discipleship of Christ!' It is not my province to speak of the spiritual nature of this connection, but in another relation I believe it is true.

"The Church of the Disciples, to which he belonged, is one of the most primitive of Christian communions, excluding every thought of distrust, competition, or advantage. It gave him a position and mission unique and generic, like and unlike that of other men. While he rarely or never referred to it himself, and might have wished at times, perhaps, to forget it, he was strengthened and protected by it. It was buckler and spear to him. It brought him into an immediate communion—a relation made sacred by a common faith, barren of engagements and responsibilities— with multitudes of other organisations and congregations, adherents and opponents, able and willing to assist and strengthen him, present or absent, at home or abroad, who dismissed aspersions on his conduct and character as accusations of Pharisees against a son of the true faith, and gave him at all times a friendly greeting and welcome, whenever and wherever he felt inspired to give the world his thought and word. All great movements and revolutions of men and nations are born of this spirit and power."

The railway along which the dead and the mourners were carried was lined with people, and strewn with flowers. Crape banners and mourning flags of every description were abundant; many of them bearing the words—"We mourn our dead President." At Cleveland immense crowds were waiting, and watched the mournful pageant with interest. A writer thus describes it:—

"While the distinguished persons were taking their seats in the funeral pavilion, carriages were seen coming into the public square. The first was drawn by beautiful white horses. The door was opened, and a young man with a mournful face alighted, and assisted to the ground a lady clad in deep mourning. These were the President's widow, and their son Harry. The other children of the President were also there; but in contrast with their youthful appearance there was another figure, bent with age, leaning on the arms of two of the President's friends, who slowly ascended the inclined plane, and took a seat near the coffin. This was the President's mother, who not many months before saw him assume his high position in Washington; and whom, in sight of everybody, he tenderly kissed on that never-to-be-forgotten day."

After an address by Dr. Errett, and prayers by the Rev. Ross Houghton and Dr. Pomeroy, the procession went to Lake View Cemetery. Flowers had been sent from legations and societies in all parts of the land. Indeed, when they arrived at the cemetery, so great were the contributions, that the ground was literally covered with flowers.

At the side of the grave Mrs. Garfield looked for a moment from the carriage-window, and then covered her face with her hands and wept. The "little white-haired mother" looked fixedly into the vault, and then drew down her veil that no one might see her grief. She felt that the one last strong tie that bound her to the earth had now been broken.

The service was very simple and very impressive. The following hymn, which had been a favourite one with the General, was sung at the grave—

> " Ho ! reapers of life's harvest,
> Why stand with rusted blade,
> Until the night draws round thee,
> And day begins to fade ?

Why stand ye idle, waiting
   For reapers more to come?
The golden morn is passing—
   Why sit ye idle, dumb?

Thrust in your sharpened sickle,
   And gather in the grain;
The night is fast approaching,
   And soon will come again.
The master calls for reapers,
   And shall he call in vain?
Shall sheaves be there ungathered,
   And waste upon the plain?

Come down from hill and mountain,
   In morning's ruddy glow,
Nor wait until the dial
   Points to the noon below;
And come with the strong sinew,
   Nor faint in heat or cold,
And pause not till the evening
   Draws round its wealth of gold.

Mount up the heights of wisdom,
   And crush each error low;
Keep back no words of knowledge
   That human hearts should know.
Be faithful to thy mission
   In service of thy Lord,
And then a golden chaplet
   Shall be thy just reward."

The stirring words of this hymn must have made many think of Garfield's own words when Lincoln was smitten down. Another worker had fallen, but God's work must be carried on all the same; and those who loved the man whom they mourned knew that for his sake, if from no other motive, they must go back to their allotted tasks, determined to toil more earnestly than before.

The band solemnly played, "Nearer, my God, to thee;"

and the Rev. H. Jones, who had been in the war with Garfield, spoke a few earnest words. They were real friends who stood around that grave; and, when it was over, and they went away to their homes, they felt that life would henceforth be more sad than ever before.

The day of the funeral was a day of mourning throughout the United States of America; and in England all classes united to keep it as a time of solemn thought. Services were held in many of the churches and chapels at the very time that the funeral was taking place at Cleveland. Among the rest was one in St. Martin-in-the-Fields, near Charing Cross, London, when the Archbishop of Canterbury delivered the following address:—

"My Christian Friends—It is a great privilege and a great responsibility to be called upon to address a few words to you at the close of this mournful day—a mournful day even in this capital, at so great a distance from the scene which we have all called to mind. Had the solemn scene taken place in some neighbouring cemetery, I doubt whether its effects would be more deeply experienced than now, when we know that it has been enacted over thousands of miles of ocean, and a vast tract of a distant continent. Why is it that the heart of this English nation, as well as that of the great American nation, has been so moved at the present time? It cannot be the mere contagion of a nation's grief, august and heartrending as is the spectacle of all the sorrow over a great man fallen. That can scarcely have travelled over sea and land to move our feelings as at this time. Neither can it be merely that we sorrow for a great career prematurely cut short. We have seen others stopped in their progress by the rude hand of death as unexpectedly—bright hopes fading away; and yet there has not been this general feeling of mourning. Neither can it have been only that during those weary weeks of suffering, borne with such Christian fortitude, the details of the sick

chamber were brought to us day by day, and we learned to admire the man who bore his fate so manfully, and to love her who, with all a woman's care, was tending through those eleven weeks the hopeless invalid. Neither can it be that there mingles with our thoughts any anxiety as to a change of policy in the great nation whose loss we mourn. Power is handed from man to man by death in all the great nations of the world, and we do not feel any great or deep anxiety; and, least of all, when we contemplate that great nation which is now mourning, do we fear lest its steady, onward course should be restrained or altered by the power of any single human will. Why is it we have been so strangely moved? First, on that July morning, when the news flashed across the Atlantic that the loved President of a great people had been smitten by a mysterious blow, I hesitate not to say that there was a feeling of consternation, not merely of dismay, throughout this community. We had read in old histories of the attempts on the life of our own Queen Elizabeth, and of the murders of Henri Quatre and of William of Orange, and we congratulated ourselves that we were not as the men who lived in those days. And when assassination revived in modern history, we turned to the barbarous monarchies of the East. We knew how thrones were vacated there, and we supposed that it was but some lingering barbarism in the great monarchies of Europe if we heard of such attempts on monarchs' lives, and we knew that this lingering barbarism concealed itself under an affectation of indignation against restraints on public liberty. But here, in the very centre of the temple of freedom, where there was no ground for any complaint, we heard of this most atrocious deed; and we thought within ourselves at first, in our alarm, that there must be in the world some vile combination against the progress of civilisation working in the dark.

"The death of Lincoln had been, at the worst, but the wild

effect of bitterness of a scarce suppressed civil war; but now we know not what might be the end if the elected chief of freemen, as much as the inheritor of a barbarous throne, were exposed to the deadly knife of the assassin without the slightest cause. A short time dispelled those fears. We learnt that the deed had its origin in vulgar avarice or ambition, thwarted by the determination of an upright chief; and then, looking calmly at the whole, our first dismay was allayed and passed away. But then we had time to think what manner of man was this over whom so great a nation was mourning from day to day, and watching the flickering life as he lay upon his deathbed. And we are told particulars which we knew not before, and what manner of man he was. We learnt that this chosen chief of fifty millions of freemen was, as it seemed, in mind as in body, a very model of what such a man should be. We learnt his early history, and all of us have traced it daily in the accounts of him which have appeared among ourselves. We learnt how, born of a race which left our own land in the *Mayflower*, to escape from the evils which a mistaken Government then brought upon freed men, he inherited the spirit of his fathers. We learnt of his early days, and that far-off and solitary farm-house in the forest; how he laboured with his hands; how the boy, full of the spirit of adventure, was seized with a desire for a seafaring life; how, when he first tasted it for a day, his pure soul was revolted by the blasphemy and drunkenness which disgraced that noble calling; how he then sought to maintain himself by day labour, as driving horses along the side of a canal; and how, when this short period passed, and sickness sent him home, he was tended by the august mother, who still survives to receive the thanks of her countrymen, for having so well, by her thrift and self-denial, earned a good education for her boy.

"All this was calculated to enlist our sympathy, and then

we were taught to trace a career, such as England knows
nothing of, and to wonder at the mode in which great men
are formed in a country, so like and yet so dissimilar from
our own—the scholar ripening into the master; the master
becoming a student in the college, a professor, a contro-
versialist, a preacher; and then, after all this strange
preparation, when the state of the country seemed to call
for it, the citizen developing himself into the colonel of a
powerful regiment, who made himself acquainted with the
practice as well as with the theory of tactics in a few weeks;
and then the able general, passing into that office from the
head of the staff, and achieving victories which seemed to
promise him the most brilliant career. Then—all this
interrupted at the call of duty—the voice of Lincoln
summoning him to take his part in the government of the
country, giving up his military career, devoting himself to
politics, and in the political life showing a bright example
of an honest, straightforward, and vigorous lover of his
country. All this, I must say, to most of us was quite
new. It opened up a picture of manhood such as in this
country we were little acquainted with, and no wonder that
our affections were drawn forth, and we felt that it was no
common man that the civilised world had lost. But then
comes the nobler and the better lesson. We know not the
secrets of the soul; we know not the exact impressions of
religion which had been made upon his heart; but we have
two signs, and we shall do well to meditate upon them—
first, how he stood forth bravely against many difficulties to
defend high character and uprightness in their dealings with
the public creditor; how he would yield to no suggestion to
trifle with what seemed to him the plain dictates of political
honesty and morality; and, secondly, that when all experiences for some time back had been in favour of making the
election to the office of President a party triumph, he
determined, at whatever cost, not to give up to party what

he owed to his country and its highest welfare—a resolution which, as far as we know, cost him his life. These lessons surely speak of a Christianity deeper than the lips, or than excited feelings. They speak of a conduct regulated through life according to Christian principles, and point an example to all public men. No wonder, then, that we recognised such a great loss as that which London is mourning to-day.

"And now, my brethren from the other side of the Atlantic, and all of us, what lessons have we to learn from this mourning, which has brought us all together so remarkably this day? Families disunited are often said to be brought together by some common sorrow. Thank God, we are not disunited, but we may be brought better to understand and love each other by our union in this common sorrow. There are many bonds to keep us together. The same blood, the same tongue, the same literature—each of us enjoying the privilege which the literature of the one race gives to the other—science in each country lending its aid to develop the industry, the prosperity, and the happiness of both. We have learned to appreciate each other. We know, here in England, my American friends, your boundless hospitality, shown to ourselves or our sons who have visited you, and who have received from you a welcome as of relations near in blood. But our union, above all, must be based upon our common Christianity. We know that the Lord God Almighty has committed to us a trust—beyond the trust He has given to any other nation of the world—to carry through the boundaries of the human race a civilisation founded upon Christianity.

"Let us learn that this union is the only true union to keep us really together in the dark ages that may be in store for the human race ; that individual, family, social, or political life must all have its cement in the gospel of Jesus

Christ. Some may think that from this country there goes forth at times an uncertain sound as to religion, and that we have received uncertain sounds from over the Atlantic; but the heart of both nations, thank God, is still truly Christian, and in the ages that are before us, may the Lord teach us both more distinctly to recognise the priceless value of that common guide, which alone can safely lead both nations—the Gospel of our Lord and Saviour, Jesus Christ."

CHAPTER XVI.

IN MEMORY OF GARFIELD.

"Forth from the dust we spring, and run
About the green earth's patient breast
Our little day. At set of sun
Into her bosom creep and rest."
—*Scribner's Monthly.*

THE number of Memorial Services held in connection with the death of General Garfield was truly remarkable. In England, as in America, his name was heard in almost all pulpits on the Sundays following the death and the funeral. In Westminster Abbey the Rev. Canon Duckworth preached to a crowded congregation from the words, "*O spare me, that I may recover my strength before I go hence, and be no more seen.*"

The sermon concluded thus :—" And can we forget to-day that convalescence—for such it seemed to be—on which millions of hearts in the New World and in the Old have so long been set with a yearning devotion ? From how many lips the fervent prayer has gone up, day by day, to Him in whose hands are the issues of life and death, "O spare him, that he may recover his strength before he goes hence and is no more seen. Morning and evening in this venerable abbey, round which, as almost the home of the race and the shrine of its grandest memories, the affections of the Western Republic twine as lovingly as our own, and in which, within recent days, a resting-place has been found for two of its noblest citizens, we have offered our public petitions for the life so dear to our great kindred, and so precious to the world. Never, perhaps, has the heart of England thrilled with deeper sympathy. From the hour when the dastardly shot was fired, one interest has been paramount throughout the length and breadth of the land—one anxiety has displaced every other. So eagerly had we awaited every telegram, so nervously had we scanned every message of hope or fear, that, when the struggle ended, and all was over, the news fell upon every English household, from that of the monarch to that of her humblest subject, with the shock of a personal bereavement. We felt as if one were taken from us whom we had long known and loved. And, indeed, in those days of deadly peril we did come to know him. Through the long agony, so gallantly borne, we watched him, we overheard many a brave and tender word; and we think we know what his country delighted to honour and trembled to lose. We recognised in him one of those rare natures which could not be hid, for God had gifted it with the prescriptive right to rule; he had made him to be a true shepherd and king of men. I have seen a description of his martyred predecessor, Abraham Lincoln, from the pen of his eloquent fellow-countryman, Phillips Brooks, and it seems to apply with singular fitness to James Garfield. 'The character by which men knew him was that character which is the most distinctive possession of the best American nature; that almost indescribable quality which we call, in general, clearness or truth, and which appears in the physical structure as health, in the moral constitution as honesty, in the mental structure as sagacity, in the region of active life as practicalness.' Striking, indeed, is the resemblance between these two great men—both emerging from the utmost obscurity and poverty by sheer force of character, by the sure, upward gravity of that genius which consists in thoroughness, moral and intellectual, both winning their way by the most legitimate efforts to the highest pinnacle of power. It would seem as if our poet-laureate had prophetically described both when he traces the rise

> 'Of some divinely-gifted man
> Whose life in low estate began,
> And on a simple village green ;
> Who breaks his birth's invidious bar,
> And grasps the skirts of happy chance,
> And breasts the blow of circumstance,
> And grapples with his evil star :
> Who makes by force his merit known,
> And lives to clutch the golden keys,
> To mould a mighty State's decrees,
> And shape the whisper of the throne ;
> And, moving up from high to higher,
> Becomes, on fortune's crowning slope,
> The pillow of a people's hope,
> The centre of a world's desire.'

" Brethren, is our faith staggered by the cruel extinction of lives like these at their very meridian of usefulness ? What is the meaning of these terrible endings which horrify the world, and render high places, though ever so nobly filled, still so perilous a trust, that it may well unnerve the bravest heart ? How comes it to pass that even the life which is richest in promise, which is fullest of self-sacrifice, and fullest of blessing, invites outrage no less than the vilest ? How is it the career on which a nation's hopes are staked can be wrecked in a moment by the infernal machine of a crack-brained fanatic or the bullet of

a disappointed place-hunter? We ask ourselves why these
things are suffered to be. Does He who rules in the affairs
of men see no pre-eminence in the man He endows so
splendidly? Does no special Providence guard those who
do their work in His name and for His glory? It cannot
be that they are less to Him than to us. He cannot cast
His divinest gifts 'as rubbish to the void;' He is ever,
be sure of it, evolving good from seeming ill. As we look
back, do we suppose that even long years of consummate
rule could have achieved more for his country than was
brought about by the tragical end of Abraham Lincoln?
We see how that end put the seal on the great work of his
life; we see that it was the death-blow of slavery, the
eternal consecration of freedom throughout the western
world. One day he stood on the field of Gettysburg,
before the graves of the thousands who had willingly
offered themselves, and he spoke words in which we read
the lesson God taught the world by his own removal.
'We cannot dedicate,' he said, 'we cannot consecrate,
we cannot hallow this ground. The brave men who
struggled here have consecrated it far beyond our power to
add or detract. The world will little note nor long remember what we say here, but it can never forget what they
did here. It is for us, the living, rather to be dedicated to
the unfinished work which they who fought here have thus
far so nobly advanced: it is rather for us to be here
dedicated to the great task before us, that from these
honoured dead we take increased devotion to that cause
for which they gave the last full measure of devotion,
that we here highly resolve that these dead shall not have
died in vain, that this nation, under God, shall have a new
birth of freedom, and that the government of the people
by the people, and for the people, shall not perish from the
earth.' But who among us here doubts that the cause for
which the speaker of these burning words perished is

reinforced now and re-consecrated by a new sacrifice? The American people are the richer this day, in all that can dignify national life, for Garfield's heroic dying. Had our prayers for him been granted, had the shattered frame revived, had the most sanguine hopes raised by his gifts and virtues been realised, it is hard to believe that he could have impressed his greatness more effectually, or done more lasting service to the nation which, with so wide a discernment, placed him at its head. Even now we see the sure beginning of good, which we trust will never pass away. While he has hovered between two worlds, all animosities have been hushed, and all divisions forgotten. The heart of the people has been bowed by that impending sorrow as the heart of one man. Is it no gain, I would ask, that all the world over, the good and law-abiding have been leagued in a closer bond by the discovery that it is not against this form of polity or against that, but against all law, and order, and authority, however constituted, that the anarchical forces of our modern society are banded together? Is it no gain that we Englishmen have been drawn, as we have never been drawn before, to our mourning kinsmen, and have made their trial our own? Is it no consolation in this dark hour that the two great peoples whom God has placed in the fore-front of this world's civilisation are knit together by one more hallowed memory, and by an interchange of sympathy never to be forgotten? And so in all humility we resign ourselves, and we commit our bereaved brethren to Him who has surely heard and answered, though He has not granted, our prayer. 'Shall I live in history?' asked that dying patriot, who will be laid at rest to-morrow. 'Yes,' was the reply, 'and in the hearts of men.' No sweeter promise ever fell upon a ruler's dying ears. He has gone hence, and will be no more seen, but his works follow him. To him may be applied the noble lines of the poet-statesman from his own land—

'Therefore I cannot think thee wholly gone—
The better part of thee is with us still.
Thy soul its hamper clay aside hath thrown,
And only freer wrestles with the ill.
Thou livest in the life of all good things.
What word thou spak'st for freedom shall not die.
Thou sleepest not ; for now thy love hath wings
To soar where hence thy hope could hardly fly.
And often from that other world on this
Some glimpses from great souls gone before may shine
To shed on struggling hearts a clearer bliss,
And clothe the right with lustre more divine.' "

If any one had told General Garfield, at the time of his visit to London, as he sauntered through the Abbey, that a sermon would one day be preached there about him, how incredulous he would have been.

The Rev. Baldwin Brown said, at the close of his address delivered in Brixton Independent Church :—" It was his long and heroic death-struggle, fighting death inch by inch, with a calmness, a courage, and a lofty sense of duty which have never been surpassed—and if, as now appears, he was himself persuaded that there was no hope, the heroism is the more conspicuous—it was this which kept on so full and tender a strain the sympathy of the whole civilised world. In England the feeling was both universal and unprecedented ; and we Englishmen are both glad and proud that such simple, tender, beautiful, and Christian expression has been given to the feeling of the nation by the messages of the Queen. The scene of his removal from Washington to the sea is one of the most pathetic and impressive in history. While two mighty emperors, whose simple fiat could put a million of men into the field in a week, were meeting in a yacht on the ocean, because there was no city in their broad dominions where they could be sure of not being blown up, this man was carried through the great country which he ruled amid a breathless hush of emotion. All the nobleness and all the tenderness of the American nature came out as his maimed and wasted form was borne by. All the traffic of the day was suspended, and the hum of its business was hushed to silence, lest a rude sound should break upon his ear, and give a new chance to death. And when at length the long sad struggle was ended, and he passed to that rest for which, under all his resolute effort, we now know that he had pined so long, there was a dimness in the eye, and a choking in the throat, of millions in America and England, as though a dear friend had been called away.

"The passage of his maimed and emaciated remains to Washington exceeded, if possible, in pathetic impressiveness, his journey to the sea. All that was distinguished in position, in reputation, in influence, in the Union was gathered to attend him. Thousands of citizens silently assembled in all the towns by which the body passed. The lads at Princetown strewed the railway thick with flowers. Along the fields the labourers lined the track. Every head was bowed, the women weeping, their tears raining on the sods, a great hush of silence over the land, broken only by the tolling of the funeral bells; cities, towns, villages, draped in mourning, the poor everywhere foremost in the expression of their grief; North and South vieing with each other in rendering honour to his memory. At Washington 130,000 passed by the bier with hushed and reverent step, to gaze for the last time on his noble but wasted features; and to-morrow, we may be well assured, amidst the most impressive funeral spectacle which the world has witnessed since our own great Duke was borne to his burial, the shattered relics of this kingly man will pass to their rest. Earth still holds more of him than the ashes which the tomb has buried from our sight. His spirit lives on, and will animate his successors. The cause for which his life was given will henceforth be consecrated by the memory of his terrible sufferings, and the service which living he would have rendered to his country, he will render more nobly by his death."

The Rev. W. M. Statham thus concluded his sermon at Hare Court Chapel, Canonbury:—" Our closing prayer is that God may guide his successor; that, with the prayers of a nation for his consecration, and the tears of a nation for his baptism, the President of to-day may take up the weapons of righteousness and truth, which have been held by two wounded, and grasped by two dying Presidents.

"They will not have died in vain if the blood of the President martyrs is the seed of a regenerated State. God bless America! The Court has departed from its old *regime*, and gone into mourning for one who is not of royal lineage. And yet he is! For every true, every pure, every noble, and every faithful man is a king's son; his coronation is on high. A preacher himself, President Garfield lived what he preached, and his last pulpit was the pulpit the age needs most—viz., the market-place, the exchange, and the parliament of the world.

" The cathedral he preached in was older than Jerusalem's Temple or the shrines of the Ptolemies, or the cathedrals of Rome and England; it was beneath the great dome that covers all the world that the President preached, 'Act the citizen as it becometh the Gospel of Christ.'

"And now he sleeps his last sleep, the pall over the countenance. The Egypt of a new civilisation goes down to bury him, a voice deeper than the moan of ocean sweeps o'er the Atlantic, and two nations clasp inseparable hands of grief and love around a martyr's tomb."

In America, preachers and poets united in honouring the memory of Garfield, by showing forth his noble life and many virtues.

The following beautiful poem was written at the time by Oliver Wendell Holmes:—

I.

"Fallen with Autumn's fallen leaf,
   Ere yet his Summer's noon was past,
Our friend, our guide, our trusted chief—
   What words can match a woe so vast?

And whose the chartered claim to speak
   The sacred grief where all have part;
When sorrow saddens every cheek,
   And broods in every aching heart?

Yet nature prompts the burning phrase
   That thrills the hushed and shrouded hall;
The loud lament, the sorrowing praise,
   The silent tear that love lets fall.

In loftiest verse, in lowliest rhyme,
   Shall strive unblamed the minstrel choir;
The singers of the new-born time,
   And trembling age with outworn lyre.

No room for pride, no place for blame—
   We fling our blossoms on the grave;
Pale, scentless, faded, all we claim—
   This only—what we had we gave.

Ah, could the grief of all who mourn
   Blend in one voice its bitter cry;
The wail, to heaven's high arches borne,
   Would echo through the caverned sky.

II.

Oh, happiest land whose peaceful choice
   Fills with a breath its empty throne!
God, speaking through thy people's voice,
   Has made that voice for once His own.

No angry passion shakes the State,
   Whose weary servant seeks for rest;
And who could fear that scowling hate
   Would strike at that unguarded breast?

He stands, unconscious of his doom,
  In manly strength, erect, serene—
Around him summer spreads her bloom ;
  He falls—what horror clothes the scene !

How swift the sudden flash of woe,
  Where all was bright as childhood's dream !
As if from heaven's ethereal bow
  Had leapt the lightning's arrowy gleam.

Blot the foul deed from history's page,
  Let not the all-betraying sun
Blush for the day that stains an age,
  When murder's blackest wreath was won.

III.

Pale on his couch the sufferer lies,
  The weary battle-ground of pain ;
Love tends his pillow, science tries
  Her every art, alas ! in vain.

The strife endures, how long ? how long !
  Life, death, seem balanced in the scale,
While round his bed a viewless throng
  Awaits each morrow's changing tale.

In realms the desert ocean parts,
  What myriads watch with tear-filled eyes ;
His pulse-beats echoing in their hearts,
  His breathings counted in their sighs !

Slowly the stores of life are spent,
  Yet hope still battles with despair ;
Will Heaven not yield when knees are bent ?
  Answer, oh, Thou that hearest prayer !

But silent is the brazen sky—
  Or sweeps the meteor's threat'ning train—
Unswerving Nature's mute reply,
  Bound in her adamantine chain.

Not ours the verdict to decide
  Whom death shall claim or skill shall save ;
The hero's life though Heaven denied,
  It gave our land a martyr's grave.

> Nor count the teachings vainly sent,
>   How human hearts their griefs may share;
> The lesson woman's love has lent—
>   What hope may do, what faith can bear!
>
> Farewell! the leaf-strewn earth enfolds
>   Our stay, our pride, our hopes, our fears,
> And Autumn's golden sun beholds
>   A nation bowed, a world in tears."

The following is from a poem by James Russell Lowell—

> "I cannot think he wished so soon to die,
> With all his senses full of eager heat,
> And rosy years, that stood expectant by,
> To buckle the winged sandals on their feet.
>
> . . . .
>
> The ship erect is prone; for ever stilled
> The winning tongue; the forehead's high-piled heap,
> A cairn which every science helped to build,
> Unvalued will its golden secrets keep.
> He knows at last if life or death be best:
> Wherever he be flown; whatever vest
> The being hath put on, which lately here
> So many-friended was, so full of cheer
> To make men feel the seeker's noble zest.
> We have not lost him all; he is not gone
> To the dumb herd of them that wholly die;
> The beauty of his better self lives on
> In minds he touched with fire, in many an eye
> He trained to truth's exact severity:
> He was a teacher: why be grieved for him
> Whose loving word still stimulates the air!
> In endless file shall loving scholars come
> The glow of his transmitted touch to share,
> And trace his features with an eye less dim
> Than ours, whose sense familiar wont makes dumb."

Among the Memorial Services held was one in the Brooklyn Tabernacle. Thousands of persons were unable to get in. Dr. Talmage took his text from Judges xvi.

30: "So the dead which he slew at his death were more than they which he slew in his life." "It sometimes occurs," said Dr. Talmage, "that after an industrious, and useful, and eminent life, in the closing hour a man will achieve more good than in all the years that preceded. My text has a very graphic illustration in the overshadowing event of this hour. President Garfield, during his active life, was the enemy of sin, the enemy of sectionalism, the enemy of everything small-hearted and depraved and impure, and he gave many a crushing blow against these moral and political Philistines; but in his dying hours he made the grandest achievement. The eleven weeks of his dying were mightier than the half-century of his living. My object this morning is for inspiration and comfort, to show that our President's expiration has done more good than a prolonged administration possibly could have accomplished. Had he died one month before he was shot down by the assassin, he would not have had his administration fairly launched. Had he died six months from now, by that time his advanced policy of reform would have destroyed the friendship of many of his followers. Had he died many years from now, he would have been out of office and in the decline of life. There was no time in the last fifty years when his death-bed could have been so effective, and there could have been no time in the fifty years to come when his death-bed could have been so overwhelmingly impressive. We talk a great deal about the faith of the Christian, and the courage of the Christian, and the hope of the Christian; but all the sermons preached in the past twenty years upon that subject put together would not be so impressive as the magnificent demeanour of our dying Chief Magistrate.

"President Garfield's death, more than a prolonged administration, has consummated good feeling between the North and the South. It is not shaking hands over a bloody chasm, according to the rhetoric of campaign documents, but it is shaking hands across and over a palpitating heart, large enough to take in both sections. He, in his dying moment, took the hand of the North and the hand of the South, and joined them ; and, with a pathos that can never be forgotten, practically said, 'Be brothers.' Ah, my friends, he has done in his death what he could not have done in all his life. Where are the flags at half-mast to-day ? At New Orleans and Boston, at Chicago and Charlestown. The bulletins of his health were as anxiously watched on the south side of Mason and Dixon's line as on the north side. Ever and anon we thought we had our own difficulties settled, and our old grudges adjusted, but the quarrel broke out in some new place. It seems now that the requiem of to-day must for ever drown out all sectional prejudices. After what we have seen during the last eleven weeks, the people of the South must be welcomed in all our Northern homes, as we of the North would be welcome in all the Southern homes. If, at any future time, some one should want to kindle anew the fires of hatred, he would find but little fuel, and no sulphureous match. South Carolina and Massachusetts, stand up and be married! Alabama and New York, stand up and join hands in betrothal! Georgia and Ohio, stand up while I pronounce you one! 'And whom God hath joined together, let no man put asunder.' No living man could have accomplished this."

Dr. Talmage went on to say, that President Garfield's death accomplished more than his life, in setting forth the truth, that when our time comes to go, the most energetic and skilful opposition cannot hinder the event; and then demanded, "Who knows but that God may make this national trouble the purification of all the people?"

"Poor Mrs. Garfield! I never read anything more pathetic in my life than what I saw in the newspapers on Friday, when they said she had gone to the White House to gather up the private property of the family, to have it taken to her home in Ohio. Can you imagine any greater torture than for her to go through those rooms in the White House, associated with her husband's kindness, and her husband's anxieties, and her husband's sufferings? You see she had, with her womanly arms, fought on his side all the way up the steep of life. She had helped him in severe economies when they were very poor ; and with her own needle she had clothed her household, and with her own hands she had made them bread. In the dark days, when slanderous assault frowned upon him, she never forsook him. They had fought the battle of life, and gained the day, and they were seated side by side at the tip-top to enjoy the victory. Then the blow came. What a reversal of fortune! From what midnoon to what midnight! Some say it will kill her. I do not believe it. The same God who has helped her on until now will help her through. The mighty God who protected James A. Garfield at Chickamauga, and in the fiery hell of many battles, will, when these members of the broken family circle come together next week, in their little home at Mentor, protect and comfort the wife, the children, and the aged mother. I invoke the grace of high heaven on those seven broken hearts.

"Ascend, thou disenthralled spirit! Ascend, and take thy place among those who have come up out of great tribulation, and had their robes washed and made white in the blood of the Lamb! This Sampson of political power, this giant of moral strength, had, in other days, like the man in the text, slain the lion of wrathful opposition, and had carried off the gates of wrong from their rusty hinges; but the peroration of his life was mightier than all that preceded. 'And so the dead which he slew at his death were more than they which he slew in his life.' While I try to comfort you to-day, there is a lesson that comes sounding from the tramp of the senatorial pall-bearers, and rolling out from the roaring wheels of the draped rail-train flying westward, and coming up from the open grave that awaits our dead President—'Put not your trust in princes, nor in the son of man, in whom there is no help. His breath goeth forth; in that very day his thoughts perish. Happy is he that hath the God of Jacob for his help.' Fare thee well, departed chieftain! Fare thee well!"

As Dr. Talmage retired from the verge of the platform, Professor Morgan played "The Dead March in Saul," and the vast assemblage, every man and woman of which was attired in plain black, slowly separated.

CHAPTER XVII.

GOOD OUT OF EVIL.

"Sun of our life, Thy quickening ray
    Sheds on our path the glow of day;
Star of our hope, Thy softened light
    Cheers the long watches of our night.

Grant us Thy truths to make us free,
    And kindling hearts will burn for Thee,
Till all Thy living altars claim
    One holy light, one heavenly flame."
              —OLIVER WENDELL HOLMES.

THE greatest sympathy was felt with the American people in all parts of the world, and there were more than a few who believed that the event of the President's death would prove exceedingly disastrous to the country. But the trouble was not without its amelioration. It must always be felt that James Garfield was never greater in his life than he was in his death. Had he remained in office until the close of the term, and died as ordinary men die, all the world would not have come, in thought, to watch by his bedside, or shed tears at his grave. It was because he proved himself so noble, so patient, so full of magnanimity, that people began to make inquiries respecting him, and to learn that his life as well as his death was worthy of study. He had been a teacher always; but the company of his scholars has grown from tens to hundreds of thousands since the shot of the assassin struck him down. His words had reached the ears of a few before; they live in the hearts of the many now. Few, comparatively, had come within the circle of his influence, until it seemed that in his weakness and death he could have no more influence to exert; and then a multitude too great to be numbered began to examine their lives by his, and to let him lead them toward higher places than before they had ever attempted to gain.

He might have said, as Joseph did to his brethren, "As for you, ye thought evil against me; but God meant it unto good, to bring to pass as it is this day, to save much people alive."

On the morning when his death was reported, two young men met for a few moments in the streets of New York, and the following conversation took place:—

"Do you sail for England to-day?"

"Yes; but I hope to be back again in two years. I will never live long out of America, for Garfield's sake."

"Ah, poor Garfield; he has succumbed at last. I am very sorry; for he was a fine man. You knew him, did you not?"

"Yes, I knew him a little. I was a Hiram boy; and I could understand what sort of men Garfield wanted for America. I am far enough from his ideal or my own wish; but I mean to be all the better because I have been acquainted with James Garfield."

"I have heard others say the same. He had a wonderful power for good over young men. We shall see, if we live long enough, other Hiram students in the White House!"

"It is quite possible; but whether it be so or not, we shall see thousands of men trying to live as grandly as he did. And I think we shall see, what I am sure he would have been glad to see, some of the abuses of our political system come to an end. The blood of Garfield, the martyred President, will purchase priceless boons for the country that he loved."

And the two men parted in the faith that it would be so.

Many people feared that Garfield's death would be the precursor of a time of lawlessness and difficulty. Such, however, was not the case. It seemed that every one remembered and acted upon the spirit of Garfield himself in regard to the assassination of President Lincoln. The nation kept itself quiet by remembering that "God reigns, and the Government at Washington still lives."

As we have already seen, the Americans, in their trouble, looked at the religious aspect of the event. There was no city that had not its commemorative meetings; and at each of them the thoughts of the people were led to Him who overrules all events. Opportunity was given to spend the excitement in prayer, as Dr. Lothrop did in Boston, in the following words:—

"Oh, help us to mingle gratitude with our thoughts as we gather here this morning, at the call and on behalf of our city, to commemorate the late President of these United States, summoned by Thee from his high place on earth to the footstool of Thy throne in heaven; and may our hearts become more and more grateful for that life, that character, that noble example, that wonderful career.

"We thank Thee, O God, that through Thy providence and his own energy and noble purpose, the youth triumphed over all the obstacles of a lowly lot, and pinching poverty, and limited opportunities; that he succeeded in the acquisition of knowledge, and the development of talents, and the formation of character, so that he became a scholar and teacher wise, and skilful, and faithful in all the highest objects of education. We thank Thee that when the exigency of the country demanded, the scholar and teacher passed into the soldier, and carried into the arena of war courage, bravery, skill, a spirit of self-sacrifice, a power of endurance, an energy of perseverance, and an aptitude and sagacity in military affairs, that showed him to be alike competent to command, and worthy to be trusted and obeyed. We thank Thee that when he was called from the camp to the capitol, from the military to the civil service of the country, he exhibited in the halls of legislation a breadth and wisdom of statesmanship, a logic and eloquence of utterance, a large and comprehensive policy, that indicated the force of his character and his principles, and secured to him respect, confidence, and trust.

"We thank Thee, O God, that when through these qualities and Thy providence, and the will of the people, he was called to the highest honour the nation could confer, and to the grandest trust it could confide to his keeping, he walked forward to that position with mingled dignity, modesty, and meekness; and that during the brief time he was permitted to discharge the duties of his office, he did so with a broad, comprehensive, and patriotic integrity of purpose. And above all, O God, we thank Thee, that when suddenly struck down by the hand of wanton folly and malignity, and left to languish, week after week, in pain and suffering, and alternate hope and apprehension, with weeping friends, an anxious nation, and an admiring world at his bedside—during all this period no murmur or complaint, no bitter thought, no harsh word, nothing unworthy of a noble soul, escaped from his lips, was written upon his countenance, or displayed in his manner; but all was calm and serene cheerfulness, submission, and trust in Thee, the exhibition of a Christian temper, and the mighty power of a Christian faith.

"And now, O God, that the end has come, amid scenes

and circumstances that make it glorious to him, but a loss and unhappiness to ourselves, we pray that Thou wouldst help us to gather up the lessons of his life, and apply them to our own characters and consciences.

"Oh, our Father, while we pray that his name, his fame, and his memory, while they abide a rich inheritance and holy consolation in the hearts of his family—the wife, and mother, and children, whom we commend to the consolation of Thy Spirit, and the guardianship of Thy love—we pray that they may dwell in the hearts of this people, that they may lie close to the consciences of this nation, and that to us, and to generations that come after us, they may ever be a guide, and inspiration, and incentive to love what is good, to do what is right, and to strive for all things noble and pure.

"Oh, our Father, sanctify unto this country this appointment of Thy providence. Grant that the life, the character, the services, and the death of our lamented President may exert a holy influence, and may serve to bind the hearts of all our people, in all quarters of this great Republic, closer together in the bonds of patriotic love and duty, so that our union may be cemented in tender ties and sympathies; so that the peace, the prosperity, the glory, the progress of this nation may endure through long generations.

"Bless all the peoples and nations of the world—this great race of humanity struggling and striving here upon earth. Help each and all to subdue the evil in the individual heart, that thus an end may come to injustice and wrong. Teach the violent, in all lands and in all classes, that the wrath of man worketh not the righteousness of God. Oh, our Father, bring all the customs, habits, institutions, all the thought and action of mankind, into a nearer and closer harmony with the spirit, the character, the teachings of Him, who coming to bear witness to Thy truth, and to proclaim Thy love unto the world, bowed His head in a grand self-sacrifice on that cross from which He has shed pardon and peace, heavenly benedictions, and holy influences upon the world. In His name we offer our prayers, beseeching Thee to forgive our sins, and to answer our prayers, and as His disciples, we ascribe unto Thee the glory, the dominion, and the praise for ever. Amen."

In the same spirit of devotion which breathed in the prayer, Boston showed no less than other cities, and perhaps not more than they, that the American people were steadily determined to carry on their own affairs in manliness and fidelity. The best among them, if not the whole nation, hoped that good might come out of evil, and the States be really strengthened and purified by the fires of affliction through which they had passed. Life is earnest, and there is little time in which to shed tears and indulge either in personal or in national grief. And when the time of mourning had passed away, the people betook themselves to the great healer—Work!

The American nation is made noble by its industry, its faith, and its hope; for it possesses all three to a remarkable degree. The Rev. Robert Collyer of Chicago shows, in a striking passage of one of his sermons, how the last two qualifications can help a man:—" Here is Cyrus Field conceiving the idea of binding the Atlantic with a cord—of making that awful crystal dome a whispering gallery between two worlds—of fulfilling afresh, in these last times, the old prophecy, that 'as the lightning cometh out of the East, and shineth even unto the West, so also shall the coming of the Son of Man be.' In carrying out his idea, the man has two servants to help him—the faith that it can be done, and the hope that he shall do it. With these aids he goes to work. Faith steadies him; hope inspires him. Faith works; hope flies. Faith deliberates; hope anticipates. Faith lets the cable go, and it breaks, and is lost. 'Nay, not lost,' cries hope, and fishes it up again. If hope had struck work in Cyrus Field, and faith alone had remained, we should not this day have had this *nexus* formed of his manhood, by which the world will be born again to a new life. But there, through the long day the noble sisters stood —faith in Ireland, hope in Newfoundland ; faith in the Old World, hope in the New. Faith threw the cord, hope caught it. And 'I saw a great angel stand with one foot on the sea, and another on the land ; and he sware by Him that liveth, that *time shall be no more.*' "

Neither industry, nor faith, nor hope had been at any time stronger in the hearts of the American people than when they betook themselves to the new administration.

There was no difficulty as to the person who was to step into the vacant place. The Vice-President was ready ; and, in accordance with custom, he took the oath of office on the day following the death of General Garfield. Mr. Arthur was the fourth Vice-President to succeed to the higher office. His address was a short one, and was delivered and listened to with emotion :—

"For the fourth time in the history of the Republic its Chief Magistrate has been removed by death. All hearts are filled with grief and horror at the hideous crime which has darkened our land, and the memory of the murdered President, his protracted sufferings, his unyielding fortitude, the example and achievements of his life, and the pathos of his death, will for ever illumine the pages of our history. For the fourth time the officer elected by the people and ordained by the Constitution to fill a vacancy so created is called to assume the Executive chair. The wisdom of our fathers, foreseeing even the most dire possibilities, made sure that the Government should never be imperilled because of the uncertainty of human life. Men may die, but the fabric of our free institutions remains unshaken. No higher or more assuring proof could exist of the strength and permanence of popular government than the fact that, though the chosen of the people be struck down, his constitutional successor is peacefully installed without shock or strain, except the sorrow which mourns the bereavement. All the noble aspirations of my lamented predecessor which found expression in his life, the measures devised and suggested during his brief administration to correct abuses and enforce economy, to advance prosperity and promote the general welfare, to ensure domestic security and maintain friendly and honourable relations with the nations of the earth, will be garnered in the hearts of the people, and it will be my earnest endeavour to profit, and to see that the nation shall profit, by his example and experience. Prosperity blesses our country; our fiscal policy as fixed by law is well grounded and generally approved; no threatening issue mars our foreign intercourse, and the wisdom, integrity, and thrift of our people may be trusted to continue undisturbed the present assured career of peace, tranquillity, and welfare. The gloom and anxiety which have enshrouded the country must make repose especially welcome now. No demand for speedy legislation has been heard; no adequate occasion is apparent for an unusual session of Congress. The Constitution defines the functions and powers of the Executive as clearly as those of either of the other two departments of the Government, and we must answer for the just exercise of the discretion it permits and the performance of the duties it imposes. Summoned to these high duties and responsibilities, and profoundly conscious of their magnitude and gravity, I assume the trust imposed by the Constitution, relying for aid on Divine guidance and the virtue, patriotism, and intelligence of the American people."

President Arthur entered very gravely into the duties of the office, and soon proved himself sagacious and wise. He did not make any immediate changes in the Cabinet, but begged the members of the ministry to retain their offices, which they did until the end of the year, when some of them resigned.

President Arthur had only been a month in the White House when a very interesting ceremony took place at Yorktown. It was the celebration of the hundredth anniversary of the surrender of Cornwallis to the army of the United States and France. The ceremonies were very elaborate, and lasted three days. Delegates from France and Germany attended to represent those countries; but these guests were not present at the whole of the festivities on account of a quarrel about precedence which occurred between them. The French objected to the position which the German flag occupied on the President's boat. The French flag was generally placed at the fore, the German at the mizen, and the American at the main. This was the case in regard to all the boats except that belonging to the President; but as that had only two masts, the German and French colours were there displayed together. This, considering all that had happened between the two nations, gave considerable offence to the French delegates, who threatened to withdraw unless the German flag came down. Mr. Secretary Blaine had to exercise some diplomatic skill, and there was much negotiation before the affair was amicably settled and the French were satisfied.

. . . .

As the rejoicings in connection with the centenary were being brought to a close a very interesting incident occurred, which proved that the most kindly feelings exist at the present time between the United States and Great Britain, feelings which Garfield's death has quickened into new life. The British flag was run up to the fore of the *Trenton*, the United States flag-ship, and was saluted by the land and naval forces of the United States. All the vessels in the harbour hoisted the British colours, and then Mr. Secretary Blaine read the following order of President Arthur :—

"In recognition of the friendly relations so long and so happily subsisting between Great Britain and the United States, in trust and confidence of peace and good-will between the two countries for all centuries to come, and especially as a mark of profound respect entertained by the American people for the illustrious sovereign and gracious lady who sits upon the British throne, it is hereby ordered that at the close of these ceremonies, commemorative of the valour and success of our forefathers in their patriotic struggle for independence, the British flag shall be saluted by the forces of the army and navy of the United States now at Yorktown, and the Secretary of War and the Secretary of the Navy will give orders accordingly."

It may be questioned if any part of the whole proceedings gave greater satisfaction to the American people than this graceful act of international courtesy. When the whole fleet fired a salute, which was answered by the guns from the batteries and camps on the shore, the people showed their approval by many demonstrations of delight and satisfaction. Loud cheers were raised, and hurrahs shouted by thousands of throats. Bands played the National Anthem, and everything was done to express and confirm all good feeling between the two nations.

"This is the American method of thanking the Queen for her messages of sympathy in reference to General Garfield," said one who stood near.

"That is so," was the response. "We are a great nation, and can appreciate greatness. Queen Victoria is a humane and Christian woman, as well as an illustrious sovereign, and we love her as much as her own people do."

"Mrs. Garfield was exceedingly gratified and comforted by the Queen's wreath and message sent to her."

"Oh, yes, she was; and there was something very touching and pathetic about the incident, too. One widow sends a kindly message to another widow. It was very good of Her Majesty, and the American people are not likely to forget it."

"It was easy to read between the lines of that telegram. It seemed to say, 'I know what the trouble is, for I have had it to bear myself, and I can feel for you. The pomp and fuss, and national signs of mourning, cannot comfort the lonely heart; only God can do that, and I pray that He will!' Queen Victoria's message meant all this, and more."

"Yes, I guess it did. She is a good woman, and I hope she will live long, and be very prosperous and happy. She has certainly, by her womanly kindness to us in our trouble, done more than a little to cement the bond of union between England and America."

"May the bond never be broken, and God save the Queen!"

"And may England and America always be friends, and thus good come out of evil."

CHAPTER XVIII.

THE END OF THE WICKED.

"Who slays a good man does a double crime,
His name shall be disgraced till end of time."

THE behaviour of murderers is never a pleasant subject of contemplation; but in the case of the assassinator of President Garfield so much occurred, that the life of one can scarcely be written without some reference to the other. From the first it was evident that the man wished to pose before the public as a political fanatic; and although it was certain that he was a murderer, he did not appear to expect a murderer's fate. His behaviour immediately after the murder is thus described:—

The excitement and indignation became so great among the crowds that were rapidly assembling in all parts of the city, that the authorities grew apprehensive for the safety of the prisoner, and in order that any attempt at lynching might be frustrated, is was determined to remove him to the district jail, and General Sherman was applied to for the assistance of the military in case of an emergency

General Sherman, after consulting Secretary Lincoln, ordered out three companies of United States artillery from the arsenal, one company being mounted as cavalry and two serving as infantry. One mounted and one foot company were stationed about the White House and grounds, and one was stationed at the jail. The district militia were also ordered to hold themselves in readiness, and remained under arms at their armouries all day. Guiteau was taken to jail in a carriage by Lieutenants Austin and Eckloff, and Detective McElfresh, of the district police. The last-named officer reports the following conversation with the prisoner while being conducted to jail: "I asked him, Where are you from?"

"I am a native-born American. Born in Chicago, and am a lawyer and a theologian."

"Why did you do this?"

"I did it to save the Republican party."

"What are your politics?"

"I am a Stalwart among the Stalwarts. With Garfield out of the way, we can carry all the Northern States, and with him in the way, we can't carry a single one."

Upon learning that McElfresh was a detective, Guiteau said, "You stick to me, and have me put in the third storey front at the gaol. General Sherman is coming down to take charge. Arthur and all those men are my friends, and I'll have you made chief of police. When you go back to the depôt, you will find that I have left two bundles of papers at the news-stand, which will explain all."

"Is there anybody else with you in this matter?"

"Not a living soul. I have contemplated the thing for the last six weeks, and would have shot him when he went away with Mrs. Garfield, but I looked at her, and she seemed so bad that I changed my mind."

On reaching the gaol, the officers of the institution did not seem to know anything about the assassination, and when taken inside, Mr. Russ, the deputy-warden, said, "This man has been here before."

The detective then asked Guiteau, "Have you ever been here before?"

He replied, "No, sir."

"Well, the deputy-warden seems to identify you."

"Yes; I was down here last Saturday morning, and wanted them to let me look through, and they told me that I couldn't, but to come on Monday."

"What was your object in looking through?"

"I wanted to see what sort of quarters I would have to occupy."

Continuing, the detective said, "I then searched him, and when I pulled off his shoes, he said, 'Give me my shoes; I will catch cold on this stone pavement.' I told him he couldn't have them, and then he said, 'Give me a pair of pumps, then.'"

The district gaol, a large brown stone structure, situated at the eastern extremity of the city, was visited by an Associated Press reporter for the purpose of obtaining an interview with Charles Guiteau, the assassin of President Garfield. The officers refused admittance to the building, stating that they were acting under instructions from Attorney-General MacVeagh, the purport of which were that no one should be allowed to see the prisoner. At first, indeed, the officers emphatically denied that the man had been conveyed to the gaol, fearing, it appears, that should the fact be made known that he was there, the building would be attacked by a mob. Information had reached them that such a movement was contemplated. The statement that the assassin's name is Guiteau is verified by the officer in charge of the gaol. The prisoner arrived, and was placed in a cell about half-past ten o'clock, just one hour after the shooting occurred. He gave his name as Charles Guiteau of Chicago. In appearance he is about thirty years of age, and is supposed to be of French descent. His height is about five feet five inches. He has a sandy complexion, and is slight, weighing not more than a hundred and twenty-five pounds. He wears a moustache and light chin-whiskers; and his sunken cheeks and eyes, far apart from each other, give him a sullen, or as the officers described it, a "loony" appearance. The officer in question gave it as his opinion that Guiteau is a Chicago Communist, and stated that he has noticed it to be a peculiarity of nearly all murderers that their eyes are far apart; and Guiteau, he said, proves no exception to the rule. When the prisoner arrived at the gaol, he was neatly attired in a suit of blue, and wore a drab hat, pulled down over his eyes, giving him the appearance of an ugly character. It may be worthy of note that two or three weeks ago Guiteau went to the gaol for the purpose of visiting it, but was refused admittance, on the ground that it was not "visitors' day." He at that time mentioned his name as Guiteau, and said that he came from Chicago. When brought to the gaol to-day, he was admitted by the officer who had previously refused to allow him to enter, and a mutual recognition took place, Guiteau saying, "You are the man who would not let me go through the gaol some time ago." The only other remark he made before being put in his cell was, that General Sherman would arrive at the gaol soon. The two gaolers who are guarding his cell state that they have seen him around the gaol several times recently, and that on one occasion he appeared to be under the influence of liquor. On one of his visits subsequent to the one mentioned, these officers say that Guiteau succeeded in reaching the rotunda of the building, where he was noticed examining the scaffold from which the Hirth murderers were hanged. Pursuant to his order from the Attorney-General, the officer in charge of the gaol declined to give any further information, nor would he state in what cell the prisoner was confined. This officer was an attendant at the old city gaol at the time of the assassination of President Lincoln.

Proceedings were commenced within a few days of the death of the President to bring a charge of murder against Guiteau. There followed a delay which, even to English minds, was almost inexplicable, and people read the newspaper accounts of the prolonged trial with weariness and impatience. Every facility was offered for the prisoner to prove that he was not guilty; and among the other pleas raised by his counsel was one of insanity. He himself published in one of the public journals a long statement of facts, and an explanation of his motives.

He said, among other things—"My conception of the idea of removing the President was this:—Mr. Conkling resigned on Monday, 16th May 1881. On the following Wednesday I was in bed. I think I retired about eight o'clock. I felt depressed and perplexed on account of the political situation, and I retired much earlier than usual. I felt wearied in mind and body, and I was in my bed about nine o'clock, and I was thinking over the political situation, and the idea flashed through my brain that if the President was out of the way everything would go better."

He proceeded to give an account of his preparation for the crime, and said he was under a pressure that he could not resist.

"I shot the President without malice or murderous intent. I deny any legal liability in this case. In order to constitute the crime of murder two elements must co-exist. First, an actual homicide; second, malice—malice in law or malice in fact. The law presumes malice from the fact of the homicide; the degree of malice depends upon the condition of the man's mind at the time of the homicide. If two men quarrel, and one shoots the other in heat or passion, the law says that is manslaughter. The remoteness of the shooting from the moment of its conception fastens the degree of the malice. The further you go from the conception to the shooting, the greater the malice, because the law says that in shooting a man a few hours or a few days after the conception, the mind has a chance to cool, and therefore the act is deliberate. Malice in fact depends upon the circumstances attending the homicide—malice in law is liquidated in this case by the facts and circumstances, as set forth in these pages, attending the removal of the President. I had none but the best of feelings, personally, towards the President. I always thought of him and spoke of him as General Garfield."

As the trial went on, the man continually interrupted the proceedings with frivolous objections and sensational exhibitions. At one time he expressed himself in the following terms:—"I propose to have all the facts bearing on this case to go to the court and the jury; and to do this I have been forced to interrupt counsel and witnesses who were mistaken as to supposed facts. I meant no discourtesy to them, or to anyone. Any fact in my career bearing on the question who fired that shot—the Deity or myself—is of vital importance in this case, and I propose that it go to the jury. Hence any personal, political, and theological record may be developed. I am glad that your honour and the opposing counsel are disposed to give an historical review of my life, and I ask the press and the public to do likewise. All I want is absolute justice, and I shall not permit any crooked work. I have an idea my counsel want crooked work. They are often mistaken in supposed facts, and I shall have to correct them. Last spring certain newspapers in New York and Washington were bitterly denouncing the President for breaking up the Republican party by improper appointments. I would like those newspapers to reprint those editorials now, and see how they would look and sound. In attempting to remove the President, I only did what the papers said ought to be done. Since the 2nd of

July they have been deifying the President, and denouncing me for doing the very thing they said ought to be done. I want the newspapers and the doctors who actually killed the President to share with me the odium of his death. I never would have shot him of my own volition, notwithstanding those newspapers, if I had not been commissioned by the Deity to do the deed. But this fact does not relieve the newspapers from the supposed disgrace of the President's removal. If he had been properly treated, he would have been alive to-day. It has been published that I am in fear of death. It is false. I have always been a religious man, and an active worker for God. Some people think that I am a murderer, but the Lord does not, for He inspired the act, as in the case of Abraham, and a score of other cases in the Bible."

The impertinence, assurance, and wickedness of these words are simply abominable.

It was not until the end of January 1882 that the weary trial came to an end. The prisoner's interruptions had been so incessant and persistent, that the judge, who had allowed him to occupy a seat by his counsel, remanded him to the dock; but even there his behaviour was no better. At length, on the 25th of January, Judge Cox delivered his charge to the jury, a masterpiece of lucidity, and exhaustive examination of facts. It concluded thus :—

" From the materials presented to you, two pictures have been drawn to you by counsel. The one represents a youth of more than average mental endowments, surrounded by certain immoral influences at the time his character was being developed; commencing life without resources, but developing a vicious sharpness and cunning; conceiving enterprises of great pith and moment, that indicated unusual forecast, although beyond his resources ; consumed all the time by unsated egotism, and a craving for notoriety ; violent in temper, selfish, immoral, and dishonest; leading a life of hypocrisy, swindling, and fraud; and finally, as a culmination of his depraved career, working himself into the resolution of startling the world with a crime which would secure him a bad eminence. The other represents a youth, born, as it were, under malign influences, the child of a diseased mother, of a father subject to insane delusions, reared in retirement, and imbued with fanatical religious views; subsequently his mind filled with fanatical theories; launched on the world with no guidance save his own impulses; evincing an incapacity for any continuous employment; changing from one pursuit to another—now a lawyer, now a religionist, now a politician—unsuccessful in all; full of wild impracticable schemes, for which he had neither resources nor ability; subject to delusions, his mind incoherent and incompetent of reasoning coherently on any subject; with an intellect so weak, and a temper so impressionable, that he became deranged, and was therefore impelled to the commission of a crime, the seriousness of which he could not understand. It is for you, gentlemen, to determine which of the portraits is the true one.

"And now, gentlemen, to sum up all I have said to you. If you find from the whole evidence that at the time of the commission of the homicide the prisoner was labouring under such a defect of his reason that he was incapable of understanding what he was doing, or of seeing that it was a wrong thing to do—as, for example, if he were under the insane delusion that the Almighty had commanded him to do the act—then he was not in a responsible condition of mind, but was an object of compassion, and should now be acquitted. If, on the other hand, you find that he was under no insane delusion, but had the possession of his faculties, and had power to know that his act was wrong; and if of his own free will he deliberately conceived the idea, and executed the homicide, then, whether his motive were personal vindictiveness, political animosity, a desire to revenge supposed political wrongs, or a morbid desire for notoriety; or, if you are unable to discover any motive at all, the act is simply murder, and it is your duty to find a verdict of guilty as indicted. Or, if you find that the prisoner is not guilty by reason of insanity, it is your duty to say so. You will now retire to your room and consider your verdict."

They did so, and in less than an hour returned into court, and in answer to the customary questions as to the verdict, answered, "Guilty." A request was then made to have the jury polled; and each man, on his name being called, pronounced the ominous word, "Guilty." The prisoner became greatly excited, and when the last man had delivered his verdict, he shrieked, "My blood will be on the heads of that jury. Don't you forget it."

It was intimated that an effort would be made to move for a new trial; and, in the meantime, Guiteau called out, in tones of desperation, "God will avenge this outrage."

Eventually a motion for a new trial was overruled, and the prisoner was sentenced to be hanged on the 30th of June 1882. This was accordingly done, and gave all the world satisfaction; for everyone felt that the deed of which he had been guilty was so dastardly and without excuse, that such a villain ought not to be allowed to remain upon the earth.

Still greater satisfaction, however, was felt in regard to another circumstance—namely, that a subscription was started in New York for the benefit of the bereaved family of General Garfield. Mrs. Garfield enjoys the interest during her life; and at her death the principal is to be divided among her children.

CHAPTER XIX.

COMRADES.

> "In the world's great field of battle,
> In the bivouac of life,
> Be not like dumb driven cattle,
> Be a hero in the strife."

THE two men whose lives we have thus pourtrayed, and the circumstances of whose births, careers, and deaths were so strangely similar, were in many respects brothers in their hearts and lives. They had both risen from the lowliest positions to the highest, by sheer force of will, to fight with adversity and win the victories of righteousness. They thought alike, and acted in harmony, and strove for the same ends in regard to all the great and important questions of the age. They were both great men, worthy to follow in the footsteps of the immortal Washington, and to finish the labours which were commenced by him. They were both violently attacked by their political opponents—and they both, if not in life, then in death, proved that "when a man's ways please the Lord He maketh even his enemies to be at peace with him."

Neither men loved war; both went into it from a sense

of right, and both faithfully obeyed the voice of duty, to follow wherever it should lead. It was during the war that the two men were brought into contact; and President Lincoln had no more loyal and hearty supporter than the man who was destined to afterwards fill his place and share his fate. In the midst of the trials that opposed Lincoln, and made his very life a burden to him, he knew that he could rely implicitly upon Garfield to be under all circumstances his most faithful ally.

And this was, not because of Garfield's interest to side with the President; but the fact that the two men had really so much in common.

We can imagine, for instance, with what pleasure and satisfaction the member of the Disciples' Church would read the following order, issued during the war by Lincoln to the soldiers and sailors of the Union :—

"The President, Commander-in-Chief of the Army and Navy, desires and enjoins the orderly observance of the Sabbath by the officers and men in the military and naval service. The importance for man and beast of the prescribed weekly rest; the sacred rights of Christian soldiers and sailors, a becoming deference to the best sentiment of a Christian people, and a due regard for the Divine will, demand that Sunday labour in the army and navy be reduced to the measure of strict necessity.

"The discipline and character of the national forces should not suffer, nor the cause they defend be imperilled by the profanation of the day, or name of the Most High. 'At this time of public distress,' adopting the words of Washington in 1776, 'men may find enough to do in the service of God and their country without abandoning themselves to vice and immorality.' The first general order issued by the father of his country, after the Declaration of Independence, indicates the spirit in which our institutions were founded, and should ever be defended. 'The general hopes and trusts that every officer and man will endeavour to live and act as becomes a Christian soldier defending the dearest rights and liberties of his country.'"

This was precisely the spirit in which both Lincoln and Garfield wished the war to be carried on. The consequences of the war itself were terrible enough without any added miseries or crimes. And yet it was one that called forth the patriotism of all the best men in the States.

There were not wanting descriptions of the war which told splendid tales of the heroism of the men and the officers who fought. But "our own correspondents" gave no more moving picture than one which was given in a sermon by the Rev. Robert Collyer of Chicago—delivered on the 2nd of March 1862, after a visit which he made to the battle-field at Fort Donelson:—"It was natural," said he, "when the news flashed into our city, that the great battle, as fierce for the number engaged in it, and as protracted as Waterloo, was turned into a transcendent victory; and when bells were ringing, banners waving, men shaking hands everywhere, and breaking into a laughter that ended in tears, and into tears that ended in laughter—that we should all remember that this victory had been won at a terrible price; and that those bells, so jubilant to us, would be remembered by many a wife as the knell that told her she was a widow, by Rachels weeping for their children, and by desolate Davids uttering the old bitter cry, 'Would to God I had died for thee, my son, my son.'

"And it was natural, too, that we should remember, that there, on that battle-field, must be vast numbers, friends and foes alike, suffering great agonies, which we could do some small thing to mitigate, if we could only get there with such medicines and surgery, refreshment and sympathy, as God had poured into the bosom of our great city.

"One incident I remember as we were detained at Cairo,

that gave me a sense of how curiously the laughter and tears of our lives are blended. I came across a group of men gathered around a soldier wounded in the head. Nothing would satisfy them but to see the hurt; and the man, with perfect good nature, removed the bandage. It was a bullet-wound very near the centre of the forehead, and the man declared the ball had flattened and fallen off. 'But,' said a simple man, eagerly, 'why didn't the ball go into your head?' 'Sir,' said the soldier proudly 'my head is too hard: a ball can't get through it.'

"A journey of one hundred and sixty miles up the Ohio and Cumberland rivers brought us to Fort Donelson, and we got there at sunset. I went at once into the camp, and found there dear friends who used to sit in these pews, and had stood fast through all the thickest battle. They gave us coffee, which they drank as if it were nectar, and we as if it were senna.

"Our ever-busy Mother Nature had already brought down great rains to wash the crimson stains from her bosom; and it was only in some blanket cast under the bushes, or some loose garment taken from a wounded man, that these most fearful sights were to be seen. But all over the field were strewn the implements of death, with garments, harness, shot and shell, dead horses, and the resting places of dead men. Almost a week had passed since the battle, and most of the dead were buried. We heard of twos and threes, and in one place of eleven, still lying where they fell; and, as we rode down a lonely pass, we came to one waiting to be laid in the dust, and stopped for a moment to note the sad sight. Pray, look out from my eyes at him as he lies where he fell. You see by his garb that he is one of the rebel army; and, by the peculiar marks of that class, that he is a city rough. There is little about him to soften the grim picture that rises up before you, as he rests in perfect stillness by that fallen tree; but there is a shawl, coarse and homely, that must have belonged to some woman; and—

> ' His hands are folded on his breast;
> There is no other thing expressed,
> But long disquiet merged in rest.'

"Will you still let me guide you through that scene as it comes up before me? That long mound, with pieces of board here and there, is a grave; and sixty-one of our brave fellows rest in it, side by side. Those pieces of board are the gravestones, and the chisel is a black lead pencil. The queer, straggling letters tell you that the common soldier has done this to preserve, for a few days at least, the memory of one who used to go out with him on the dangerous picket-guard, and sit with him by the camp fire, and whisper to him, as they lay side by side in the tent through the still winter night, the hope he had before him when the war was over, or the trust in this comrade if he fell. There you see one large board, and in a beautiful flowing hand, 'John Oliver, Thirty-first Illinois,' and you wonder for a moment whether the man who has so tried to surpass the rest was nursed at the same breast as John Oliver; or whether John was a comrade, hearty and trusty beyond all price.

"And you will observe that the dead are buried in companies, every man in his own company, side by side; that the prisoners are sent out after the battle to bury their own dead; but that our own men will not permit them to bury a fellow-soldier of the Union, but every man in this sacred cause is held sacred even for the grave.

"And thus, on the crest of a hill, is the place where the dwellers in that little town have buried their dead, since ever they came to live on the bank of the river. White marble, and grey limestone, and decayed wooden monuments tell who rests beneath. There stands a grey stone, cut with these home-made letters that tell you how William N. Ross died on the 26th day of March 1814, in the twenty-sixth year of his age; and right alongside are the graves, newly made, of men who died last week in a strife which no wild imagining of this native man ever conceived possible in that quiet spot. Here, in the midst of the cemetery, the rebel officers have pitched their tents, for the place is one where a commander can see easily the greater part of the camp. Here is a tent where some woman has lived, for she has left a sewing machine and a small churn. Not far away you see a hapless kitten shot dead; and everywhere things that make you shudder, and fill you with sadness, over a wreck and ruin of war.

"Here you meet a man who has been in command, and stood fast; and when you say some simple word of praise to him in the name of all who love their country, he blushes and stammers like a woman, and tells you he tried to do his best; and when we get to Mound City we shall find a man racked with pain, who forgets his sufferings in telling how this brave man you have just spoken to not only stood by his own regiment in a fierce storm of shot, but, when he saw a regiment near his own giving back, because their officers showed the white feather, rode up to the regiment, hurled a mighty cry at those who were giving back, stood fast by the men in thickest fight, and saved them; and, says the sick man, with tears in his eyes, 'I would rather be a private under him than a captain under any other man.'

"I notice one feature in this camp that I never saw before; the men do not swear and use profane words as they used to do. There is a little touch of seriousness about them. They are cheerful and hearty, and in a few days they will mostly fall back into the old bad habit so painful to hear; but they have been too near to the tremendous verities of hell and heaven on the battle-field to turn them into small change for every-day use just yet. They have taken the Eternal Name for common purposes a thousand times; and we feel as if we could say with Paul, 'The times of this ignorance God passes by.' But on that fearful day, when judgment fires were all aflame, a voice said, 'Be still, and know that I am God;' and they are still under the shadow of that awful name."

The troubles of a nation are often, more than anything beside, the bringers of strength and real nobility of character. The war left its traces in many thousands of darkened homes; and yet the very children that have since grown up in the homes have been more heroic because their fathers were heroes. In any case, we in England feel that although the cause of slavery was not wiped out except at an awful cost, the liberty of God's creatures was worth it all.

It was seen then, and understood for the first time, how many really great men enriched the United States. There were not a few, but many heroes. Take, for example, the character of General Thomas, who fought with Garfield, and on whose character he pronounced the following among many eulogistic words:—

"Thomas's life is a notable illustration of the virtue and power of hard work; and in the last analysis the power to do hard work is only another name for talent. Professor Church, one of his instructors at West Point, says of his student life, that 'he never allowed anything to escape a thorough examination, and left nothing behind that he did not fully comprehend.' And so it was in the army. To him a battle was neither an earthquake, nor volcano, nor a chaos of brave men and frantic horses, involved in vast explosions of gunpowder. It was rather a calm, rational concentration of force against force. It was a question of lines and positions, of weight of metal and strength of battalions. He knew that the elements and forces which bring victory are not created on the battle-field, but must be patiently elaborated in the quiet of the camp, by the perfect organisation and outfit of his army. His remark to a captain of artillery, while inspecting a battery, is worth remembering, for it exhibits his theory of success: 'Keep everything in order, for the fate of a battle may turn on a buckle or a linch-pin.' He understood so thoroughly the condition of his army and its equipments, that when the hour of trial came he knew how great a pressure it could stand, and how hard a blow it could strike.

"His character was as grand and simple as a colossal pillar of chiselled granite. Every step of his career as a soldier was marked by the most loyal and unhesitating obedience to law—to the laws of his Government, and to the commands of his superiors. The obedience which he rendered to those above him he rigidly required of those under his command.

"His influence over the troops grew steadily and constantly. He won his ascendancy over them neither by artificial, nor by any one act of special daring, but he gradually filled them with his own spirit, until their confidence in him knew no bounds.

"His power as a commander was developed slowly and silently; not like volcanic land lifted from the sea by sudden and violent upheaval, but rather like a coral island, where each increment is a growth—an act of life and work."

The same words might have been spoken by some one else upon James Garfield himself; and also, as far as they relate to character rather than to circumstance, upon Lincoln too. Both men were alike in their chivalry and tenderness towards women. Garfield was doubtless the more refined of the two. His wife and mother were women of so high and excellent a type, that few have equalled them; and his love and reverence for them made Garfield the more gallant and chivalrous to all women for their sakes. And Lincoln showed that he, too, could appreciate the noble qualities of the American women.

He was on one occasion, and only a short time before he died, speaking at a fair held on behalf of the soldiers. "This extraordinary war," he said, "in which we are now engaged falls heavily upon all classes of people, but the most heavily upon the soldier. For it has been said, 'All that a man hath will he give for his life;' and while all contribute of their substance, the soldier puts his life at stake, and often yields it up in his country's cause. The highest merit, then, is due to the soldier.

"In this extraordinary war, extraordinary developments have manifested themselves, such as have not been seen in former wars; and among these manifestations nothing has been more remarkable than these fairs for the relief of suffering soldiers and their families. And the chief agents in these fairs are the women of America. I am not accustomed to the use of the language of eulogy. I have never studied the art of paying compliments to women, but I must say that, if all that has been said by orators and poets, since the creation of the world, in praise of women were applied to the women of America, it would not do them justice for their conduct during this war. I will conclude by saying, 'God bless the women of America.'"

The men were, indeed, comrades in arms! They fought together against Wrong, and Slavery, and Sin, and Oppression, as in their younger days they had fought against Poverty, Ignorance, and Want. They fought under one Master, for both loved and served Jesus, and obeyed Him as their Captain. Let us give thanks for their lives, and be glad that the brave soldiers have gone to their reward, and have received the Master's "Well done!"

CHAPTER XX.

WHAT MADE THEM HEROES?

"Live not for thyself alone !
  Know that God made all men brothers ;
  Therefore let thy deeds be done
  Ever for the good of others."

WHY do we give the name of Hero to each of the two men whose lives are before us?

Every man who honestly works his way from a lowly position to a higher one has something heroic in him ; and measured by this test, Lincoln and Garfield were certainly heroes. The great Washington, whom all the world delights to honour, and America most of all, was of gentle blood, and represented the higher intellectual and social phase of American life. His education, and the circumstances of his family, made him rather the representative of the aristocratic class than that of the self-made men. But Lincoln and Garfield, statesmen and patriots both of an exceedingly high order, were from the ranks of the people, and illustrated in themselves the marvellous possibilities of American citizenship. From the most illiterate to the most refined condition, from the poorest position to the most honourable, from the wooden stools and hard beds of the poor to the pictures and luxurious accessories of wealth, from the log-hut to the executive mansion, need not necessarily be a very long journey in America.

In England there are wonderful opportunities for determined young spirits. We have our Dick Whittingtons and our Livingstones, our mayors and artists, our wealthy merchants and famous literary men, who have won their own way in the world. To the young who are at the bottom of the social ladder, whose homes are poor, and who have to work hard, it ought to be an encouragement to read of two heroes who had to pass through the same difficulties. Look at the early days of the two men, Lincoln first :—

"After a seven days' journey through an uninhabited country, their resting-place at night being a blanket spread upon the ground, they arrived at the spot selected for their future residence, and no unnecessary delays were permitted to interfere with the immediate and successful clearing of a site for the cabin. An axe was placed in Abe's hands, and with the additional assistance of a neighbour, in two or three days Mr. Lincoln had a neat house of about eighteen feet square, the logs composing which being fastened together in the usual manner by notches, and the cracks between them filled with mud. A loft in this hut was Abe's bedroom, and there, night after night for many years, he who afterwards occupied the most exalted position in the gift of the American people, and who dwelt in the White House at Washington, surrounded by all the comforts that wealth and power could give, slumbered with one coarse blanket for his mattress and another for his covering."

The same contrast was seen in the case of Garfield as of Lincoln :—

"The country was nearly all wild, and the new farms had to be carved out of the forest. The dwelling of the Garfields was built after the standard pattern of the houses of poor Ohio farmers in that day. Its walls were of logs, its roof was of shingles split with an axe, and its floor of rude thick planking, split out of tree-trunks with a wedge and maul. It had only a single room, at one end of which was the big cavernous chimney, where the cooking was done, and at the other end a bed. The younger children slept in a trundle bed, which was pushed under the bedstead of their parents in the daytime, to get it out of the way, for there was no room to spare; the older ones climbed a ladder to the loft under the steep roof. In this house James A. Garfield was born 19th November 1831."

But poverty of itself never made heroes. There must be the spirit of self-denial and determination, and then the poverty will prove no hindrance to a man's advancement.

The persistent resolve to succeed in that to which they put their hands was seen in nothing more plainly than in the manner of gaining an education which characterised both Lincoln and Garfield. The rail-splitter and the tow-path lad were alike awake to the fact that ignorance does nothing, and learning helps to the accomplishment of all things.

Of Lincoln we are told:—"The lad had an offer which promised to afford him employment during the long monotonous evenings; a young man who had removed into the neighbourhood having offered to teach him how to write. The opportunity was too fraught with benefit to be rejected, and after a few weeks of practice under the eye of his instructor, and also out of doors with a piece of chalk or charred stick, he was able to write his name, and in less than twelve months could, and did, write a letter. Six months of instruction within the walls of an insignificant school-house was all the school education that Abraham Lincoln received during a long life-time, the greater part of which was spent in public positions, where ability and talent were indispensable requisites."

And of Garfield we are told :—" He studied hard, often walked alone in the roads or fields, and attended to all his duties with promptness. During his collegiate course he tried to earn small sums of money by teaching evening writing-school, but never secured a very profitable number of scholars. He dressed very plainly and cheaply, and was compelled to economise in every way. But Garfield's student days appear to have impressed him as but a portion of a whole life of study."

It was the self-helpfulness which both men possessed in such an unusual degree that was the secret of their success in educational, as in all other matters. They exercised the native talents with which God had endowed them; and in circumstances comparatively unfavourable, they both manifested the sterling worth of character that is more valuable than gold or silver.

And there was something heroic in the way in which both men were willing to acknowledge in their prosperity the uses and blessings of their adversity. The flat-boat builder and the plank-planer never grew too proud to speak of their humble origin. They never forgot that they were of the people, and that they shared with the people an identity of experiences and interests. Both men were wise enough to appreciate the power which their early poverty gave them over the nation of which they became the leaders. In gladness or sorrow they could sympathise with them. They knew how surely happiness and prosperity spring from the great principles of justice and humanity.

Both men were full of kindness of heart towards the poor. A Washington correspondent said, that when he entered the President's office one afternoon, he found Mr. Lincoln busily counting greenbacks.

"This, sir," said Lincoln, "is out of my usual line."

"Do you mean that a President of the United States has very little to do with money?"

"No, not that. But a President of the United States has a multiplicity of duties not specified in the Constitution or Acts of Congress. This is one of them."

"How is that, sir?"

"This money belongs to a poor negro who is a porter in the Treasury Department, at present very bad with the small-pox. He is now in hospital, and could not draw his pay because he could not sign his name. I have been at considerable trouble to overcome the difficulty and get it for him, and have at length succeeded in cutting red tape, as you newspaper men say. I am now dividing the money, and putting by a portion labelled in an envelope with my own hands, according to his wish."

Mr. Lincoln went on with his work, and indorsed the package very carefully.

"No one," added the correspondent, "witnessing the transaction, could fail to appreciate the goodness of heart which prompted the President of the United States to turn aside for a time from his weighty cares, to succour one of the humblest of his fellow-creatures in sickness and sorrow."

President Garfield was not less kind than President Lincoln, though the stories told of him are somewhat different. One of his former pupils said, "No matter how old we were, Garfield always called us by our first names, and kept himself on the most familiar terms with all. He played with us freely, scuffled with us sometimes, and talked with us in walking to and fro; and we treated him, out of the class-room, just about as we treated one another. Yet he was a most strict disciplinarian, and enforced the rules like a martinet. He combined an affectionate and confiding manner, with respect for order, in a most remarkable degree. If he wanted to speak to a pupil, either for reproof or approbation, he would generally manage to get one arm around him, and draw him close up to him. He had a peculiar way of shaking hands, too, giving a twist to your arm and drawing you right up to him. This sympathetic manner has helped him to advancement. When I was a janitor he used sometimes to stop me, and ask my opinion about this and that, as if seriously advising with me. I can see that my opinion could not have been of any value, and that he probably asked me partly to show me that he felt an interest in me. I was certainly his friend all the firmer for it."

There are not many records of meetings and conversations between the two men; but one rather amusing one is told of some remarks made by Lincoln to Garfield on one occasion.

"By the way, Garfield," said Mr. Lincoln, "you never heard, did you, that Chase, Stanton, and I had a campaign of our own? We went down to Fortress Monroe in Chase's revenue cutter, and consulted with Admiral Goldsborough as to the feasibility of taking Norfolk by landing on the north shore, and making a march of eight miles. The Admiral said, very positively, there was no landing on that shore, and we should have to double the Cape and approach the place from the south side, which would be a long and difficult journey. I thereupon asked him if he had ever tried to find a landing, and he said he had not. 'Now,' said I, 'Admiral, that reminds me of a chap out West who had studied law, but had never tried a case. Being sued, and not having confidence in his ability to manage his own case, he employed a fellow lawyer to manage it for him. He had only a confused idea of the meaning of law terms, but was anxious to make a display of learning, and on the trial constantly made suggestions to his lawyer, who paid no attention to him. At last, fearing that his lawyer was not handling the opposing counsel very well, he lost all patience, and springing to his feet, cried out, 'Why don't you go at him with a *capias*, or a *surre-butter*, or something, and not stand there like a confounded old *nudum pactum!*'"

Abraham Lincoln seems never to have spoken to any man without telling him a tale of some kind. Doubtless, if the future could have been foreseen at the time when these two men were together, more incidents and conversations and stories would have been forthcoming.

Both were cheerful, and even merry; and both were good. A writer who knew Lincoln says of him :—

"Mr. Lincoln could scarcely be called a *religious* man, in the common acceptation of the term, yet a sincerer *Christian* I believe never lived. A constitutional tendency to dwell upon sacred things; an emotional nature, which finds ready expression in religious conversation and revival meetings; the culture and development of the devotional element, till the expression of religious thought and experience becomes almost habitual, were not among his characteristics. Doubtless he felt as deeply upon the great question of the soul and eternity as any other thoughtful man, but the very tenderness and humility of his nature would not permit the exposure of his inmost convictions, except upon the rarest occasions, and to his most intimate friends. And yet, aside from emotional expression, I believe no man had a more abiding sense of his dependence upon God, or faith in the divine government, and in the power and ultimate triumph of Truth and Right in the world. In the language of an eminent clergyman of this city, who lately delivered an eloquent discourse upon the life and character of the departed President, 'It is not necessary to appeal to apocryphal stories in circulation in the newspapers—which illustrate as much the assurance of his visitors as the simplicity of his faith—for proof of Mr. Lincoln's Christian character.' If his daily life and various public addresses and writings do not show this, surely nothing can ever demonstrate it."

Another writer, Mr. Noah Brooks, in *Harper's Magazine*, gave the following reminiscence:—"Just after the Presidential election he said, 'Being only mortal, after all I should have been a little mortified if I had been beaten in this canvass before the people; but that sting would have been more than compensated by the thought that the people had notified me that all my official responsibilities had been lifted off my back.' In reply to the remark that he might remember that in all these cares he was daily remembered by those who prayed, not to be heard of men, as no man had ever before been remembered, he caught at the homely phrase, and said, 'Yes, I like that phrase, "Not to be heard of men," and guess it is generally true as you say; at least I have been told so, and have been a good deal helped by just that thought.' Then he solemnly and slowly added, 'I should be the most presumptuous blockhead upon this footstool, if I for one day thought that I could discharge the duties which have come upon me since I came into this place, without the aid and enlightenment of One who is stronger and wiser than all others.'"

James Garfield was a more decidedly pronounced Christian than Abraham Lincoln. Dr. Errett, in his funeral address, gave the following information:—"When James Garfield was yet a mere lad, in this county a series of religious meetings were held in one of the towns of Cuyahoga County by a minister by no means attractive as an orator, possessing none of the graces of an orator, and marked only by entire sincerity, by good reasoning powers, and by earnestness in seeking to win souls from sin to righteousness. The lad Garfield attended these meetings for many nights, and after giving earnest attention to the sermons, he went one day to the minister and said to him, 'Sir, I have been listening to your preaching night after night, and I am fully persuaded that if these things you say are true, it is the duty and the highest interest of

every man of respectability, and especially of every young
man, to accept that religion and seek to be a man. But,
really, I don't know whether this thing is true or not. I
can't say that I disbelieve it, but I dare not say that I truly
and honestly believe it. If I were sure that it was true, I
would most gladly give it my heart and my life.' So, after
a long talk, the minister preached that night on the text,
'What is truth?' and proceeded to show that, notwithstanding all the various and conflicting theories and opinions
in ethical science, and notwithstanding all the various and
conflicting opinions in the world, there was one assured and
eternal alliance for every human soul in Jesus Christ; that
every soul was safe with Jesus Christ; that he never would
mislead; that any young man giving Him his hand and
heart, and walking in His pathway, would not go astray;
and that whatever might be the solution of ten thousand
insoluble mysteries, at the end of all things the man who
loved Jesus Christ and walked after the footsteps of Jesus,
and realised in spirit and life the pure morals and the sweet
piety, was safe, if safety there were in the universe of God;
safe, whatever else was safe; safe, whatever else might
prove unworthy and perish for ever. And he seized upon it
after due reflection, and came forward and gave his hand to
the minister in pledge of his acceptance of the guidance of
Christ for his life, and turned his back upon the sins of the
world for ever. The boy is father to the man; and that
pure honesty and integrity, and that fearless spirit to
inquire, and that brave surrender of all the charms of sin
to convictions of duty and right, went with him from that
boyhood throughout his life, and crowned him with the
honours that were so cheerfully awarded to him from all
hearts over this vast land. There was another thing—he
passed all through the conditions of virtuous life between
the log cabin in Cuyahoga and the White House; and in
that wonderfully rich and varied experience, moving up

from higher to higher, he has touched every heart in all this land at some point or other, and he became the representative of all hearts and lives in this land; not only the teacher, but the representative of all virtues, for he knew their wants and their condition, and he established legitimately the ties of brotherhood with every man with whom he came in contact. I take it that this vow, lying at the basis of his character, this rock on which his whole life rested, followed up by the perpetual and enduring industry that marked his whole career, made him at once the honest and the capable man, who invited and received, in every act of his life, the confidence, and trust, and love of all who earned to know him."

The truest Christians are the greatest heroes. Garfield's family coat of arms, "*In cruce vinco*"—"By the cross I conquer"—may have supplied him with the motive power of his life. He knew and trusted the greatest Hero the world has ever known, and his fellowship with Him made him philanthropic, merciful, gentle, and righteous.

Both Lincoln and Garfield proved themselves heroes by the way in which they met death. Neither was afraid to die. In the one case, however, the man must have lived in almost constant remembrance that his life had been threatened; while in the other there could have been little expectation or fear. There was something remarkable, too, in the fact that the one who, knowing how often he had been threatened, had plenty of time for preparation, was shot, if not dead on the spot, so murderously that he did not speak afterwards; while the other, who had received no warning, lay for more than two months between life and death. Lincoln was no coward. He once said, "It would never do for a President to have guards with drawn sabres at his door, as if he were, or were trying to be, or were assuming to be, an emperor." He said, too, "Soon after I was nominated at Chicago I began to receive letters threatening my life. The first one or two made me a little uncomfortable, but I came at length to look for a regular instalment of this kind of correspondence in every week's mail, and up to inauguration day I was in constant receipt of such letters. There is nothing like getting *used* to things."

He did not want to die suddenly, and always declared that he would be a coward in front of a gun. But the fear of death never prevented him from doing that which he believed to be his duty. And if he had known beforehand that there would come to him the shot of the assassin, it would have made him none the less resolute to do the right according to the light that was given him.

Neither did Garfield want to die. There is no doubt, indeed, that his hope and longing to recover helped in part to make the last struggle uncertain for so long. Garfield loved the beautiful earth, with all its flowers and sunshine, its friendships and joys. He would have got well if he could. Had he not a mother who loved him, a wife who was devoted to him, and children and friends who revered him? And it was in the summer time that he was smitten down; and while he lay in pain and weakness, alternating between life and death, he could hear the gentle voices of those who fain would have spoken words of comfort to him, he could hear the twitter of birds upon the lawn, and the *lap* of the sea as it broke upon the shore. Sweet scents came to him as he lay, to remind him of the charms which the world possesses. As one beautifully said at Chicago :—

"He wanted to the very last to live, and said so, and scanned the poor thin face for some sign that it might be so, and was no more resigned to go than we were to have him go; and felt as we do, that, so far as we can understand the divine love which encircles all our lives, it was not God's will that he should perish. Now, nothing he has done seems more beautiful to me than the grand soldierly resolution to hold on to his life, and have the whole worth of it, for his own sake and for ours. Life was dear to him. He loved the world. It was a beautiful world. When he had taken the great solemn oath, standing before all the people, the first thing he did was to turn to his old mother and his wife, and kiss them, sealing in that grand simple way the oath he had taken to serve us well. In some men that would have been the merest clap-trap; in James Garfield it was the fine flower of his whole manhood. They took the sacrament when they were crowned in the great old lands: that was his sacrament; and the noble old mother blessed her son, and the sweet, true wife her husband, and the children's hearts beat quick and proud for their father; and surely since the world was made we have seen nothing more sacred than this, in which the old home-life flashed out for an instant in that new beatitude. And so the home and the home treasures were what the good President fought for through the weakness and the pain. How could he submit if there was any help on earth or in heaven? He saw the fear in the face that had challenged him once out of all the world, and heard it in the voice to which his heart answered, and heard it in the sobs of the children; and there the instinct of a true man, who has all these treasures to guard, rose towering like some great angel over the threat of dissolution."

But though this was so, the hero was ready to die. There is a well-known picture by Sir Noel Paton. which represents a knight passing through death to immortality. More than a few people must have thought of Garfield in connection with it, or it in connection with him. The hero has fought his life's battles well, but the end has come now. He has been brave, but now he is weary, and lifts his white face with a smile as he sees that death is only an angel of light. He has fought a good fight, he has finished his course, he has kept the faith; henceforth there is laid up for him a crown of life.

CHAPTER XXI.

THE LESSONS OF THEIR LIVES.

> " Lives of great men all remind us
>   We may make our lives sublime,
> And departing, leave behind us
>   Footprints on the sands of time ;
> Footprints that perhaps another,
>   Sailing o'er life's chequered main,
> Some forlorn or shipwrecked brother,
>   Seeing may take heart again."

LINCOLN and Garfield, the New World Heroes, were living illustrations of the inspiring words of their own poet, Longfellow. They were really great men, and they have left " footprints on the sands of time" which will not soon be obliterated. We may hope that the story of their humble beginnings, their political achievements, and their soldier-like end, may fire the hearts of thousands of the boys in England to try and follow in their steps.

What are the chief lessons to be learnt from the histories of these two men ?

The first is, that *no poor boy is compelled to grow into a poor man.*

In these days, especially, everything depends, not upon the circumstances in which a man is born, but upon the mettle of which he is made—the spirit that is in him If Lincoln and Garfield, without a penny to start them in life, without a friend in a good position to stretch out a helping hand, could rise to the very topmost step of the social ladder, what may not any boy do? Look at them in the first years of their life; what do they possess? No clothes, no education, no money, no friends. What are their possessions? They have none. And yet they had! They were young, they were strong, they were industrious, they were persistent, they were masters of themselves. And so they possessed the best qualifications for success in life that could be enjoyed by any. After reading their biographies, let no boy say, that because his parents lived in poverty and obscurity he, too, must be poor and obscure for the whole of his life. Not at all! He has, perhaps, even a better chance of rising in the world, and doing well with his life, than if he had been the inheritor of riches. Any observer of the habits and lives of the people of England to-day will be struck by seeing how frequently young men who come into the substance gathered by their fathers waste it in a few years.

Who does not know of instances in which a man has commenced business in a humble way and without capital, has worked up the small business to a large one, and gradually but steadily accumulated property, until he has become known as a successful merchant, who retires from the business, which he hands over to his son, and himself spends the later years of his life in the enjoyment of leisure, wealth, and municipal honours? while the son, in his turn, sees the business dwindle, the income fall below the expenditure, and not many years after his father's death has to go through the humiliation of bankruptcy and the trouble of ruin? Such occurrences are so common that every one knows of them; so common, that they may lead us to wonder whether a young man who starts in life with nothing but his own clear brains, his own clever hands, and his own strong heart, has not a better capital than he who inherits a good business and plenty of money without them.

Let no one be discouraged because he is poor. Poverty is not necessarily a great stumbling-block to progress. It may be used as a stepping-stone from the lowly places to the heights of ambition. And every British boy has now the one thing which, above all others, gives a man a start in life. There is no need now for a boy to write his sums on odd pieces of wood, or study the sign-posts in order to learn to read. An education is to be for ever in the future of England the birthright of her children. And having this, the world is free to any boy. He will find that life is a battle; but it will be quite open to him to win. It is a competitive examination all through; and always the best equipped, the most clever, and the most persevering, will carry off the prizes. Any young man, therefore, may aspire to wealth and honour. In England, perhaps, not less than in America, people can make their own fortunes, or lose those that their fathers made. It depends upon themselves whether they shall be, in the fierce battle that is being fought, the victors or the vanquished. Let them, therefore, resolve with their whole heart as to what they will do and be, and carry their purpose through all obstacles.

But the second lesson taught by the lives of Lincoln and Garfield is, that *although success is possible to all, only a few win it.*

What of those who were companions of the two boys who became heroes? The world has never heard of them. Why not? The upward path was as free to them as to these. They, too, could have borrowed books; they, too, could have thought wisely; they, too, could have spoken and acted. Why have not their words come down to us, their actions won renown?

We know that there is another power than his own which every man has to feel. "The blessing of the Lord maketh rich." "Except the Lord build the house, they labour in vain who build it." But still a great deal depends upon the man himself. Many people fail who might rise, because they are hindered by their own weaknesses. Self-indulgence is at the source of much that spoils a life. It is more pleasant to pamper than to vigorously deny self, and most people do the more pleasant thing as far as they can. To be always at work requires a strong whip, and we are not at all disposed to whip ourselves. No one succeeds in life who only does just what he is compelled. Incessant industry is a condition of success. If Lincoln had contented himself with splitting a dozen instead of a hundred rails at a time; if Garfield had risen late, and gone to bed early when it was free for him to choose which he should do, we should never have heard of either. Their habit was to work, and to keep on working, and to make the work tell. Some people work by fits and starts only—they are never the most successful men; it is those who are always in earnest, who are painstaking enough to look again and again at the same thing, and to give to it unwearied attention, who succeed. And a great deal depends upon the patience with which a man attends to all the details of his work. If he does not give time and thought to little things as well as great, he will not be as successful as he might be. But if his work is to him more than his ease, and more than his comfort, more, indeed, than all beside, he will not only succeed in it, but rise by it. And each can measure himself by these tests, and so know at once whether he will be one of the few who triumph or of the many who are defeated.

Another lesson which these men teach is, that *in every great life, character is an important element of success.*

These men were great because they were good. They were truthful. Even as boys they would not lie. They gave their word as an honourable bond, and neither would break it. And because they were trustworthy they were trusted. The nation discovered, what individuals had learnt, that the most implicit confidence could be placed in them. While they were yet young it was known that they would work as well in the master's absence as if his eyes were upon them. And as they grew older, and filled more important positions, the same repose of mind was felt in regard to them. They both illustrate the saying of Jesus, "He that is faithful in that which is least is faithful also in much." And this quality of faithfulness contributed more than a little to their prosperity. We shall find it the same in every instance. Those who are not to be relied upon cannot hope to prosper. Many fail because the fiat has gone forth—"Unstable as water, thou shalt not excel." These men succeeded because they were steadfast, firm, and faithful, and also because they were self-controlled. They had conquered themselves, and therefore they were masters of others. The rulers of their own spirits, they became also rulers of men. If this element be absent, there is a blemish in the character that will prevent it from becoming really great. Only weakness allows itself to be overcome.

And, then, there was another element in the character of these two men that had much to do with their excellence. "He is the greatest of all who is the servant of all." They were both ministers to the people. It was for services that they had rendered to others that they were so honourable and honoured. No selfish person can be great. No one who strives for place and power, that he may gratify his own ambition, can ever rise to the highest attitudes of human excellence. But such were not these men. "I do not wish for it myself; but if I can be useful, I am willing to occupy the position." This was the spirit that actuated both men, and this is the spirit out of which the world's real philanthropists are made. It is those who "are at leisure from themselves" who are the best servants; and it is these men who become benefactors, liberators, heroes.

And there is one more lesson which the lives of Lincoln and Garfield teach, and it is, that *the Christian is the highest type of man*. Let all who wish to do the best with the life that has been given them, turn away even from our New World Heroes to Him who is the Light of the World, and whose life was the most beautiful, the most perfect the world has ever known. And was not He also martyred? The lessons of the lives of the Presidents are the more impressive, insomuch as they were copies of Him; and their deaths do but faintly show forth the same grand truths of fidelity and devotion to the very end; for *greater love hath no man than this, that a man lay down his life for his friends*.

Printed by WALTER SCOTT, "*The Kenilworth Press,*" Felling, Newcastle-on-Tyne.

www.ingramcontent.com/pod-product-compliance
Lightning Source LLC
Chambersburg PA
CBHW030346230426
43664CB00007BB/550